Are We Not Men? Unstable
Masculinity in the Hebrew Prophets

Are We Not Men? Unstable Masculinity in the Hebrew Prophets

RHIANNON GRAYBILL

OXFORD
UNIVERSITY PRESS

OXFORD
UNIVERSITY PRESS

Oxford University Press is a department of the University of Oxford. It furthers the University's objective of excellence in research, scholarship, and education by publishing worldwide. Oxford is a registered trade mark of Oxford University Press in the UK and certain other countries.

Published in the United States of America by Oxford University Press
198 Madison Avenue, New York, NY 10016, United States of America.

Library of Congress Cataloging-in-Publication Data
Names: Graybill, Rhiannon, 1984– author.
Title: Are we not men? : unstable masculinity in the Hebrew prophets / Rhiannon Graybill.
Description: New York : Oxford University Press USA, 2016. |
Includes bibliographical references and index.
Identifiers: LCCN 2015043885 (print) | LCCN 2016031873 (ebook) |
ISBN 9780190227364 (hardcover : alk. paper) | ISBN 9780190227371 ()
Subjects: LCSH: Men (Christian theology)—Biblical teaching. | Bible. Prophets. |
Bible. Old Testament—Criticism, interpretation, etc.
Classification: LCC BS1199.M34 G73 2016 (print) | LCC BS1199.M34 (ebook) | DDC 224/.06—dc23
LC record available at https://lccn.loc.gov/2015043885

9 8 7 6 5 4 3 2 1
Printed by Sheridan Books, Inc., United States of America

To my parents

Contents

Acknowledgments

THERE ARE MANY people who made this book possible. The project began at the University of California, Berkeley, as my doctoral dissertation in Near Eastern Studies. I am grateful to Robert Alter, Daniel Boyarin, Chana Kronfeld, and Celeste Langan for their guidance, as well as their trust. At Berkeley, I also owe a debt of gratitude to Benjamin Porter and John Hayes. At Rhodes College, this book was nourished into its present form. My colleagues in Religious Studies supported the project, and me, from the beginning. In the department, I have found sympathetic listeners, critically engaged readers, and conversation partners, all of whom helped refine the book and its arguments. In particular, John Kaltner and Steven L. McKenzie provided me with a number of valuable comments and suggestions. Karen Winterton helped in many ways; Kenan Padgett assisted me in obtaining a number of research materials. The Dean's Office provided me with a research leave to complete the manuscript, for which I am deeply appreciative. I am also grateful for my students, their enthusiasm, and their curiosity—they have asked all manner of questions, many of which made this a stronger book.

At Oxford University Press, I have been lucky to work with Steve Wiggins, a wonderful editor. I am also appreciative of the feedback from three anonymous reviewers. An early version of chapter 4 was published in *The Bible and Posthumanism*; I would like to thank Jennifer Koosed for including the piece, and for her comments. An early version of chapter 1 likewise appeared in the journal *Biblical Interpretation*; Tat-siong Benny Liew and two reviews provided helpful feedback that shaped the final version of the piece.

Multiple audiences also heard and commented on early versions of this work. Chapter 1 was first presented to the AAR Body and Religion group in 2011. Chapter 2 benefited from multiple audiences, including the Gender, Sexuality, and the Bible session at SBL (2013), and audiences at the University of Mississippi (2014) and Centenary College (2015). An early form of chapter 3 was presented at the 2010 SBL annual meeting to a joint session of Gender, Sexuality, and the Bible, and LGBT Hermeneutics; this chapter was also the basis of a 2013 lecture at Washington University in St. Louis. I presented versions of chapter 4 at the 2010 SBL Annual Meeting (Reading, Theory, and the Bible) and to the Arts Research Center at UC Berkeley, where I was selected as an ARC fellow (2011). I am grateful to each of these audiences for the opportunity to share my work.

A number of wonderful readers and friends have offered comments, critiques, and reassurance at multiple points in the writing process. Kurt Beals has supported me in so many ways from the very beginning. Lena Salaymeh gave each chapter a careful and attentive reading; her comments improved the book immensely. Early on, Rachel Havrelock, Nathaniel Deutsch, Mark Wallace, Helen Plotkin, and Thomas R. Lee all provided me with encouragement. I would also like to express my gratitude to Kent Brintnall, Angela Frederick, Raphael Graybill, Judith Haas, Alison Joseph, Shorena Kurtsikidze, Sarah Levin, Yosefa Raz, Emily Regier, P. J. Sabo, Krista Spiller, SherAli Tareen, Renee Thompson, Caki Wilkinson, and Emily Wistar. Finally, I want to thank my family, especially my parents, Jessica Crist and Turner Graybill, for their unwavering support.

Abbreviations

AIL	Ancient Israel and its Literature
AThANT	Abhandlungen zur Theologie des alten und neuen Testaments
AYB	Anchor Yale Bible
BASOR	*Bulletin of the American Schools of Oriental Research*
BCT	*The Bible and Critical Theory*
BDB	*Brown-Driver-Briggs Hebrew and English Lexicon*
BibInt	*Biblical Interpretation*
BIS	Biblical Interpretation Series
BMW	Bible in the Modern World Series
BTB	*Biblical Theology Bulletin*
ContC	Continental Commentaries
FCB	Feminist Companion to the Bible
GCT	Gender, Culture, Theory
HALOT	*Hebrew-Aramaic Lexicon of the Old Testament* (Kohler-Baumgartner)
HBM	Hebrew Bible Monographs
HS	*Hebrew Studies*
HSM	Harvard Semitic Monographs
HTR	*Harvard Theological Review*
ICC	International Critical Commentary
JBL	*Journal of Biblical Literature*
JR	*Journal of Religion*
JSOT	*Journal for the Study of the Old Testament*
JSOTSup	*Journal for the Study of the Old Testament*, Supplement Series
LHB/OTS	Library of the Hebrew Bible/Old Testament Studies
LXX	Septuagint
MT	Masoretic text
NICOT	New International Commentary on the Old Testament
OBT	Overtures to Biblical Theology

OTL	Old Testament Library
RRBS	Recent Research in Biblical Studies
SBL	Society of Biblical Literature
SBLDS	Society of Biblical Literature Dissertation Series
SBLSS	Society of Biblical Literature Semeia Studies
SBLSym	Society of Biblical Literature Symposium Series
SBTS	Sources for Biblical and Theological Study
SiBL	Studies in Biblical Literature
TS	*Theology and Sexuality*
TWOT	*Theological Wordbook of the Old Testament*
VT	*Vetus Testamentum*
ZAW	*Zeitschrift für die alttestamentliche Wissenschaft*

Introduction

THIS IS A book about men and their bodies. More specifically, it is about a particular group of men (the Hebrew prophets) and a particular set of experiences surrounding the male body. Most of these experiences are peculiar, troubling, painful, or otherwise outside of the ordinary. The chapters that follow offer a series of encounters with these male bodies and body parts: with prophetic hands and feet, hearts and lips, mouths and genitals. There is much to see, and to say, when we turn our critical inquiry to the bodies that inhabit prophetic texts and narratives.

These are not the bodies (or indeed the men) that appear most frequently when we talk about or think about bodies in the Hebrew Bible. Neither are they the bodies that seem to receive the most attention from the text itself. Instead, the bodies that attract description are those touched with beauty or engaged in action. The body of David, for example, receives a good deal of attention. We know of his ruddy complexion (1 Sam. 17:42), his youth, his relatively slight stature. The text gives multiple details about the body of Samson (Judg. 14:6–9, 15:9–18, 16:3, 16:13–30), whose strength is matched only by his great head of hair (and, eventually, by an unwanted haircut). There are the bodies of Adam and Eve, whether gloriously naked or newly clothed and lingering on the edge of Eden (Gen. 2:25, 3:7, 3:21). There is the handsome body of Joseph, drawing hungry looks from Potiphar's wife (Gen. 39:6–8), and jealous ones from his brothers (especially when his body is adorned in the famous cloak, Gen. 37:3). Even though the biblical text is notoriously thrifty with details concerning appearances, these bodies (David, Samson, Adam and Eve) summon readers' attention, whether by creating pleasure in their description, advancing the narrative in their actions or both. Given this, it is not really surprising that these are the sorts of bodies favored in artistic renderings of biblical scenes.

The prophets are a stranger bunch by far. Perhaps the most famous visual representation of a prophet's body is Charlton Heston as Moses in Cecil B. DeMille's *The Ten Commandments* (1956)—arms raised, gray beard billowing, the waters parting before him. But this representation of Moses' body as a source of power and authority, however much it resonates with certain contemporary notions we attach to the term "prophet" (many of them informed, consciously or unconsciously, by works such as DeMille's film), does not really match the portrayals of prophets and their bodies in the Hebrew Bible itself. The prophets' bodies appear surprisingly frequently in the text, but their appearances are often perplexing or unsettling. Elisha spreads his body over a dead boy to bring him back to life (2 Kgs. 4). Ezekiel lets his body lie on the banks of the river Chebar, bound, for more than a year (Ezek. 4). When specific body parts appear, their appearance is hardly more reassuring or familiar, introducing uncircumcised lips (Exod. 4:10; Isa. 6:5–7) and fiery bones (Jer. 20:9).

As a way of entering into the question of the prophetic body, I want to begin with an example from the book of Isaiah. There are many bodies in Isaiah—the bodies of the people of Judah, the bodies of seraphim, the metaphorical body of daughter Zion, the bodies of children (which often function as signs), even a glimmer of the body of Yahweh. The body I wish to consider, however, belongs to Isaiah himself. It appears in chapter 20, in the midst of the text's Sargon of Assyria's capture of Ashdod. The passage reads:

> At that time, Yahweh had spoken to Isaiah ben Amoz, saying, "Go and remove the sackcloth on your loins and the sandals from your feet," and he had done so and walked naked and barefoot. Yahweh said, "As my servant Isaiah walks naked and barefoot for three years as a sign and a portent against Egypt and against Ethiopia, so will the king of Assyria drive away the Egyptians as captives and the Ethiopians as exiles—young and old— naked and barefoot, with exposed buttocks, to the shame of Egypt. And they will be dismayed and ashamed because of Ethiopia their hope and of Egypt their boast." (Isa. 20:1–5)[1]

Here, nestled among the prophecies, warnings, and narrative interludes that fill the book of Isaiah, the body of the prophet suddenly appears—unclothed and exposed. Isaiah is undertaking prophecy, but not through words. Instead, this is prophecy by means of bodily exposure. The prophet's nakedness is humiliating, even shocking; it is also necessary to the working of the prophecy. A naked male body is effective as a sign insofar as its lack of clothing is disruptive and disturbing. Lest we pass too quickly over its significance, the text describes the naked body at least twice, both in narrative prose and in a quote from Yahweh (this quote, moreover, includes double reference to the naked body). The latter description even compels us to consider, if briefly, the prophet's "exposed buttocks."

That the book of Isaiah contains such a naked male body is—to some readers, at least—shocking, and perhaps humiliating as well. It is tempting to move
quickly and shift the emphasis from the prophet's actions to their meaning, to
resolve the metaphor from its *vehicle* (the naked body) to its *tenor* (what this
nakedness signifies). Historically oriented readers often stress the political context of the passage, as well as the significance of Egypt and Assyria.[2] In this reading, the action of Isaiah taking off his clothes and shoes is easily explained as a sign
of the futility of allying with Egypt and Ethiopia against the Assyrian threat. But
naked bodies are never just neutral signs. This is especially the case when questions of politics or faith are at stake. And so instead of hurrying past the embar-
rassing site of Isaiah's naked, not-quite-young flesh to reach what "really matters,"
I want to remain with the prophet's body.

First, there is a great deal of pain in this small story, though it goes unaddressed
by the text. Isaiah is to walk naked and barefoot for three years. This command
does not simply use the body to make a point; it also causes significant physical
pain in the process. Yahweh's message depends directly on Isaiah's suffering. And
yet this suffering is also denied recognition in the text. In *The Body in Pain*, Elaine
Scarry takes up the entangled questions of pain, language, and recognition. She
argues that the "unsharability" of pain amplifies the intensity of the experience of
suffering.[3] The book of Isaiah does not even acknowledge the experience of pain
that three years of nakedness inflicts, let alone attempt to give it voice. It is both
unsharable and voiceless. It is an intense but unnamed suffering for which the text
knows no empathy.

The complement to pain in Isaiah 20 is shame. Unlike pain, which remains
unmentioned, shame appears directly: the point of the prophet's nakedness is to
stage humiliation. Isaiah's nakedness is shameful, and in its shamefulness it anticipates the humiliation that Assyria will bring onto Egypt and Ethiopia. The humiliated body stands as a protest against any alliance with these powers. Yet as in the
case of pain, the abstract sign of shame depends upon the specific shaming of the
prophet's body, through its exposure, its vulnerability, and its suffering. When we
think about the body of Isaiah as a sign, we risk forgetting the specificity of the
prophet's body. There is no generic, abstract, neutral body. Isaiah's nakedness has
specific consequences for his experiences of masculinity and embodiment. What
Isaiah does with his body troubles expectations of what a male body ought to do,
and how it ought to appear. Visual and textual evidence from the ancient Near
East shows that male nakedness and vulnerability are linked, for example, to the
humiliation of prisoners of war.[4] Such humiliation also activates gender categories and understandings of gender performances: humiliating a man is frequently
linked to stripping away his culturally recognized masculinity.

Beyond pain and shame, this scene of prophetic nakedness is also rather queer. The term "queer" has, of course, many meanings; I return to these in greater detail below. For now, I want simply to offer some brief reflections, drawing on Sara Ahmed's discussion of the term and its range of meanings in *Queer Phenomenology*. As Ahmed notes, queer offers a "way of describing what is 'oblique' or 'off line'"; it may likewise refer to "specific sexual practices" and "nonnormative sexualities."[5] The term *queer* accommodates both of these sets of meanings, without, however, collapsing one into the other. And both meanings come into play in understanding the incident in Isaiah 20. As a prophetic action, Isaiah's nakedness bears an oblique relation to more typical forms of prophecy, such as speech. While it is not wholly separate, or even separable, it follows a different trajectory of meaning making, one that is not always immediately intelligible to the intended audience. Frequently, the meanings of symbolic actions are difficult for the intended audience to grasp—yet another sense of "oblique."[6] And yet this scene is also queer in that the action of prophecy depends upon not just any symbolic action, but specifically upon the exposure of the male buttocks. To have one's nakedness made the subject of the gaze is humiliating; this is one of the central points of the story of Noah's exposure to Ham (Gen. 9). That this gaze is directed to the buttocks is likewise challenging to the norms of heteronormativity in the text. It is queer in more than one way that Isaiah should act out his prophecy by exposing his posterior.

It is not only Isaiah who acts queerly, or who has a queer experience of the body. Hosea, Jeremiah, and Ezekiel all use their bodies to perform symbolic actions, and rather queer ones—Hosea's involves marrying a promiscuous woman (Hos. 1), Jeremiah's centers on a dirty loincloth (Jer. 13), and Ezekiel's, as I will show in detail, depends upon the "unmanning" of the body (Ezek. 4–5). At other points, the bodies of prophets seem to have a queer power (again, understood both as generally peculiar and as specifically sexually other). They may, for instance be involved in healing: Elisha spreads his body over a dead boy to bring him back to life (2 Kgs. 4:32–35); Elijah performs a similar healing (1 Kgs. 17:19–22). In these stories, the prophet's therapeutic work depends upon the touch of his body—a touch, moreover, that is frequently between men and other men, or men and children. In still other narratives and prophetic scenes, it is the prophet's bodily appearance that is queer. Elijah, clothed in animal skins and feasting on locusts, cuts a memorable figure, such that John the Baptist and many others are compelled to imitate his unusual dress. (Timothy Koch, equally memorably, calls Elijah a "hairy leather-man," a description that captures some of the queer valences of his actions and adornment alike.)[7]

The body may also be queer in the way it deviates from the norm, whether Moses' many bodily difficulties (including weakness, illness, and a queerly glowing face) or the seeming absence of the body from other prophetic texts, such as Second Isaiah. This is a queer relation to norms of the body as complete, sufficient, capable, and present.[8] When specific body parts appear, their appearance is hardly more reassuring or familiar. Moses and Isaiah each complain of uncircumcised lips; Moses is rewarded with a "prosthetic mouth" in the form of his brother (Exod. 4:14–16), while Isaiah receives a fiery coal to the mouth (Isa. 6:5–7). Ezekiel opens his mouth, takes God's scroll into his body, and tastes honey (Ezek. 3:1–3). Jeremiah also tastes sweetness, but there is fire in his bones (Jer. 15:16, 20:9).

Returning to Ahmed's double description of "queer" as oblique trajectory and nonnormative sexuality, I suggest that both figure into the biblical representation of masculine prophetic embodiment. There is no single norm of the prophetic body, no ideal exemplar against which all other prophets (or parts thereof) are compared. The book of Deuteronomy insists upon the specialness of Moses, claiming "there was never again a prophet like Moses" (Deut. 34:10)—a claim I return to in some detail in chapter 1. But even Moses functions less as an ideal than as one of series of examples of the disturbances, bodily and textual, of prophecy. The prophetic body may be deficient or excessive, or perhaps even both at once. Frequently it tends toward the *queer*, in one or more of the senses of the term. The work of *Are We Not Men?* is to trace these prophetic bodies, to draw out both their similarities and their particularities. While the bodies of the prophets are articulated against the background of biblical norms of embodiment, they do something very different. Exploring this difference—or better, differences—is one emphasis of this book.

A Brief Statement of Argument

The body is essential to prophecy. The body of the prophet is not simply a vessel that is filled with the prophetic word, or a channel through which prophecy passes. Instead, prophecy is staged on and through the body, and cannot occur without it. Prophecy is embodied practice. But however much prophecy depends upon the body, it also makes demands upon it. The prophets do not pass through prophecy unaltered.

Prophecy is an act of survival, and the prophet's body is a site of suffering—though also, at points, of pleasure, as well as transformation. In particular, the masculinity of the prophet is put under pressure by the demands of prophecy and becomes unstable. While the prophets of the Hebrew Bible are, with few exceptions, male, masculinity is a cause of some difficulty for prophetic bodies. To read the prophetic narratives with close attention to the body is also to perceive a series of challenges to the norms of masculinity and masculine embodiment. This challenge does not always occur in the same way, or with the same effects. Each prophetic text offers a somewhat different response, though there are certain commonalities. Thus, tracing the question of masculine embodiment in prophecy means pursuing a pattern of disturbances and instabilities across the texts. Masculinity is unstable in prophecy, and especially as manifested in and through the body of the Hebrew prophet.

These two initial claims, that the body is essential to biblical prophecy and that prophecy disturbs the prophet's masculine embodiment, are essential groundwork for the third component of the argument. I propose that the prophetic body is a queer body. This identification of the prophetic body as queer builds upon the description of masculinity as unstable while also extending beyond it. Queerness, I suggest, describes a particular sort of destabilizing of the prophetic body, its actions, and its desires. "Queer" has ascended to some prominence in the past decades, even in a field as traditionally oriented as biblical studies. As much queer scholarship notes (and as I have already indicated above), the term has multiple, sometimes contradictory meanings. "Queer theory" was originally proposed by Teresa de Lauretis as an alternative to "gay and lesbian studies." De Lauretis sought to create an alternative phrase that was at once broader and more radical.[9] Since then, "queer" has been employed in a wide range of ways: as an updated form of LGBT and other related acronyms, as shorthand for a wide range of nonheteronormative sexualities, as a marker of a particular politics or relation to power, as a verb to describe specific forms of scholarly and hermeneutic activity (as in the now common expression "to queer the text").

My aim in this book is not to pick a side in this ongoing debate over the meaning of "queer," but rather to draw on this multiplicity of meanings to understand the prophetic body in its own multiplicity of instabilities and queer trajectories. I am not invested in adjudicating definitions, but rather in seeing how they might be used. *Are We Not Men?* will trace the ways in which various forms and definitions of queerness influence, intersect with, and productively contaminate each other. I am interested in what sort of work naming the prophetic body as a queer body can do, how it can open up new perspectives on understanding prophecy and embodiment. To borrow from Deleuze and Guattari, "The question . . . is not 'What does it mean?' but rather '*How does it work?*'"[10] This is a reading practice on the side of the possible, if not the proper.

In describing how queerness "works" in prophetic embodiment, Ahmed's work on queerness and phenomenology is instructive. She describes queer phenomenology's project as double, explaining, "To queer phenomenology is also to offer a queer phenomenology. In other words, queer does not have a relation of exteriority to that with which it comes into contact."[11] Building on Ahmed, I suggest that *the queer prophetic body* (as an object) and *queering the prophetic body* (as a critical practice) are not fully separable. Instead, they are entangled objects, practices, and acts. The work of *Are We Not Men?*, then, is twofold: to trace the prophetic body as a queer object and to queer the prophetic body. I want to show both *why* it is productive to describe the prophetic body as queer and *how* we might explore new ways of reading.

In particular, I wish to trace a specific queer object, the prophetic body. Of queer objects, Ahmed writes,

> Queer objects support proximity between those who are supposed to live on parallel lines, *as points that should not meet*. A queer object hence makes contact possible. Or, to be more precise, a queer object would have a sur-face that supports such contact. The contact is bodily, and it unsettles that line that divides spaces as worlds, thereby creating other kinds of connec-tions where unexpected things can happen.[12]

Ahmed's language of unsettling links up with instability of the prophetic body that I have already described. This instability opens a space of queer poten-tial; as with the queer object Ahmed describes, it "makes contact possible." Like the naked buttocks of the prophet Isaiah under the watchful gaze of the Judeans (and the text's readers), the prophetic body brings about queer proximities, unit-ing *points that should not meet*. The surface of the prophetic body makes all kinds of contact possible, as does, at points, the body's interior. And the queerness of the prophet's body is queer precisely in the ways in which "it unsettles the line that divides spaces as worlds" and thereby renders other organizations and trajec-tories conceivable.

Rereading Isaiah's Nakedness, Reimagining the Prophetic Body

In Isaiah's unmasculine, uncomfortable, and humiliating nakedness, it is also pos-sible to trace the beginnings of something else. To begin to explore the space of possibility in the text, I want to turn, briefly, from biblical criticism and queer theory to another form of response: Anne Carson's poem "The Book of Isaiah." Carson's is one of a handful of literary texts to take seriously the nakedness of the prophet (William Blake's *The Marriage of Heaven and Hell* is another).[13] Carson's poem offers a loose narrative about the prophet Isaiah, drawing events and images from the biblical text. Though her text is not explicitly queer, it directs atten-tion to the prophet's body in ways that allow us to think productively about the body, unstable masculinity, and even queerness. Carson imagines Isaiah as caught in a painful, dynamic, transformative struggle with God and Israel alike. Carson opens her account as follows:

> Isaiah awoke angry.
>
> Lapping at Isaiah's ears black birdsong no it was anger.
>
> God had filled Isaiah's ears with stingers.
>
> Once God and Isaiah were friends.
>
> God and Isaiah used to converse nightly, Isaiah would rush into the garden.
>
> They conversed under the Branch, night streamed down.
>
> From the sole of the foot to the head God would make Isaiah ring.
>
> Isaiah wanted a name for the pain, he called it sin.[14]

"The Book of Isaiah" begins with the prophet waking in anger. His body, already present in the opening lines, remains essential throughout the text. Body parts, bodily affects, and theological anxieties mingle uneasily. This is a body taken over, transfixed, and transformed by prophecy. Its pains are at once divinely caused and radically personal, linking the prophet to the deity via—as another line of the poem describes—"a great attraction between them—which Isaiah fought (for and against) for the rest of his life."[15] As the poem unfolds, drawing on events and images from the biblical book of Isaiah (including the incident of the prophet's nakedness), the representation of the prophet gradually evolves into a richer, transformed understanding of prophetic masculinity. Nakedness, vulnerability, and pain are all a part of this transformation.

Over the course of poem, Isaiah's body even becomes feminine—or at least other than ordinarily masculine—as it is overtaken by the divine and filled with milk:

> Isaiah felt sensation below the neck, it was a silk and bitter sensation.
>
> Isaiah looked down.
>
> It was milk forcing the nipples open.
>
> Isaiah was more than whole.
>
> I am not with you I am *in* you, said the muffled white voice of God.
>
> Isaiah sank to a kneeling position.

New pain! said Isaiah.

New contract! said God.

Isaiah lifted his arms, milk poured out of his breasts.

Isaiah watched the milk pour like strings.

It poured up the Branch and across history and down into people's lives and time.

The milk made Isaiah forget about righteousness.[16]

In Carson's (re)vision of Isaiah, the body is physically altered. Here, this alteration takes the form of milk, the maternal fluid forcefully altering male breasts. This prophetic body is labile, unstable, violated, and transformed by the divine word. It is also off-kilter, peculiarly oriented, *queer*. Ahmed writes, "Bodies become straight by tending toward straight objects, such that they acquire their 'direction' and even their tendencies as an effect of this 'tending toward.' "[17] If this is the case, what do we make of the body of a prophet that tends—against its own will—toward a God who enters the body as milk? Certainly there is something queer about this body, in both its secretions and its orientations.

As with Carson's Isaiah, so too with the Hebrew Bible. Many of the poem's most striking images are drawn directly from the text of Isaiah. With her image of the lactating prophet, for example, Carson adapts and repurposes a series of maternal images from Isaiah 40–55. The naked prophet, the prophet's wife, and the reluctant people of Judah are all likewise figures familiar from the book of Isaiah. But it is not simply the inventory of images and metaphors that mark Carson's poem as deeply biblical. Instead, her writing picks up on an important current of the biblical text: the centrality of the prophetic body, as well as its peculiarity. She sets into play the categories of masculinity, prophecy, and the body in a manner already familiar from the biblical authors.

What would it mean to take Carson's reading seriously as an account of the prophetic body? Unlike in Carson's poem, in the biblical text the body of Isaiah appears only occasionally in the text. The text begins with a brief superscript labeling itself as the vision of Isaiah son of Amoz (Isa. 1:1) and jumps immediately into prophetic speech; it is not until the prophet's calling in chapter 6 that his body draws the text's attention. While the call scene is carefully couched as a vision, the bodies contained within it are vividly present. Isaiah sees Yahweh sitting on a throne (6:1); his eyes are drawn from the edge of the divine garment to the seraphim that attend to the deity (6:2–3). Unlike Yahweh's, their bodies are the object of a detailed textual description;

it is only after attending to their wings and voices that Isaiah turns to his own body, bemoaning his "unclean lips" (6:5). A scene of purification using a hot coal follows; it is only after this intervention that the prophet, and his body, are deemed fit for prophecy. As in Carson's version of Isaiah, the body of the prophet is the site of negotiation between the human and the divine. It is subjected, moreover, to painful transformation—by milk, for Carson, by a coal, in Isaiah 6. And as in the poem, there is a certain erotic charge here. Isaiah's eyes are drawn to the edge of Yahweh's garment, but no further (this is in contrast to Ezekiel and his gaze on the divine body, as I take up in chapter 4). The seraphim cover themselves for modesty's sake, and yet this action, too, draws attention to what is covered as much as it defers it. There are no women here; Isaiah's female companion will not appear for another two chapters. But in this wholly masculine space, even the touching of a man's mouth becomes an erotically charged act. Isaiah cannot look; Isaiah must be touched—not directly, but by tongs. (Perhaps the role of these tongs is to enforce a distance between bodies, to diffuse the intimacy of the touch.) While Isaiah's body is not feminized in his calling, it is rendered queer or "unmanned" (to anticipate a term I use in chapter 4) through its openness to the male deity.

There is also a strangeness that attends to the body. Isaiah's bodily transformation with the coal is immediately followed by a command to stop up the eyes and ears of the people to whom the prophet is sent (Isa. 6:9–10). The bodies of the people undergo radical (and forced) modification to become their own obstacles. As I have argued elsewhere, there is a denial of understanding in this moment that (1) hinges on the body and (2) cannot be fully explained by the historical failure of prophecy. Instead, we have an affective excess, tied to the peculiarity of the bodies in question.[18] To further complicate matters, Isaiah himself is a Judean, and thus belongs, as well, in the category of those to whom he is sent to prophesy, and who refuse his message. Isaiah is his own obstacle; his body is part of the national and political body that opposes him.

In the scenes that follow, Isaiah's body appears only occasionally, though the appearances are notable ones—he fathers a child with a female prophet and gives the baby a symbolic name (Isa. 7); there is also the aforementioned nakedness (20:1–5). The prophet's body is useful, perhaps even essential, to his message, and yet it is also difficult and peculiar. When he acts, he is alternately cartoonishly masculine (the fathering of children as a sign of the efficacy of prophecy, 8:1–4) and humiliated (wandering naked, 20:1–5). There is also a skittishness around maternity and the maternal body. While Second Isaiah (40–55) famously contains a number of maternal images, these appear in the text only at the moments when the prophetic body is almost entirely absent. Carson's retelling aside, the body of the prophet almost never appears in Isaiah 40–55, where these images are concentrated.[19]

While there are only a few key narratives involving Isaiah's body, these moments reflect, as well, connections to other prophetic bodies. Isaiah's difficulty with his mouth echoes Moses (Exod. 3–4).[20] Isaiah's fathering of children mirrors Hosea's (Hos. 1).[21] Isaiah's nakedness anticipates Ezekiel's sign acts (Ezek. 4–5).[22] Thus, Carson's linking of Isaiah's body to other biblical texts and moments is itself reflective of the forms of the prophetic body in the biblical texts. Carson herself will return, briefly, in chapter 3. Though my approach in that chapter will differ from Carson's poetic reworking, especially in figuring Yahweh, certain figures reappear: fluidities, the female body, the (unwillingly) transformed masculine. What Carson captures in her version of Isaiah is not limited simply to that prophet. Instead, I suggest that similar currents circulate in and around other prophetic bodies in the biblical text as well. It is the very difficulties that prophets experience with their bodies—nakedness, suffering, pain—that render these bodies queer, while also holding forth the promise of transformation, even a transformation of the very experience of masculinity.

Masculinity and Prophecy

I have already traced, within broad parameters, the argument for the instability and queerness of the prophetic body. Before shifting to offer an overview of the chapters that follow, I want to address two additional important and related issues: masculinity and prophecy. These concepts play a key role in this book. The questions *Why masculinity?* and *Why prophecy?* anticipate the importance of the male body of the prophet in destabilizing and queering the experience of masculinity. *Why masculinity?* calls us to investigate gender as an analytic category and interpretive difficulty. *Why prophecy?* directs attention to the prophet as figure, to prophecy as a social phenomenon, to "prophetic literature" as a body of texts, and to the literary representations of each of these. I consider both of these questions in greater detail below.

Why Masculinity?

Are We Not Men? focuses on masculinity and male bodies as part of a broader interest in analyzing sex and gender in the Bible. Until recently, work on these topics typically concerned women. As several generations of feminist critics have pointed out, the Hebrew Bible is filled with problematic and deeply troubling representations of women. Much of the text involves men; when women appear at all, it is generally in order to bear children or to be used to negotiate power relations between men. In addition, women are frequently the victims of violence, especially sexual violence (for example, Gen. 34; 2 Sam. 13); even the use of feminine metaphors is almost always negative (for example, Hos. 2; Jer. 3:20–25; Ezek. 16, 23). This dismal state of affairs has led to important and insightful scholarly work on women and femininity in the text, which continues to be produced by scholars writing today. In fact, it is this very body of work that led me (and others) to the study of masculinity.

Masculinity has more recently become a topic of great interest in biblical studies.[23] The study of masculinity is often discussed as complementary to, but not necessarily coterminous with, feminist critique.[24] From my perspective, however, the issue of masculinity is a deeply feminist one. So long as "gender" remains a stand-in for "women" or even "female representation and experience," men and masculinity are allowed to pass unproblematized and unconsidered. Men remain ungendered, and the "neutral," unmarked subject remains implicitly masculine. There is nothing neutral, however, about allowing the masculine to pass as an unsexed neutral subject. As Luce Irigaray (an important influence at multiple points in this book) writes, "Everyone claims neutrality without noticing that he is talking about *one* neuter, *his* neuter, and not an absolute neutrality."[25] Elsewhere, Irigaray makes the point even more strongly: "We can assume that any theory of the subject has always been appropriated by the 'masculine.' "[26] Much of her work is dedicated to pushing back against this false neutrality of the masculine; Irigaray seeks to create alternate spaces and orders of meaning "between women." I want to suggest that another important component of this work is gendering the masculine in order to break the link between masculinity and neutrality. My work in masculinity grows out of this feminist commitment to sex the masculine.

The very act of turning the scrutinizing gaze onto the bodies of men is a feminist act, insofar as it challenges the neutrality of the masculine. Much has been written about the female body as an object to be looked at, about scopophilia and the phallic gaze, about the dynamics of the fact that, in the simple but compelling words of John Berger, "men act, women appear."[27] And so when we as readers and theorists, male or female, turn our gaze onto the male prophet's body, onto the *masculine*, this is already a political and critical act. This redirection of the gaze also makes possible a queer reading and a queer male body. So long as gender and sexuality are marked as topics pertaining exclusively to female bodies or male-female heterosexual dynamics, a queer gaze remains invisible. Sexing the masculine thus opens new directions of possibility for gender and sexuality alike. *Are We Not Men?* seeks to think critically about masculinity, but always informed by a feminist perspective. Approaching masculinity queerly is one way to undertake this critical work.

Queer approaches hold much promise for this work. The promise of the queer should not, however, come at the expense of the ground feminist scholarship has fought to gain. In biblical studies as in other disciplines, feminist and queer methods have an uneasy history of coexistence, occasionally slipping into competition. Though they share concerns with sex, gender, sexuality, and the body, they approach these concerns differently. Feminist scholarship is sometimes suspicious of the emphasis on masculinity and male sexuality that tends to dominate queer reading; lesbian-informed approaches offer a possible alternative.[28] A queer approach, meanwhile, may find the feminist methods insufficiently attuned to sexuality, or overly bound up in heterosexual relations between men and women. Still, there is the possibility of common ground. *Are We Not Men?* is intentionally positioned as both feminist and queer. I draw from, and engage with, both critical traditions. Indeed, I would even suggest that doing justice to the prophetic body *demands* a queer and feminist reading. This book offers such a reading.

Why Prophecy?

While masculinity has begun to be a topic of some interest in the study of the Hebrew Bible, most of this work has neglected prophecy.[29] This is unfortunate because prophecy is an especially interesting place to think about masculinity. In the Hebrew Bible, the prophets—dozens, even hundreds of them—are almost entirely men. Just five women are described as prophets in the text: Miriam (Exod. 15:20), Deborah (Judg. 4:4), Huldah (2 Kgs. 22:14 and 2 Chr. 34:22), Noadiah (Neh. 6:14), and the unnamed female prophet in Isaiah (Isa. 8:3). Both Noadiah and Miriam, moreover, are criticized by male prophets (Nehemiah and Moses, respectively) for their prophecies. Not only are the prophets of the Hebrew Bible almost entirely male, but their world, too, is a world almost entirely of men. When women enter this world, it is generally to introduce conflict, to sleep around, or to die. Thus Elijah, for example, battles with the Phoenician queen Jezebel (1 Kgs. 18), the "whoring wife" becomes a favored metaphor across the prophetic writings (for example, Hos. 2, Jer. 3, Ezek. 16), and Ezekiel complains about false female prophets (Ezek. 13:17).

The general nastiness of prophecy toward women has been well documented.[30] But what does masculinity look like when we direct attention to its thoroughly masculine context? Is it stable, or threatened? How is masculinity articulated and contested between men, particularly when some of those men are prophets? One of the first scholars to take up this question, David J. A. Clines, described the prophets as "he-prophets." Clines posits—and I would agree—that "prophecy in the Hebrew Bible is essentially a masculine project"; he goes on to argue that prophetic masculinity is a sort of hypermasculinity: prophets as he-men.[31]

In this book, I identify another sort of answer to this question. I am interested in prophetic masculinity particularly because prophecy is the point at which the ordinary representations of biblical masculinity break down. Prophecy can be read as a series of failures of masculinity—or, alternately, as transformations to the very representation of "masculinity" as a category. Of the biblical prophets, Elijah perhaps comes closest to the "he-prophet." But mostly, the prophets fail to act in a very traditional or accepted masculine way at all, as the following chapters will show. Prophecy presents a series of crises for the category of masculinity. And yet these crises also contain the potential of a masculinity conceived otherwise. Like the milk that forces itself from Isaiah's breasts in Carson's retelling, prophecy forces open the body, challenging its experience of masculinity and threatening its margins with fluidity—sometimes literally so, as in Carson's prophetic lactation. Thus exploring prophetic masculinity means exploring, as well, the possibility of breaking it down and reconfiguring the male body.

An Overview of the Bodies to Follow

The chapters that follow offer an exploration of prophecy, masculinity, and embodiment in the Hebrew Bible. Chapter 1 begins with Moses, purported to be the ideal prophet (Deut. 34:10). But what is happening with Moses' body? All kinds of strange things. The first chapter, "The Materiality of Moses: The Prophet's Body in Trouble," explores the particularities and problems of Moses' body, while setting them against the norms of masculinity that appear elsewhere in the biblical text. Moses' body is *queer*, in many senses of the word. And it is here that we first encounter prophetic masculinity as an alternative to the dominant norms of gender and embodiment found elsewhere in the Hebrew Bible. The prophetic body emerges at once pained and glorious, disabled and celebrated, rendered unmasculine and yet all-too-excessive in its vitality. The body of Moses opens the possibility of conceiving of prophetic masculinity queerly.

The next three chapters of the book offer case studies of prophetic masculinity in three of the literary prophets: Hosea (chapter 2), Jeremiah (chapter 3), and Ezekiel (chapter 4).[32] This collection of chapters crosses the traditional boundaries between "major" and "minor" prophets; it is also not a historical-critical account. Instead, my interest is in exploring the intersections of masculinity and prophecy; these texts each contain especially rich moments to unpack this theme. To draw out the significant moments of masculinity and embodiment, I have also assembled an eclectic set of critical texts and tools, many of them borrowed from outside biblical studies.

The case studies begin in chapter 2, "The Horror of Hosea: Female Bodies and Masculine Anxieties in Hosea 1–3," which brings together the biblical text with horror film. Hosea 1–3, the account of Hosea's marriage, is infamous for its violent representations of female bodies—so infamous that at times it seems there is nothing left to say. This chapter moves beyond this impasse by bringing the biblical text in conversation with the horror film (and in particular, the possession film). Drawing on Carol Clover's theorization of gender and horror, particularly the possession film, this chapter argues that the female body figures masculine anxiety. The text of Hosea 1–3 is fixated on open female bodies as a material ground to work through the problems of masculinity. The male body is a problem for Hosea (and for Yahweh), but it is a problem that is displaced onto the female body. Reading Hosea with and through horror—and in particular, *The Exorcist*—directs attention to the difficulty of embodied prophetic masculinity, as well as the text's attempts to circumvent this problem.

From Hosea, I turn to the prophet Jeremiah, and to a specific extension of his body: his voice. More than any prophet, Jeremiah complains to Yahweh about prophecy, and his complaints frequently invoke the suffering of his body. These protests and laments occur at multiple points in the book but are especially concentrated in a series of passages known as the "Confessions," scattered throughout Jeremiah 12–20. In chapter 3, "The Hysteria of Jeremiah: Gender and Voice in the Confessions," I read Jeremiah's use of voice through the model of hysteria. Hysteria, a disturbance of voice and body primarily associated with female patients, has been an important concern in psychoanalysis, from Sigmund Freud and Josef Breuer's *Studies in Hysteria* and Freud's case study of "Dora" to more recent feminist scholarship. Drawing on this body of work, I argue that the prophet adopts the forms of sound traditionally marked as feminine, even as his body gives voice to what cannot be spoken in language. Like hysteria, Jeremiah's vocal disturbances subvert both the performance of gender and the organization of meaning by offering an alternate, nonmasculine gender performance through sound. But while hysteria destabilizes gender, it does not allow the prophet to escape from it.

From Jeremiah, I shift to Ezekiel, and in particular to Ezekiel 1–5. In these opening chapters of the book of Ezekiel, the prophet experiences a theophany, swallows a scroll, and then embarks upon the "sign acts," a series of bizarre performances. Ezekiel's actions, which include lying on his side for over a year (Ezek. 4:4–6) and eating bread baked on excrement (4:9–13), are dramatic; they are likewise ineffectual and perplexing. Chapter 4, "The Unmanning of Ezekiel: The Prophet's Body Voluptuous and Shattered in Ezekiel 1–5," treats Ezekiel 1–5 as a drama of "unmanning," a term I borrow from Daniel Paul Schreber. Schreber, a German judge, experienced a nervous breakdown in 1893; after several years of institutionalization he gained his freedom and authored a text entitled *Memoirs of My Nervous Illness* (1903). His *Memoirs* describe his calling as a prophet and messiah whose body must be feminized and divinely sexually penetrated to save the world. Since their publication, the *Memoirs* have been an important touchstone for theories of sexuality, embodiment, and desire; I use them to read Ezekiel and to illuminate the demands prophecy places upon masculinity and the male body. Along with hysteria, unmanning provides a useful model for thinking through prophecy, both in the suffering it imposes on the body and in the queer openness and transformation it makes possible. The unmanned body is a new way of understanding the prophetic body.

Chapter 5, "The Queer Prophetic Body," brings together the specific arguments of chapters 1–4 into a general description of the prophetic body. I return to the argument already stated in this introduction, that is, the prophetic body is a queer body, sketching out some major tendencies of queer prophetic embodiment. In addition to the case studies set forth in chapters 1–4, I briefly introduce two additional prophetic bodies, Jonah and Miriam. These examples serve to refine further the description of the prophetic body. Building on the example of Miriam, this chapter attends to the pain of the prophetic body, linking such pain to questions of the legibility of queer life and the coercive demands of happiness. It likewise considers, briefly, the possibility of reading the prophetic body as queer assemblage. The aim of these engagements is twofold: first, to illustrate some specific connections between the prophetic body and contemporary theoretical work, and second, to demonstrate the value of the prophetic body—and indeed biblical texts, objects, and concepts more generally—for contemporary scholarship beyond the traditional boundaries of biblical scholarship. The book concludes with a concise chapter of final reflections.

Some Brief Comments about Method

With the overview of the chapters set forth, I want to offer some brief comments on my method. The pursuit of prophetic masculinity has led me to explore uncommon juxtapositions and intertexts. Often, I have found a modern parallel illuminating in ways that either ancient texts or conventional forms of biblical scholarship are not. I have already suggested that Carson's poetic response to Isaiah both complicates the text and opens a new space for critical engagement. Carson is a poet and classicist, not a biblicist—and yet it is her distance from the biblical text, as much as her intimacy with it, that gives her reading its power. In the studies that follow, I have looked even further afield for intertexts. Some are artistic, some critical, some pathological or perverse; often, they cross classifications and categories. All function to destabilize and challenge the seeming stability of the biblical text.

Frequently, my method tends toward playfulness; I am less interested in an orthodox application of "theory" to "text" than in placing various forms of text together to see what might emerge. Here, an important touchstone for my method is Brian Massumi's *Parables for the Virtual*. Massumi argues that simply applying one text or discipline to another is both totalizing and unproductive. Instead, he proposes that scholars embrace a model of "shameless poaching," oriented toward connections and attuned to affect. Setting aside preoccupations with fidelity and good faith reading creates unexpected effects, "producing a creative tension that may play itself out in any number of ways."[33] Concepts are mobile, but their relocation from one context is never perfect. Instead, an affective residue clings to uprooted concepts. And this lingering affect produces unexpected effects, generating what Massumi terms "conceptual struggle" and "creative tension," as well as new configurations impossible to predict beforehand. All this is implied in the language of "poaching"—an act that assumes that something of the original context remains with the object even as it is removed from this context. Poaching is illicit, improper, and dangerous; it is also thrilling. This holds true when the object of this poaching is conceptual.

Massumi's concern is with science and the humanities; I propose adopting a similar understanding of the relationship between "theory" and the Bible. In bringing together the prophetic texts of the Hebrew Bible with texts from contemporary theory (both center and margins), my aim is to engender a "creative tension" similar to what Massumi describes. This tension is produced, in part, through the collision of affects. It is also important to note that the relation works in two directions. The export of theoretical concepts to the world of biblical prophecy does not leave these concepts unchanged. Instead, there is a bleed.[34] Ahmed describes affects as "sticky," clinging to words and objects.[35] This idea of stickiness offers another way to set into words the unexpected consequences of bringing together biblical and nonbiblical texts. Thus while my focus will remain on the biblical side of this relationship, I occasionally attend to the ways in which the contemporary texts are touched.

There is one other feature of my method that I wish to address: my use of psychoanalysis and psychoanalytic texts. A majority of the chapters in *Are We Not Men?* engage with psychoanalysis, in varying ways. At points, I turn to Freud himself, though I do not always use his texts in the ways that he—or the psychoanalytic orthodoxies that emerged in his wake—intended (more shameless poaching here). I am particularly interested, for example, in Freud and Breuer's *Studies in Hysteria*, which contains ideas that Freud himself later rejected (most famously the "seduction theory"). In other cases, I turn to the voices of Freud's patients (such as Dora) or subjects (Judge Schreber, whom Freud never met but whose memoir furnished the father of psychoanalysis with much material). By leveraging these suppressed or alternative voices against the "master narratives" of psychoanalysis, I aim to show new ways in which the "texts" of psychoanalysis, broadly understood, may be used to read biblical texts.

Taken together, these various moments of engagement suggest a broad spectrum of possible ways to read *with* psychoanalysis. This multiplicity of possible responses is itself reflective of the range of engagements between queer theory and psychoanalysis. As queer theories or biblical scholars—or both—we can read with Freud, or against him. We can privilege the silenced voices against the master narrative. We can even turn the prophets against Freud, taking their words and bodies not as symptoms or objects of study, but as radically other hermeneutics. As should now be clear, there is no single theory of psychoanalysis and biblical texts here. Instead, I have aimed to show the breadth of the terrain, the many and complex possibilities of engagement. Indeed, the use of psychoanalysis throughout *Are We Not Men?* provides a model for bringing together biblical texts and theory. As with psychoanalysis, so too with other critical and theoretical discourses. This, in turn, parallels the additive, generative method of scholarship described by Massumi. Shameless poaching, sticky fingers, but in the pursuit of new configurations of knowledge and desire, and a new way of understanding the prophetic body.

Details to Watch out For

In addition to close readings *of* prophetic bodies, the chapters that follow will sketch a number of parallels *between* prophetic bodies in the text. These are brought together in greater detail in chapter 5, "The Queer Prophetic Body." However, I want to anticipate the most significant here.

The Body Disturbed

The chapters that follow argue that the disturbance of the body is a necessary part of prophecy. The body of the prophet cannot pass unaltered or untouched. Nor does the body serve simply as a conduit for prophecy, transmitting the prophetic message from Yahweh to the prophet, or perhaps even onward to the people. Instead, the very entry into the space of prophecy is an entry into bodily alteration. In some cases, this transformation of the body is a specific, punctual event, as when Isaiah's mouth is purified by a fiery coal (Isa. 6:6–7). In other narratives, the alteration or disturbance of the body is an ongoing process, as in Ezekiel's sign acts, the subject of my chapter 4. In still other cases, the body experiences a shifting sequence of afflictions and alterations, as Jeremiah describes in his Confessions (chapter 3). What these moments share is an emphasis upon the body not as epiphenomenon, but as essential part of prophecy. There is no prophecy without the body.

The Use of Women

A second theme that recurs across these chapters is the use of women. Prophecy is largely an affair by and for men, at least in the biblical world (or more accurately, the world that the authors of the Hebrew Bible imagine). There are not many women to be found, still fewer in the prophetic texts. When they do appear, it is frequently in the form of sexualized or maternalized fantasies of whores, wives, and mothers. Another occasional occurrence of women is as opponents to male prophets, whether religiously, as in the case of the female prophets that Ezekiel decries (Ezek. 13:17), or politically, as in the case of Jezebel (1 Kgs. 16:29–34, 18:17–40, 19:1–3.) Still, this relative absence of women does not mean that the text is uninterested in women—to the contrary. The *figure of woman*—and here I intentionally describe not real women, but rather their representation in a masculine economy of fantasy—is highly productive for thinking through questions of prophecy, embodiment, and masculinity. As Irigaray writes, "Theoretically there would be no such thing as woman. She would not exist. The best that can be said is that she does *not exist yet*."[36] Woman's lack of existence, however, is no obstacle to her being used as raw material to be formed into masculine discourses, ideologies, and fantasies.

Repeatedly, biblical texts use female bodies "to think with," to provide an occasion or ground to work through other issues. At times, the female body represents a displacement of masculine anxiety; I argue this is especially the case in the opened female bodies of Hosea. At other points, the male prophet attempts to claim for himself a feminized body or feature of embodiment, an argument I introduce with Moses (chapter 1) and trace further in reference to Daniel Paul Schreber in chapter 4. Masculinity is negotiated in and on the bodies of women; not infrequently, this negotiation is violent. The use of women thus surfaces as a concern throughout *Are We Not Men?*

Hysteria, Unmanning, and Other Structures of Understanding

At multiple points in this text, I draw on nonprophetic models to offer an understanding of the prophetic body. Two of the most significant of these are hysteria (discussed in chapter 3) and unmanning (discussed in chapter 4). Notably, each of these chapters engages with a major text or texts from the history of psychoanalysis: Freud and Breuer's *Studies in Hysteria* and Freud's subsequent case history of "Dora," formally titled "Fragment of an Analysis of a Case of Hysteria," and Daniel Paul Schreber's *Memoirs of My Nervous Illness*, respectively. In each case, I argue that the text stands in meaningful relation to biblical prophecy and helps illuminate its structure. Using the *Studies in Hysteria* and the Dora case, I argue that *prophecy is structured as hysteria*. From Schreber's memoir, meanwhile, I adopt the concept of "unmanning"—Schreber's term for a radical transformation of his male body into something totally other—to suggest that *prophecy unmans the body*.

While psychoanalytical texts are central to these arguments, the engagement is not straightforward. My use of hysteria, for example, draws less on Freud and Breuer's work than on the case studies themselves as textual objects of interest. Frequently, my readings run against the grain of Freud and Breuer's original works; in doing so, I contribute to an already substantial feminist literature on hysteria. With Schreber, meanwhile, my engagement is emphatically not with Freud's reading, but with Schreber's own words. I suggest, moreover, that Schreber's memoir can be read as a sophisticated and meaningful negotiation of the problem of embodied masculine subjectivity confronted with an aggressive male deity. In approaching these texts, *Are We Not Men?* models a pliant, flexible, and playful form of engagement, one in which biblical texts and unruly prophets have a great deal to say to the "master discourse" of psychoanalytic textuality.

Fluidity and Openness

Masculine embodiment is not simply conceived in the prophetic texts; it is also reimagined. The challenges and difficulties of the male body are not without their own fantasies of new and alternate forms of masculine embodiment. While some of these new orders of masculinity depend upon the subjection or subjugation of the feminine (as anticipated in "The Use of Women," above), others originate in the *male* body. I suggest, in particular, that fluidity and openness offer a number of possibilities for reconceiving of the male prophetic body. The opening of the male body occurs at multiple moments, and in multiple ways, in the text. At times, it is primarily symbolic, as when the word of Yahweh comes to the prophet (a frequent opening line in the prophetic books). At other moments, it is fiercely literal, as in Isaiah 6:5–7, Ezekiel 3:1–3, and several other instances this book will explore. Openness functions doubly: both as an event experienced on or by the prophetic body, and as a figure for the "opening up" of the category of masculinity.

Openness is also linked, in my reading, to fluidity. In using the term *fluidity*, I refer both to the metaphorical possibility of change and transformation and to the literal instances of fluids in the text. Ezekiel's self-imposed refusal to drink notwithstanding (Ezek. 4:11),[37] all sorts of liquids circulate in and around the prophetic bodies. Blood, water, tears, and semen all appear. Fluidity also offers a way of highlighting the materiality of the body. The prophet's body is more than voice and gesture; it is also a messy, leaky assembly of blood and bones, wounds and pains. Emphasizing fluidity and openness in and around the prophetic body is one way of noting, and attending to, this materiality. Materiality is also key to the possible transformation of the masculine. I have already alluded to Irigaray's critique of the "neutral" masculine; this is linked, as well, to a critique of the bodiless male subject. In response, Irigaray and other feminist philosophers have argued that attending to the male body as *body* is essential to any reimagining of masculinity.[38] And this means taking seriously the fluids in and around the male body, as well as that body's openness.

The opened male body is a body that breaks with the norms of embodiment. No longer closed off, the body becomes vulnerable. Insofar as identity is predicated on a solid, impermeable masculinity, it too is threatened by the opening of the body. This threat also contains the possibility for new forms of masculinity to emerge. Insisting upon the fluidity of the male body counters a masculinity predicated on borders, separations, and a repudiation of the feminine. Instead, the open, fluid body may become a queer prophetic body. Without appropriating the bodies of women—a risk at multiple points in biblical attempts to rethink masculinity—it envisions another sort of masculine embodiment as possible. This is masculinity as labile, unstable, and in flux. By arguing that prophetic masculinity opens up to, at moments, masculine embodiment as fluidity, this book will also suggest that prophetic texts about embodiment are a valuable source for the larger contemporary theoretical issue of rethinking and working through embodiment.

Why This Study Matters

Queer bodies, queer masculinities, prophets, problems, potential transformations—there is a great deal swirling around here, and a great deal at stake. Framing the prophetic body as queer adds to the growing body of literature bringing together biblical texts with queer theory and related work. While the prophetic literature has been largely underrepresented in these developments, *Are We Not Men?* addresses this lack. At the same time, understanding the prophetic body as queer offers a new way of understanding the specifics of prophetic embodiment. Queerness, as both an obliqueness and a sexuality, illuminates the prophetic body.

The queer reading of the prophet's body and the reading of the prophet's body as queer are projects that emerge together, supplementing and supporting each other.

Thinking about the male body, and not simply masculinity as such, is also an important critical gesture. Gendering the masculine, refusing to let it pass as neutral and unmarked, offers a corrective to prior texts and reading practices alike. No longer should the female body alone be forced to bear the weight of gender, to be figured as a deviation from the original, unsexed (masculine) norm. Thinking squarely about male bodies, and male prophetic bodies in particular, provides an opportunity to rethink what male embodiment means. Against a dominant narrative, ancient and modern, of the male body as whole, complete, and self-contained (and frequently strong, abled, and *hard* as well), the Hebrew prophets demand, and contain, alternate forms of masculinity. The bodies of the prophets are opened, pained, and fluid; they stand in opposition to and ultimately queer an image of masculinity as a strict control of the body. As such, they are a crucial, underdeveloped resource for thinking about masculinities, in the Bible and after it.

This altered and opened understanding of masculinity can also lead to new understandings of prophecy. Prophecy is not simply a performance of power. Neither is it simply a virtuoso act of transmission from divine words to human ones. Instead, prophecy is an embodied practice, one that is located on and through male bodies. Too often, the body seems to get in the way. But if we start with the body, instead of treating it as an aftereffect or a nuisance that interferes with the practice of (or proper study of) prophecy, we find the text opened to new possibilities and orders of meaning, even as we find the body itself increasingly queer. We can reconceive of biblical prophecy as a deeply embodied practice, one that pains, transforms, and alters the gender performance of the body.

All told, the biblical text does not exist in a vacuum. The text has significant influence over modern understandings, inside and outside of scholarly and religious communities. This is especially true when the issues at stake are as fraught as gender, bodies, and what it means to be a man. To this end, I hope this book will contribute, as well, to these conversations—not simply by offering a set of answers, but also by offering a model for reframing questions. What does it mean to have a body, to be a prophet, to perform masculinity? What sorts of alternate masculinities does the biblical text contain, hidden away in its pages? What might we do with these masculinities, how might we use them? These are questions that we can begin to ask, and that this book may help to answer.

1

The Materiality of Moses

THE PROPHET'S BODY IN TROUBLE

NO ONE KNOWS where Moses is buried. There is a lengthy and famous midrash that describes the prophet Jeremiah learning to mourn the destruction of the Temple. As part of this process, he is commanded to raise the patriarchs and Moses from their graves to testify against Israel. The patriarchs pose no difficulty, being easily located in the Cave of Machpelah. But Moses—where is Moses to be found? Jeremiah protests to God, who provides a workaround, the most famous of prophets is raised, and the midrash continues.[1] Still, this moment points to an important feature of the biblical Moses narrative—the prophet's grave remains a secret; as Deuteronomy has it, "no one knows his burial place to this day" (Deut. 34:6).

Moses' missing body is often taken as a sign of his power. At the same time, the fact that his burial place is unknown is a convenient means to prevent its veneration. If there is no location, there can be no shrine erected upon it. And yet the absence of Moses' grave is only one in a series of complications and difficulties involving his body. In the account of his death, we are assured that Moses' body is flawless, with perfect vision and sustained vigor (Deut. 34:7). At other points in the text, however, his body is described in quite different terms. From birth onward, Moses' body is perceived by onlookers as different, special, frightening, *other*. This judgment, first passed by the prophet's mother (Exod. 2:2), follows him until his death. Moses possesses "a heavy mouth and heavy tongue" (4:10), which threaten his vocal performance. At the time of his prophetic calling, he is afflicted with a scaly skin disease (4:6–7); later in his life, he is forced to veil his face, which has begun to glow and terrify the people he serves (34:29–35). In between these events, Moses' life is threatened by Yahweh and saved by the blood of his son's circumcision (4:24–26). He also channels divine power in battle, yet finds himself unable to hold up his own hands without assistance (17:11–12).

At almost every moment that his body enters into the text, it is marked as somehow *other*. Moses' body is at once glorious and insufficient, wounded and excessive, threatened and threatening. The difficulties he will experience as prophet—and for Moses, these difficulties are many—are written on his body. Indeed, his somatic problems are constitutive of his status as prophet. And yet they also point beyond simply difficulty. In its weakness, vulnerability, and difference, Moses' body is in many ways a queer body, even as the stories that swirl around it queer the notion of prophecy and the forms of masculine embodiment it engenders.

While the other chapters of this book position the prophetic body against contemporary contrasts and analogues, this chapter is concerned wholly with Moses. "There was never again a prophet like Moses," Deuteronomy 34:10 insists. Given such insistences, it seems a bit unsporting to demand parallels. Instead of positioning Moses against other bodies, I will read the prophet's body against itself, drawing out the multiple representations of body parts and embodiment more generally that vie uneasily in the text. I will begin with a brief description of the norms of masculinity and embodiment, norms against which the text articulates Moses' difficult body and troubled masculinity. This, in turn, leads to a detailed analysis of the many peculiarities of Moses' body from birth to death, from good baby to beautiful corpse—but with all sorts of strangeness and even terror in between. In its weakness, vulnerability, and difference, Moses' body breaks with the hegemonic masculine norms of the text. Instead, Moses presents an alternate performance of masculinity and an alternate mode of masculine embodiment. The final work of this chapter is to trace the contours of this reconfigured masculinity, as well as to anticipate its influence on other prophetic bodies. The example of Moses suggests that prophecy at once depends upon, disturbs, and alters the body of the prophet. If prophecy is written on the body, then the body also displays the transformation of prophetic masculinity.

The text does not tell us where Moses is buried. But even if his grave is missing, his body is all too present (and often, all too strange) in the biblical text. Let us, then, turn to this body.

Prolegomena: Masculinity, the Male Body, and the Hebrew Bible

In order to understand how the narrative of Moses disrupts the norms of masculinity and embodiment, it is first necessary to establish what these norms are. I will not offer a comprehensive survey of biblical masculinity studies or biblical masculinity here. I do, however, wish to highlight a few important points to set up the discussion of Moses that follows. In the Hebrew Bible, masculinity is not the necessary and inevitable consequence of a male-sexed body; neither is it a rigid binary identity. Instead, as elsewhere in the ancient Near East and

Mediterranean, masculinity is centrally a matter of degree. It is established relationally, as part of what Virginia Burrus terms "a dynamic spectrum or gradient of relative masculinities."[2] The relations of sexual penetration offer one way of determining relative masculinities, with the active, penetrative partner (ordinarily male) establishing his masculinity over and against the penetrated partner (male or female).[3] However, the performance of masculinity does not depend exclusively on sexual practice or object choice, any more than it depends upon biological sex. Instead, masculinity is a complicated and shifting negotiation of body, sex, sexuality, and performance.

Academic studies of masculinity often describe a plurality of masculinities within a specific cultural context. Among these masculinities, there is a particular importance granted to "hegemonic masculinity," a term that first appears in sociology but is quickly borrowed into other disciplines. "Hegemonic masculinity" describes a culturally specific and culturally valued form of masculine performance.[4] While the theory has undergone refinement since its introduction in the 1980s—the complexity of the relationship between hegemonic and subordinated masculinities, and between masculinities and femininities, has been increasingly acknowledged by scholars[5]—it remains significant. Hegemonic masculinity furnishes a cultural ideal of masculine performance. It simultaneously sustains a specific hierarchy of gendered power relations and provides fringe benefits to male bodies that do not themselves achieve the hegemonic ideal. This concept has proven to be a useful analytic category for biblical studies as well, particularly in assessing how the biblical text constructs and enforces norms of masculinity.[6] The hegemonic masculine subject in the Hebrew Bible is aggressive, dominating others (violently as well as perhaps sexually); he is also deeply concerned with honor. Sexual potency and the fathering of children (particularly of sons) also function as important demonstrations of masculinity.[7]

The hegemonic masculine ideal evokes, in turn, a specific sort of male body. The norms of domination, virility, and paternity elevate strength, agility, and power as bodily ideals. The bodily ideal is likewise of an abled body, as work on disability studies and gender by Thomas Hentrich and Carole Fontaine has shown.[8] There is also a concern that the body not be overly open or leaky. The regulation of sexual activity and accompanying concern with purity is linked to two discourses of the body: the investment in (male) bodily wholeness, which is breached by fluids and discharges (Lev. 15:1–18), and the concern with avoiding association with the female body, which is leaky, unstable, and contaminating (15:19–30). Bodily wholeness—itself associated with male bodies and not female ones—is a major concern of the purity laws and the legal texts more generally.[9] Beauty has also sometimes been associated with hegemonic masculinity, most notably by David Clines, though this claim has not passed without complication and critique.[10]

In spite of the power of hegemonic masculinity as an ideal in the text (and as a textual object for interpreters), it is not the only type of masculine performance along the gradient of masculinities. Instead, hegemonic masculinity is negotiated over and against other masculinities. Nor is the hegemonic position intrinsically stable. Instead, the contrary holds true. As Roland Boer writes,

> Despite the effort in the Bible to present a series of overlapping ruling and dominating perspectives, all the way from social organization to sexuality, not to mention religion, they are very shaky indeed. Or to put it even more forcefully, the very act of asserting dominance is inherently unstable. Subversion lurks in every murky doorway and under every bed. Hegemony is continually undermined from within and without.[11]

The text simultaneously constructs hegemonic masculinity as an ideal and places this ideal under pressure. There is no simple dominant form that masculinity assumes. Instead, as Boer indicates, instabilities and difficulties are present in the text from the beginning. Masculinity in the Bible, even hegemonic masculinity, is unstable—"shaky indeed."

My reading of the body of Moses traces a specific shakiness in the representation of biblical masculinity, one that is bound up with the premier prophet himself. Moses is sometimes taken as a model of hegemonic masculinity in the biblical narrative.[12] However, when we examine Moses more closely—and in particular Moses' body—the prophet's masculine performance appears increasingly unstable. His body does some very strange things in the course of the text.

Moses' Body

There is no single difference or peculiar feature that marks Moses' body as radically other. Instead, the effect of Moses' body—and the resulting challenge prophetic embodiment poses to hegemonic masculinity—is cumulative. This bodily otherness is hinted at when Moses is born and again at his death; it also appears at multiple moments within his lifespan. It is likewise dispersed across the prophet's body, emphasizing both specific body parts (hands, face) and a more general bodily condition. And so before theorizing Moses' body as a whole I will consider the essential moments in his experience of embodiment. What follows is an account of the most important features of Moses' prophetic body.

The Good Baby

Moses' body is special from birth. When he is born, his mother immediately observes that he is "good" (*ṭôḇ*):[13] "The woman conceived and bore a son; and when she saw that he was good, she hid him three months" (Exod. 2:2). Moses' mother's words are unusual; the quality of babies is not frequently remarked upon in the Bible. When information is given at the time of a child's birth, it generally marks a present or future narrative significance, as in the births of Jacob and Esau (Gen. 25:22–26), Peleg (Gen. 10:25), and Ichabod (1 Sam. 4:21–22). Unlike these other narratives, however, the details given about Moses' birth do not serve to explain either his name or the general condition of the world at the time. Thus the mention of Moses as *ṭôḇ*, while brief, is not simply a literary mechanism:[14] in addition to telling us something about the narrative, the identification of the infant Moses as *ṭôḇ* tells us something about the prophet's body as body.

Moses is born at a moment in the Exodus narrative when Pharaoh has ordered the death of all Hebrew boys (Exod. 1:22). This imbues his mother's identification of her newborn child as "good" with pathos. What makes this boy child "good"? *Ṭôḇ* may refer to the infant Moses' moral or ethical goodness or to his appearance; *ṭôḇ* can refer to good looks, though usually it bears this meaning when used in conjunction with a longer description or phrase.[15] It may also predict Moses' future importance, which his mother somehow perceives as she looks upon his infant form. Or *ṭôḇ* may mean not "good" or "good-looking" but simply "viable," implying that the infant Moses is less exceptional than (barely) acceptable. This is the reading advanced by S. Levin, who has argued that something about the physical appearance of the baby created initial doubt—perhaps a cleft lip or palate, given Moses' own descriptions of his "heavy tongue" subsequently in the narrative.[16] In Levin's reading, Moses' mother's words are less a celebration than an assessment of visible bodily difference or even deformity.

This last reading, while provocative, seems a stretch—the mother who looks at her newborn child and callously pronounces him "viable" is perhaps a better fit for dystopian science fiction. However, it is valuable insofar as it directs attention toward Moses' body as body. Too often an emphasis on Moses' *goodness* (whatever this goodness should mean) overwhelms any attention paid to Moses' *embodiment*. Whatever their specific meaning, Moses' mother's words are triggered by the sight of the infant boy. Furthermore, her judgment suggests that there is something other about this child, and about the child's body. This suggestion gains credibility when the prophet's body reappears two chapters later, in adult form. When Moses receives his prophetic calling, his body, already marked as *ṭôḇ* by his mother and the text, is again brought under scrutiny.

Heavy Mouth, Heavy Tongue

The most famous of Moses' bodily afflictions are his "heavy mouth" and "heavy tongue" (*kᵉḇaḏ-peh ûkᵉḇaḏ lāšôn*, Exod. 4:10). These difficulties with the prophet's mouth first figure in his call story, when Moses raises his difficulty in producing intelligible speech as an objection to Yahweh's call (4:10–16). Later, he repeats the description, but with the variation of "uncircumcised lips" (*ʿᵃral śᵉp̄āṯāyim*, 6:12, 6:30). The precise meanings of a "heavy mouth" and a "heavy tongue" are ambiguous. Mouth (*peh*) and tongue (*lāšôn*) refer to parts of the body, but may also be used as metonyms for "speech." Heavy (*kᵉḇaḏ*) refers to some sort of malfunction; what exactly this malfunction is remains unclear.[17] The problem may be a difficulty with enunciation (such as a stutter or soft or slurred voice),[18] or it may indicate a physical deformity, perhaps a cleft palate.[19] It is also possible that the meaning of the phrase is metaphorical, indicating a lack of eloquence (Moses is an inferior public speaker) or of linguistic competence (Moses is unable to speak Hebrew and/or Egyptian, or at least unable to do so fluently).[20]

Let us take these variant readings in turn. If "heavy mouth" and "heavy tongue" suggest a physical disability such as a cleft palate, then they mark the otherness of Moses' body. Jeremy Schipper has demonstrated the existence of "a meaningful conceptual category regarding physical difference" in the ancient Near East.[21] Visible physical disability thus sets the prophet apart, separating him from the Israelite norm of embodiment even as it draws attention to his own othered body. This particular interest in Moses' body does not diminish if we follow the second reading and take "heavy of mouth" and "heavy of tongue" to refer to a difficulty in speech or enunciation. Such a difficulty with speech represents the interference of the body in the transmission of meaning. An affliction such as a stutter signals the stubborn materiality of the body, its refusal to surrender and vanish, leaving only pure voice.[22] Instead, the body is present, and the body presents trouble. Even if Moses' difficulty lies in linguistic competence (though this reading seems least likely),[23] we can still see the difficulty with language production directing attention to the body, which produces sound but no meaning.

What is really at stake here is not the specifics of Moses' condition but rather the more general status of Moses' body as an insufficient body. The text strongly suggests that Moses is not simply offering an idle protest of his own lack of rhetorical skill. Yahweh himself acknowledges Moses' assessment of his powers of speech as valid. Instead of refuting or dismissing Moses' complaint, he provides Moses with a solution: a prosthetic mouth in the form of his brother Aaron, "who shall speak for you to the people; he shall serve as a mouth for you, and you shall serve as God for him" (Exod. 4:16). This response validates Moses' assessment of his own bodily lack without, however, healing or otherwise altering it. Whatever bodily problems precede prophecy will last within it; unlike Isaiah (Isa. 6:5–7),

Moses will not have his mouth purified or restored. Instead, his body is metaphorically and functionally extended into the body of his brother, Aaron, who will become his "mouth." The prophet receives his own prophet, his own earthly oral prosthesis. This doubling of the structure of prophecy—Aaron is to Moses as Moses is to Yahweh—further thematizes the strangeness of the prophet's body, at once central and inadequate, necessary and displaced.

A Scaly Hand, Faltering Arms

In the course of his prophecy, Moses' body is also struck by disease and difficulty. While his heavy tongue is a permanent affliction (though not one, it seems, that seriously interferes with the practice of prophecy—Moses talks a great deal after his original complaint to God and interview with Pharaoh), other problems afflict him intermittently. In the call story, the prophet is afflicted with *ṣāraʿat*, "scale disease," rendering his body abject. The abject describes that which is disgusting, excluded, loathsome. Wounds, bodily secretions, excrement, and decay are all forms of the abject; as Julia Kristeva notes, they mark the borders of life and death.[24] The abject defiles "the self's clean and proper body," just as scale disease marks Moses.[25]

The scale disease is sent by Yahweh, part of an attempt to persuade Moses of his prophetic calling. After Moses expresses reluctance, Yahweh instructs him to place his hand in his cloak; and "and when he took it out, his hand was scaly, like snow" (*mᵉṣōraʿat kaššāleg*, Exod. 4:6). Like so many of Moses' bodily problems, the precise meaning of the words is uncertain. The participle *mᵉṣōraʿat* from the verb *ṣrʿ* refers to a skin disease with a wasting effect. While numerous specific ailments have been proposed (including leprosy—known in modern times as Hansen's disease—vitiligo, psoriasis, or some other rash or fungal infection), the condition does not seem to correspond to any specific disease.[26] The term *ṣāraʿat* suggests scaliness and so, following Jacob Milgrom, I will translate it with the intentionally general "scale disease"; its primary signification is of impurity staged on the body.[27]

Moses' *ṣāraʿat*, while temporary, thematizes the alterity, abjection, and power of his body. Scale disease marks Moses' body as impure and threatening. Whatever is afflicted with scale disease—people and body parts but also houses—must be set apart, removed from the community until it is purified (Lev. 14). Thus the transformation of Moses' hand portends Moses' exclusion from his community as prophecy increases his difference, as well as the repeated alterity of his body. At the same time, the scales on Moses' hand are a marker of his own power. Drawing attention to the scale disease that strikes Miriam (Num. 12), Propp even suggests, "Within the Elohistic source, *ṣāraʿat* appears to be the specific penalty for doubting Moses' authority."[28] In Exodus 4:6, the particular twist is that Moses occupies both roles: the divinely empowered prophet and the divinely punished doubter. Ṣāraʿat is a sign of the prophet's power, even when the unfortunate bearer of the sign is Moses himself.

The motif of Moses' body as afflicted medium returns in new form after the prophet's great success in leading the Israelites out of Egypt. In Exodus 17, the Israelites fight the Amalekites at Rephidim, and Moses' body is directly implicated in the struggle. The text recounts,

> Whenever Moses held up his hand, Israel prevailed, but when he lowered his hand, Amalek prevailed. But Moses' hands grew weary; so they took a stone and put it under him, and he sat on it. Aaron and Hur held up his hands, one on one side, and the other on the other side, so his hands were steady until the sun set. (Exod. 17:11–12)

The Israelites' success in battle depends directly upon the postures of Moses' body. And yet it is beyond Moses' capacity to maintain his body in the proper form. He is forced to rely upon the assistance of others, to sit while others hold up his hands. And it is Joshua, not Moses, who actually leads the Israelite army into battle—another bodily extension that recalls Moses' earlier dependency on Aaron, his prosthetic mouth.

On the surface, this story of the battle with the Amalekites is one of passing weakness—Moses is able, with assistance, to lift his hands; the Israelites win their battle, and Moses commemorates the victory by erecting an altar. And yet the moment of weakness in the middle of the narrative is as significant as the triumphant conclusion.[29] Moses' drooping arms suggest not just weakness but also emasculation. Furthermore, the prophet's struggle to hold up his hands recalls his previous struggles with speech. As Marc Shell notes, difficulties in speech and difficulties in mobility—paradigmatically, the stutter and the limp—are often mapped onto each other.[30] Furthermore, the text figures both problems as heaviness—first a heavy mouth and heavy tongue, now heavy (kᵉbēdîm) hands (Exod. 17:12). These two tropes of bodily difficulty resonate with each other and reinforce the overarching representation of Moses' body as both weak and extraordinary, a conduit for divine power that requires assistance of its own. Shell writes, "God as ventriloquist needed a spokesman because He was unable to speak directly to the people. We will see that the dummy Moses, whom he called on to speak for Him, was both too much and too little like God to do the job."[31] Here again, Moses' body is called into the service of the prophetic message and, at the same time, altered by it. Prophecy occupies and overtakes the body. The prophet is at once powerful and powerless, an architect and an instrument of the victory. At the same time, the power of Moses is also what undercuts his masculinity.

The Body Radiant and Veiled

The scale disease that Moses experiences in his call story is a temporary affliction. Though it prefigures the transformations, both physical and social, that prophecy will bring upon Moses, it does not permanently alter his body. And yet prophecy does have permanent bodily consequences. Moses spends forty days on Mount Sinai without eating or drinking (Exod. 34:28). This feat of restraint presages a still greater bodily transformation. When he descends from Mount Sinai, beams of light stream from Moses' face, frightening the people until they hear his voice and recognize him:

> As Moses came down from Mount Sinai, with the two tablets of the covenant in his hand coming down from the mountain, Moses did not know that the skin of his face radiated light [*qāran ʿôr pānāyw*] from speaking with him. When Aaron and all the Israelites saw Moses, the skin of his face was radiating light [*wᵉhinnê qāran ʿôr pānāyw*] and they were afraid to come near him. But Moses called to them; and Aaron and all the leaders of the congregation returned to him, and Moses spoke with them. Afterward all the Israelites approached, and he instructed them in all that Yahweh had said to him on Mount Sinai. (Exod. 34:29–32)

The text presents a scene of terror as well as transfiguration. The radiance of Moses' face distances him from the other Israelites, socially and physically, and makes him more like Yahweh.[32] Moses and Yahweh speak face to face (Deut. 34:10); it is fitting that it is Moses' face that is transformed. This transformation, moreover, is not simply an increase in brightness, but also a physical change. The Hebrew verb *qrn*, which is used to describe the light streaming from Moses' face, is used elsewhere to mean "to sprout horns."[33] The semantic range of the term thus suggests that the light beaming from Moses' visage has some kind of solidity and heft to it. This materiality of light occurs in other ancient Near Eastern texts, as in the *melammu*, a blinding mask of light possessed by the Akkadian gods, "a somatic mark of divine rulership."[34] As Seth Sanders has demonstrated, these conceptual categories hold for ancient Israel as well. Sanders writes, "Moses' face could, quite literally, radiate horns, and the need to translate the term as either divine radiance or physical protuberance is merely a side-effect of our conceptual categories, irrelevant to ancient Israelite ideas."[35] Thus the light that streams forth is corporealized in Moses, becoming an extension of his body. Unlike the normative modification of the male Israelite body, the cut of circumcision, here bodily transformation is additive.[36]

And yet Moses' face does not merely stand as a marker of Yahweh's presence among the Israelites. Instead, the prophet chooses to cover his face whenever he is among the people:

> When Moses had finished speaking with them, he placed a veil [*masweh*] on his face. Whenever Moses went in before Yahweh to speak with him, he would remove the veil, until he came out. When he came out, he told the Israelites what he had been commanded. The Israelites would see the face of Moses, that the skin of his face was radiating light; and Moses would put the veil on his face again, until he went in to speak with him. (Exod. 34:33–35)

This veiling further sets Moses apart. No longer able to wear his own face, neither can he display the radiant face of divine encounter in the midst of the Israelites. In the streaming light of Moses' face, we thus have two forms of transformation: the divine glow of the prophet's face, and the opacity of the covering he places over it. The first moves the prophet closer to Yahweh, almost blurring the divine-human boundary with its radiance (even as this blurring comes at the expense of Moses' human identity and appearance). The second moves the prophet away from the category of the normatively masculine. In covering his face, Moses further erases the specificity of his identity. He also makes his body into a concealed, private, interior space, thereby suggesting a move outside of ordinary masculine performance and self-presentation. And yet this veiled face also signals an intimacy of *voice*, shared between Moses and Yahweh.[37] Above all, the body of Moses is altered, a change at once transformative and terrifying, and one that marks his altered relations to the community itself.

The word used for Moses' facial covering, *masweh*, occurs only in this passage.[38] The singularity of the term perhaps reflects the singularity of the moment—Moses' self-concealment is unlike any other moment of self-concealment in the text, just as Moses is singular among the prophets. And yet the act of veiling also implies certain thematic parallels. In the Hebrew Bible and the ancient Near East, veiling is a predominantly feminine practice. Significant narrative moments involving veiling or covering the head or face nearly always concern female characters, such as Tamar disguising herself as a prostitute (Gen. 38:14) or Rebekah veiling herself upon meeting her future husband Isaac (24:65). While head coverings are not explicitly required of women in the Hebrew Bible, the act of covering the head is culturally legible as a feminine action.[39] The text thus invites us to see at least the traces of a displacement of gender in Moses's veiling; Jennings goes so far as to call Moses' veil a "feminizing mark" and links it to "the wounding of patriarchy."[40] Whether it is patriarchy that is transformed or only Moses' face, the text suggests, at a minimum, a move outside of normative masculine embodiment.

"Did I Conceive This Entire People?"

If Moses' veiling opens the *possibility* of reading the prophet's body as feminized, then Moses himself forces the question of feminization by describing his own body as female. Exhausted by the demands of mediating between an intractable God and a rebellious people, Moses protests:

> Moses said to Yahweh, "Why do you treat your servant so badly? Why am I unable to find favor in your eyes, that you put the burden of this entire people upon me? Did I conceive this entire people? Did I give birth to them, that you say to me, 'Carry them on your breast like a nurse carries a nursing child, to the land which I have promised to their fathers'? Where will I get meat to give to this people, because they cry to me, 'Give us meat and we will eat!' I cannot carry this entire people alone, for they are too heavy for me. If this is how you are going to treat me, just kill me—if I have found favor in your eyes—so I will not see my misery!" (Num. 11:11–15)

Struggling to express the depth of his frustration, Moses figures his body as female. He likewise imagines a feminine role for himself, bearing, carrying, and caring for children. And yet tellingly, his apparent auto-feminization occurs exclusively through rhetorical questions, which disavow the feminine even as they draw on its figurative power. His complaint is also unstable in the categories of female bodies it employs. Almost as soon as the maternal body is introduced, it is displaced, as the prophet shifts his comparison from mother to nurse ('*ōmēn*, "nurse," "attendant," or "nanny"; the masculine form of the noun is used). This shift removes the sexual specificity of the reproductive female body in favor of the nurturing role, gendered but not sexed, which is shared by mother and nurse. And yet even this role proves undesired and unsustainable; Moses claims to prefer death. Though the prophet has just described himself as a mother or perhaps a nurse, *he would prefer to die* than to play that role. The feminine and the maternal are abject, perhaps deadly. It is even more remarkable if we consider Moses' self-description to be wholly confined to the realm of figurative speech: even as *metaphor*, the feminine-maternal is destabilizing, perhaps deadly. As at many other points in the text, the female body, even figurative, quickly slips toward danger and death (cf. Prov. 5:3–23).

Thus while it is tempting to read Moses' complaint as a statement of the feminizing effects of prophecy, such a reading ignores the profound negativity surrounding the female body, as well as the lengths Moses will go to avoid it. What is at stake in this moment in Numbers 11 is not the embrace of the feminine, but rather an anxiety over the masculine body of the prophet. For Moses, prophecy complicates the experience of masculine embodiment without, however, offering a simple resolution into femininity or the female body. His angry metaphors push up against hegemonic masculine embodiment. But there is no resolution for the prophet's body—not, at least, until death.

The Body in Death

The closer Moses draws to Yahweh, the more his body is transformed. The shining face of the prophet anticipates his further alienation from ordinary forms of masculine embodiment. This reaches a peak in the account of Moses' death. At the end of Deuteronomy, Moses is buried "in the land of Moab, opposite Beth-peor, and no one knows his burial place to this day" (Deut. 34:6). In describing Moses' death, the text also goes to pains to underscore his vitality: "Moses was one hundred twenty years old when he died; his sight was unimpaired and his vigor had not abated" (34:7). Moses' body, subjected to so many pains and difficulties in his life, is returned to wholeness in the account of his death. Lēḥa, "vigor," evokes virility,[41] as does the mention of the prophet's undimmed vision (it is worth noting here the phallic symbolism of the eyes).[42] This body is not a terrifying body or a body marked as Other, but a body that fits a cultural ideal of masculine embodiment. The prophet achieves in death what he could not in life: a whole and robust body. And this body, it seems, maintains a power and an appeal, such that its location must be deliberately obscured.

The celebration of Moses' body in death works to underscore its peculiarity in life. Moses' vigor and undimmed vision are signs of bodily wholeness and power, and thus of hegemonic masculinity. Privileging these features of the prophetic body is a way of straightening the previously queer trajectory of prophetic embodiment.[43] Vigor and vision, privileged in death, offer a different sort of narrative of the prophet's body than the text to this point has constructed. While alive, however, Moses repeatedly breaks with hegemonic masculinity. His body is queer, both in its excesses and in what it lacks. This is especially true of the surfaces of Moses' body, his skin and face, as well as his mouth. Moses' body also displays a disturbing tendency to extend beyond the prophet himself. He cannot lift his hands without the assistance of others; he speaks with Aaron as an external mouth; light radiates outward from his face and requires a permanent veiling. These prosthetic additions are matched by the lack inherent in the prophet's own body: his heavy tongue and lips hinder his speech. Moses' body, already unusual at birth, is pained and altered by prophecy. The result is a prophetic body that breaks with the norms of biblical embodiment. But to what end?

Thinking Masculinity and Embodiment with Moses

Ordinarily, as we have seen, the biblical texts privilege a male body that is complete, whole, and normatively abled. And yet Moses' body is alternately weak, afflicted, and radiant. It is also curiously unbounded, depending upon and extending into the bodies of others: from Aaron, who serves as Moses' prosthetic mouth, to Hur and Aaron, who lift the prophet's faltering arms, to Yahweh, whose conversations leave Moses with a terrifying glow. Prophecy changes the body, in ways that stand in uneasy relation to the accepted norms of text and community. I will briefly trace three ways of understanding this transformation: as disability, as feminization, and as queering of embodiment.

Moses as Disabled

One way to understand the body of Moses is through the category of disability. Over the course of his life, Moses embodies multiple forms of disability. His problems with his mouth and lips, which he fears will disqualify him from prophecy, suggest either a physical disability or another form of impairment linked to the production of speech. Unlike Isaiah, Moses is not relieved of this difficulty when he is called as a prophet (contrast Isa. 6:5–7). In addition to this congenital difficulty, Moses experiences several forms of temporary disability. His arms are struck with weakness in the battle against the Amalekites, requiring the assistance of others. He is also temporarily afflicted with scale disease. There is also the question of his face, which is permanently transformed. Though this transformation is never explicitly described as a disfigurement, it prompts reactions of fear and repulsion; disfigurement and even ugliness are linked conceptually with the larger category of disability in the biblical text.[44] Taken together, these various features represent Moses' body as a disabled body.

What does it mean to understand the prophetic body through a hermeneutics of disability? Disability has a complex relationship to the norms of embodiment in the Hebrew Bible, as work in disability studies has shown.[45] In the case of Moses (and the prophet's speech in particular), Nyasha Junior and Jeremy Schipper argue that Moses deploys disability strategically. For Junior and Schipper, "Moses uses his disability . . . as a rhetorical strategy for coping with questions of group loyalties or commitments," which "allows him to circumvent questions about his group identity."[46] They argue that Moses is indeed disabled, as indicated by the biblical text, but that his disability also provides him with unique opportunities for leadership of the people. In this reading, disability is not simply something done to or passively experienced by the prophet. Instead, Moses intentionally foregrounds his disability as a guarantee of the success of his prophecy.[47] Disability secures leadership. This reading suggests, moreover, new ways of understanding other moments of disability in the Moses narrative, without relying upon the tired and sometimes offensive biblical tropes of the utopian erasure of blindness, lameness, and other bodily "defects."

Read in this way, disability is neither secondary feature nor regrettable affliction. Instead, it is fundamental to prophecy. No longer is disability something to be corrected (as in the Bible's own utopian visions, which promise an end to blindness, deafness, and other forms of disability, and which have been critiqued by disability studies readings for this reason); instead, it is helpful or even essential to prophecy's function. The association of disability with the prophetic body, in turn, challenges the representations of both categories and pushing back against the normative. But while embodiment is clearly challenged, this reading does not, at least at first pass, appear to reconfigure gender. For this, we need to bring together the disability critique with a reading of the prophet's body as feminized.

Moses as Feminized

Moses' body is not only disabled; it is also feminized. There is also an assortment of textual evidence associating Moses' body with the female body. The veiling of his face is the climax in a sequence of actions that challenge and confound hegemonic masculinity; it is also an act ordinarily performed by women. His affliction with scale disease is likewise feminizing in associating him with Miriam, and with the broader trope of the female body excluded from the community for exceeding its bounds. Female embodiment in the biblical world is problematic, in part, because of the ways that the female body breaches its own boundaries, through discharges, fluidities, and so forth. The margins of the female body are *messy*— and so too with Moses, whose body so often exceeds the ordinary or blurs into the bodies of others.

Even the disabling of Moses' body can be read as a feminization, an association substantiated by reference to other ancient Near Eastern texts. Fontaine describes the feminizing of male warriors in biblical texts and other Near Eastern iconography as a means of disabling the foe. She writes, "The message (and hope) is clear: men can be disabled as warriors simply by regendering them."[48] Hentrich likewise argues that disability overtakes gender in the Hebrew Bible, with disabled male bodies viewed as demasculinized.[49] Still, while there are certain overlaps between the representations of femininity and disability, they remain distinct. Saul Olyan, for example, cautions that the feminization of disabled men is thus "a seldom attested strategy at best."[50] Thus Moses' disability does not explain (or explain away) his embrace of feminine imagery; neither do his flirtations with the female body erase his bodily disability. Instead, each represents a distinct, if interrelated, movement outside the category of normative masculine embodiment. While femininity and disability are both excluded from the ideal of the male body, they are not identical.

Further, while Moses' body may be feminized, it is also worth noting that the prophet himself resists this association. While Moses uses the female body to describe his own experience of prophecy, it is couched in the language of repudiation. (*Did I give birth to this people?* the prophet asks, but his question demands a negative answer.) Moses' words may reflect a sensitivity to his own precarious masculinity, a last-ditch effort to shore up masculine privilege. But nevertheless, there is a distinction to be maintained between speaking of the feminine and becoming feminine. As I will demonstrate at length in the chapters that follow, the female body is often useful to "think with"—to work through and negotiate questions of masculinity. Keeping this in mind, it is important to avoid accepting Moses' feminized body at face value, or equating this body with a woman's body. Instead, what appears as a feminization represents a reconfiguration of the masculine and a move toward an alternate form of prophetic masculinity.

Moses as Queer Assemblage

In addition to femininity and disability, it is also possible to read Moses' body as queer. This becomes especially clear in the "bridegroom of blood" episode, which I will consider in a moment. But even in the scenes of embodiment already considered above, there is something queer about the prophet's body. The combination of beauty, difficulty, and nonnormative trajectories of embodiment all point to the possibility of reading the prophetic body of Moses as a queer body. Returning to Sara Ahmed's description of queer as both oblique and sexually divergent,[51] Moses' body is queer both because it follows an oblique trajectory and because it manifests nonnormative relations to sexuality and identity. There is an intimacy between Moses and Yahweh,[52] one that can be read from his body (beginning with his face). There is also Moses' double attraction to and repulsion from the female body that he claims as his own, only to repudiate—this gesture may well be feminizing; it is also rather queer.

Further, the queerness in the text may extend not simply to specific features or actions by Moses, but to the prophetic body as queer *assemblage*. The notion of the assemblage comes from Deleuze and Guattari; it has been developed in relation to queerness and queer hermeneutics by Jasbir Puar. In *Terrorist Assemblages*, Puar proposes reading the bodies of the terrorist and of the turbaned Sikh man, among others, as "queer assemblages" that oppose the dominant organization of sexuality, surveillance, and power she terms "homonationalism." For Puar, the queer body as assemblage makes it possible to move beyond thinking of queer as a binary identity; it also opens a greater flexibility for both bodies and reading practices. Queer embodiment becomes not a fixed identity, but a dynamic assemblage "within which bodies interpenetrate, swirl together, and transmit affects and effects to each other."[53] This description speaks as well to Moses, whose bodily difference consistently emerges between bodies—his face contagiously illuminated from Yahweh's face, his arms sagging in Hur's and Aaron's hands, his infant goodness as judged by his mother's gaze (and perhaps in relation to other bodies and babies as well). Moses' body likewise transmits affects, beginning with the terror his face engenders in whoever looks at him.

Conceiving of the body as a queer assemblage also foregrounds the question of intensity. Puar writes, "Assemblages allow us to attune to movements, intensities, emotions, energies, affectivities, and textures as they inhabit events, spatiality, and corporealities."[54] In this way the assemblage sets forth intensity an alternative to intersectionality, which models identity as constructed through intersecting vectors of class, race, gender, sexuality, and so forth. What intersectionality misses, however, is *intensity*. To describe Moses as *male*, *Hebrew*, and perhaps *disabled* or *feminized* is to offer a description that is at once accurate and insufficient. It minimizes the strangeness of the prophetic body, its degree of deviation from normative modes of embodiment. And it forecloses the possibility of transformation, of a body changed and changing. But it is necessary for any theory of Moses' body to encompass that body's ongoing changes. Queer assemblage thus both takes seriously the ongoing emergence and dynamism of Moses' body and makes possible an understanding of the prophetic body that encompasses femininity, disability, and other axes of identity, without, however, being bound to them. It also suggests the possibility of understanding Moses' pain and suffering through the affective lens of *intensity*.[55]

I raise these possibilities not to advocate definitively for them, but rather to give a sense of the space of possibility surrounding the body of the prophet. I return to this reading of the prophetic body as queer assemblage in greater detail in later chapters. For now, the goal is only to give a sense of the breadth of possibility in understanding Moses' body. These interpretations converge in their shared understanding of the prophet's body as exterior to the normative representation of biblical masculinity. There is something *other* about Moses' embodiment, whether this otherness is interpreted through more traditional categories, such as gender and disability, or through Deleuze and Guattari's assemblages.

What is crucial is the movement beyond the norms of masculinity. The prophetic body has become a queer body.

The Male Body and the Bridegroom of Blood

In tracking and exploring this movement beyond the norms of biblical masculinity, I want to turn to one additional, essential moment in Mosaic embodiment: the narrative of the "bridegroom of blood" (Exod. 4:24–26). This narrative, I will suggest, brings together transformation, openness, and fluidity in a constellation of ideas and tropes that presages a transformed prophetic body and a queer, non-phallicized prophetic masculinity.

This fragmentary incident occurs shortly after Moses' call story, as he returns to Egypt with Zipporah and their sons. The text reads,

> On the way, at a place where they spent the night, Yahweh met him and tried to kill him. But Zipporah took a flint and cut off her son's foreskin, and touched his "feet" [*wattagga' l'raglāyw*] with it, and said, "Truly you are a bridegroom/son-in-law of blood to me!"[56] [*ḥᵃtan-dāmîm ʾattā lî*]. So he left him alone. It was then she said, "A bridegroom/son-in-law of blood by circumcision" [*ḥᵃtan dāmîm lammûlōt*].[57] (Exod. 4:24–26)

The passage, despite its terrific brevity, is fraught with textual difficulties, mostly concerning the antecedents of the masculine pronouns and object suffixes. The first instance, "Yahweh met *him* and sought to kill *him*," seems fairly clearly to refer to Moses, who is the object of Yahweh's address in the previous verse. The foreskin likewise clearly belongs to Moses' and Zipporah's son (though which son is unclear).[58] But whom does Zipporah touch with the foreskin, and where? There is a textual question concerning the dual noun *raglayim*, which I have translated as "feet" but which can also refer to the legs or the genitals. There may also be a deliberate metonymy or doubling of meanings in the text. But whatever the specific referent here, the passage is clearly genitally charged. The central event is a circumcision; the text is likewise concerned with the blood it produces. Whether this blood is applied to the penis or some other lower extremity on the male body is a secondary concern—the narrative is queer either way.

A second question is whose "feet" are these—Moses', Yahweh's, or the son's? The confusion is longstanding; the Talmud takes up the difficulty:

> One said, "It was at the feet of Moses."
> Another said, "It was at the feet of the angel."
> The third said, "It was at the feet of the child."[59]

Among modern commentators, Propp argues that the feet belong to Moses, "since it is Moses' crime that is being atoned"—here the crime refers to Moses' previous manslaughter of an Egyptian.[60] Hans Kosmala, however, argues that the blood is applied, prophylactically, to the body of the son.[61] And Christopher B. Hays suggests that the feet belong to Yahweh, and that Zipporah's smearing of the blood is apotropaic, seeking the protection of her family.[62]

If the blood is applied to Moses' body, then its application serves as a reminder of the fleshliness and vulnerability of Moses' own bodily form. If the blood is applied to Moses' son, meanwhile, the text thematizes the vulnerability not of Moses' body but of his genealogical line—second-degree sterility, narrowly avoided. This reading is perhaps bolstered by the death of Ezekiel's wife (Ezek. 24:16–25) and the prohibition against marriage for Jeremiah (Jer. 16:2), both of which suggest the sterilizing effects of prophecy. Making the son's body central to the scene also displaces Moses, destabilizing the paternal power balance. But perhaps it is not essential to distinguish between the body of Moses and the body of his son. Instead, in this brief passage, the bodies of father and son function as a single symbolic unit. The son represents the continuation of Moses' line; his blood saves Moses' life. Just as circumcision serves, in general, as the bodily sign of the covenant, so does the son's circumcision, in particular, furnish as a bodily sign of the relationship between Moses and Yahweh. And the blood this circumcision releases binds Moses and his son, both momentarily and historically. In this moment of relation, the masculine body is constituted through its fluids, and through the fluids of others applied to it.

There remains a third possibility, that the blood is applied to *Yahweh's* feet. If this is indeed the intended reading, then Exodus 4 offers a striking example of what Howard Eilberg-Schwartz terms a "God sighting,"[63] a moment when the body of God appears in the text. This does not, however, resolve the problem of the male body, or of Moses' male body in particular. Instead, as Eilberg-Schwartz's work demonstrates, whenever such a "God sighting" occurs, its effect is to destabilize human masculinity.[64] If the body where Zipporah places the blood is Yahweh's body, then Moses' masculinity is under threat.

Under each of these readings, the human male body is a site of vulnerability, of potential (for Moses) and prophylactic (for the son) wounding. The opening of the son's body saves the father's. The cutting of the son's genitals—the symbolic wounding or cutting (off) of Moses' line—allows Moses himself to live. The blood of the son's penis evokes the body—and the bodily vulnerability—of the father, wherever it is smeared. The fact that Zipporah performs the action on her son, while Moses is the recipient of the shed blood, reinforces the passivity of the prophet and his body. This passivity, moreover, is a reversal of the ordinary expectations of biblical masculinity and confirms Moses' break with hegemonic masculine embodiment. The play with fluidity, openness, and wounding also suggests the possibility of imagining alternate forms of masculine bodies. If the stutter and/or cleft palate suggested a body outside the domains of the "normal," and the scaly hand suggests a body outside the bounds of the community, then the bloody penis in this story of the bridegroom of blood further pushes the body out of the ordinary organization of bodily masculinity.

Thus while Exodus 4:24–26 centers on circumcision, it offers a productive starting point for a non-phallicized masculinity. The penis is indeed central to the text: Zipporah's flint cuts her son's foreskin, and there is blood; as a result, Moses is allowed to live. Even with the ambiguities of the text, these details are incontrovertible. But this penis does not signify the phallus. In a reversal of the ordinary formulations made familiar by psychoanalysis, it is the penis and not the phallus that is critical. What phallic power there is belongs to Zipporah, who administers the critical cut. The male bodies, for their part, are represented as bloody and vulnerable. The significance of the penis depends upon its opening and its wounding—the genitals as site of vulnerability instead of locus of phallic power. Deliverance comes in the form of a cut. This is a queering of the normative category of masculinity. It ushers in a new way of understanding masculinity and male embodiment, one that foregrounds openness and vulnerability over phallic domination of the other.

Fluidity, Openness, and a New Mosaic Masculinity

I want now to push a bit further in considering the significance of fluidity as it relates the male body of the prophet Moses. The blood of circumcision in Exodus 4:24–26, wherever it is smeared, is one in a series of fluid moments in the life of Moses, from his watery deliverance as a baby (Exod. 2) to his death overlooking the Jordan River (Deut. 34). Moses parts the waters of the Sea of Reeds to allow the Israelites to escape Egypt (Exod. 14:21–27). Water, too, figures in Moses' inability to enter the land of Canaan—he is punished for striking the rock twice to cause it to release water (Num. 20:9–13). Fluidity is a recurring theme throughout the life of the prophet. And in the bridegroom of blood narrative, it is intentionally associated with Moses' body. Fluidity does not simply serve to mark the passage of the prophet's life, however. Instead, it also suggests the opening up of the prophet's masculinity, both theoretically and, in the case of Exodus 4:24–26, literally.

Writing beyond the boundaries of biblical studies, feminist philosophers and theorists have suggested that openness and fluidity are crucial to conceiving of male embodiment in ways that do not perpetuate violence. Luce Irigaray, for example, has argued that the bodiless masculine subject of philosophy is a fiction predicated on the erasure of the feminine.[65] As she writes in *The Forgetting of Air in Martin Heidegger*, "The Being of man will be constituted on the basis of a forgetting."[66] This forgetting includes the forgetting of both the maternal-feminine, which makes the male subject possible, and of the subject's own body. Representing the male body as closed off and self-contained is one step in this process toward the fantasy of a bodiless masculine subject.

Irigaray does not simply diagnose the problem of the disembodied, "neutral" masculine, however. Instead, she also suggests that it may be possible to conceive of masculine subjectivity and embodiment differently. This requires, to begin, acknowledging that the masculine subject is not bodiless, but rather possesses a body.[67] This body, moreover, is both material and vulnerable. In *Speculum of the Other Woman*, one of her earliest and still most influential works, she suggests, if briefly, that the wounding of the male body represents an opening up of masculinity. As Amy Hollywood notes, Irigaray's *Speculum of the Other Woman* praises the "glorious slit" of the wound in Christ's side.[68] This praise represents a reimagining of the body to offer an alternative to penetrative, phallic, sealed-off masculinity (though not one that Irigaray herself pursues).[69]

The opening up of the male body has also been taken up by Elizabeth Grosz, a feminist philosopher influenced by Irigaray. Her book *Volatile Bodies*, a study of feminist theory, embodiment, and philosophy, concludes with an urgent call to recognize the specificity and materiality of the male body. Grosz writes,

> Perhaps the great mystery, the great unknown, of the body comes not from the peculiarities and enigmas of female sexuality, from the cyclically regulated flows that emanate from women's bodies, but from the unspoken and generally unrepresented particularities of the male body . . . what remains unanalyzed, what men can have no distance on, is the mystery, the enigma, the unspoken of the male body.[70]

Grosz, however, is not willing to let the male body maintain its double status as universal bodiless norm and mysterious embodied enigma. Building upon Irigaray's work, she insistently pursues the male body and its fluids, concluding that the male body is in fact a fluid body, but its fluidity remains largely disavowed. She criticizes "the reduction of men's bodily fluids to the by-products of pleasure and the raw materials of reproduction," which masculine subjects undertake to avoid association with the feminine and the feminine body.[71] In its place, she looks forward to a moment "when men take responsibility for and pleasure in the forms of seepage that are their own, when they cease to reduce it to its products, when they accept the sexual specificity, particularity, and limit that is their own."[72]

Reconceiving of the male body, meanwhile, has significant consequences. In Irigaray's work, these are not clearly spelled out, and appear only elliptically. In the case of Grosz, it is clearer that an embrace of messy corporeality, especially fluidity, makes possible a new conception of masculinity. As she writes,

> A different type of body is produced in and through the different sexual and cultural practices that men undertake. Part of the process of phallicizing the male body, of subordinating the rest of the body to the valorized function of the penis, with the culmination of sexual activities occurring, ideally at least, in sexual penetration and male orgasm, involves the constitution of the sealed-up, impermeable body. . . . A body that is permeable, that transmits in a circuit, that opens itself up rather than seals itself off, that is prepared to respond as well as to initiate, that does not revile its masculinity (as the transsexual community does) or virilize it (as a number of gay men, as well as heterosexuals tend to do) would involve a quite radical rethinking of male sexual morphology.[73]

In Grosz's analysis, conceiving of the male body as fluid and permeable provides a much-needed alternative to the phallicized male body that valorizes penetration and repudiates flow. It is possible (perhaps even necessary) to imagine a different model of masculinity, one that is permeable, labile, and open. For Grosz (and perhaps Irigaray as well), this alternate ideology of masculinity has its origins in the materiality of masculinity—the form of the male body.

Grosz's argument is specifically addressed to contemporary masculinity, not to the biblical text. And yet the body of Moses in many ways fits her requirements for a "radical rethinking" of masculinity beyond the hegemonic, phallicized ideal. Moses' body is passive, permeable, open. Instead of exercising a monopoly of phallic power, it is a body acted upon by (divine) others, a body altered, open, and fluid. The bridegroom of blood is only the most graphic enactment of this dynamic of opening and fluidity. The messiness of Moses' body and its boundaries is especially thematized in this passage, which also offers a striking example of a nonhegemonic Mosaic masculinity, a masculinity centered on the fluid, open male body.[74]

Conceptualizing the body as fluid opens new possibilities for understanding the text. On a basic level, it offers a solution to the problem of the bridegroom of blood narrative. The body, it seems, is not simply the object of random divine violence or of an archaic account of circumcision. Instead, it is reconfigured as a fluid body. Zipporah's cutting of the son (the extension of Moses) as well as her smearing of the blood underscore this point. No longer are the margins of the body, previously a matter of such importance—and such difficulty—the central concern. Instead, it is in fluidity, in the body that at once is and is not a body, that we can best imagine the possibility of alternate orders of being in the text. So, too, does the fluid destabilize the dominant norms of masculinity in the Hebrew text. Other ways of conceiving of the prophet's male body slip in around the margins and sluice through the openings that fluidity itself creates. Moses' bloody, threatened body becomes a queer object, while destabilizing the already unstable performance of prophetic masculinity.

Non-phallicized Masculinity beyond the Moment of the Cut

Exodus 4:24–26 introduces the possibility of an alternative configuration of masculinity, embodiment, and prophecy. This text is fundamental to understanding Moses' performance of masculinity. The opened, bloody, non-phallicized male body renders the representation of masculinity. The challenge that Moses' body poses to hegemonic masculinity, visible at multiple moments in the Moses narrative, appears most clearly here, even as the textual ambiguities effect a blurring between the bodies of father and son. This is a different sort of male body: wounded, opened, vulnerable, non-phallic. And it entails a different sort of masculine performance than that of hegemonic masculinity—what we might call Mosaic masculinity.

When we take this moment as essential to understanding prophetic masculinity, it opens new possibilities for understanding the other peculiarities of Moses' embodiment. Moses' difficulty with his mouth and tongue is not simply an impediment to his practice of prophecy; instead, it represents another site of bodily openness and non-phallicized masculinity. The mouth that struggles to voice words and the lips that are marked with heaviness are an alternative to the confident, dominant speech that corresponds to norms of masculinity. Moses, to be sure, speaks well; he also speaks through difficulty. Taking the bridegroom of blood as the privileged entry point into the text makes clear that this paradoxical relation to the body—as necessity, as difficulty—is not supplemental, but fundamental to prophecy. The same is true of Moses' heavy arms, which are less a prophetic failure than a fundamental part of his prophecy. So too the glowing face, a necessary terror that also marks the prophet's transformation. Reading with Exodus 4:24–26 to the fore makes clear that these moments—the disabling, the wounding, the affliction, the transformation—of Moses' body are not secondary or supplemental. Instead, they are a crucial part of the prophetic body, a body which is vulnerable, necessarily so. This is a body that Yahweh seeks to kill; a body that is saved not by military valor but by female hands that apply the blood of another. All the norms of hegemonic masculinity break down here. Instead, we have something else, a body whose masculinity is not centrally organized around the phallus.

It is possible, furthermore, to consider the non-phallicized masculinity in the bridegroom of blood incident as part of a larger constellation of queer masculinity in the text. The body of Moses does not simply fail to uphold hegemonic masculine norms. It also presents a radically other form of masculine embodiment that we might describe as queer. Moses' body is vulnerable and opened; it is likewise potent and powerful. The ordinary logic of masculine norms do not apply. Viewed from one perspective, the body is a deficiency and lack; from another, it is a dazzling fullness and assemblage. The repudiation of the closed-off, invulnerable body that the bridegroom of blood incident provides helps to bring together these multiple ways of reading Moses—as feminized, as disabled, as desired and desiring—together the broader paradigm of the "queer body." It is important, of course, to recall that "queer" and "non-phallic" are not identical; the queer may also be phallic or even hyperphallic. Instead, the point is here that the vulnerable, non-phallic masculinity of Exodus 4:24–26 stands in meaningful relation to the other scenes of bodily peculiarity and difficulty, suggesting, overall a queered prophetic body. There are two important points to highlight here: first, the body is disturbed by prophecy, and second, the fluid opening of the prophet's body suggests the possibility of reconfiguring embodied masculinity in the case of Moses.

Significantly, the wounded, opened, and afflicted body of Mosaic masculinity is never criticized by the text. Nor does the feminization of Moses' body brought about by the veiling of his face and the smearing of blood by Zipporah come under fire. Instead, the text is at pains to emphasize Moses' exemplary status ("there was never again another prophet like Moses"). At the same time, the narrative of Moses suggests that the hegemonic norms of masculine embodiment in the Hebrew Bible are less singular than they at first seem, and other, queerer, forms of masculine embodiment are possible and indeed occur without censure. This raises a final important question—is it only Moses who has this experience of the body? Or does Moses' complex embodiment of masculinity extend to other prophetic bodies?

Coda: The Prophetic Body after Moses

The text is careful not to leave Moses without a successor. Moses anoints Joshua to follow him and transmits his authority (Num. 27:18–20); the opening of the book of Joshua likewise identifies the leader as the chosen successor (Josh. 1:1–9). Given the many disturbances in the body of Moses, what can we say about the masculinity of Joshua? Though he is not as great as Moses (according, at least, to the text), he is presented as a successful leader. Joshua first appears in the text in the battle against Amalek (Exod. 17); he later draws attention as one of the fourteen spies Moses dispatches to the land of Canaan (Num. 13–14). In the latter narrative, only Joshua and Caleb are undaunted by what they encounter there (that is, giant fruit and giant inhabitants). Their calls for the people to conquer the land, though drowned out by the protests of the others, are rewarded, as Yahweh allows these two alone among their generation to survive to enter the Promised Land. Upon entry, Joshua proves to be a more than able leader, leading the Israelites in a string of military conquests, recounted in the book of Joshua.

In many ways, Joshua reinscribes the very norms of biblical masculinity suspended in the narrative of Moses. His body is not vulnerable; he does not suffer from disease, weakness, or difficulty in speech. His many victories in conquest inscribe a military vigor that is a marker of "successful" or hegemonic biblical masculinity. "There was never again a prophet like Moses," but, if we take the text at its word, the transition from Moses to Joshua marks a reassuring reinstatement of textual norms of masculinity. Still, there are a few moments in the narrative that seem to suggest glimmers of an alternate configuration of gender and embodiment. The passing of prophetic authority from Moses to Joshua—not a transfer from father to son, but rather across lines of kinship—is, in its way, a moment of intimacy. From one perspective, this masculine transfer of power, conducted wholly without women (unlike in traditional filiation, a woman is not even needed to bear the child), reinscribes patriarchy. From another, we might consider the touching of bodies, the closeness, perhaps even the queerness of the moment.[75]

While Joshua is Moses' literal successor in Deuteronomy and the Deuteronomistic History, it is the literary prophets who assume his mantel in the canon more broadly. Prophecy in the Deuteronomistic History is filled with games of power. Perhaps more than any other prophet in the Hebrew Bible, Elijah fulfills Clines's description of the "he-prophet" (though Clines is careful to distinguish between the writing prophets, who he claims are "no doubt, are on the whole pretty harmless individuals," and the significantly more threatening Elijah).[76] The difficulty of Elijah's body, if there is one, is a difficulty of excess—*too much* masculinity, virility, divine spirit, power. Elijah offers us a vision of prophetic subjectivity as intrinsically excessive. It is, rather, the literary prophets who are the clearest heirs to Moses' prophetic difficulties. There is a complex web of relations between these texts and the Pentateuchal texts describing Moses. I am less interested, however, in directional vectors of influence (a repeated concern in studies of prophetic texts) than in the shifting relations of the body, masculinity, and the male prophet. The literary prophets considered in the chapters that follow each experience a disturbance of the norms of masculinity and embodiment. The work of the remainder of this book is to draw out the difficulties and complexities of the bodies of the literary prophets.

The problem with which this chapter began—the mysterious location of Moses' body after death—has become the more fundamental question of the prophet's body. How is Moses' body to be understood? After tracing both a number of bodily strangenesses and multiple ways of understanding this body, I have argued for reading Moses' body as positioned in excess of the norms of hegemonic masculinity and masculine embodiment. As an exemplar of the norms of biblical masculinity, Moses' body fails. But as a prophet, Moses succeeds, and succeeds like no one else. This success, moreover, occurs not in spite of but through the prophetic body. The prophetic body becomes both queer and exceptional, its material form reflecting the demands of the prophetic calling. In the case of Moses, the prophet's exceptional body has multiple significances in the text. It serves as sign (and symptom) of his prophetic vocation. At the same time, it challenges the norms of hegemonic masculine embodiment. This challenge comes not, on the whole, through the feminization of the body, but rather through a reconfiguration of the masculine.

There was never again a prophet like Moses, or a prophetic body like Moses' body. And yet the negotiations of masculinity and embodiment in the Moses narratives play a central role in understanding the unstable and even queer prophetic body. Moses' burial place may be hidden, but his body has much to show.

2

The Horror of Hosea

FEMALE BODIES AND MASCULINE ANXIETIES
IN HOSEA 1–3

THE FAMILIES OF the prophets do not frequently appear in the prophetic books. This omission does not mean that all is well—what we do know hardly inspires confidence. Jeremiah is forbidden to marry or have a family (Jer. 16:2). Ezekiel has a wife, but only until Yahweh kills her as an object lesson for the people (Ezek. 24:14–25). Isaiah has a wife (perhaps, herself, a prophet)[1] and several children, though they appear in the text only briefly, as part of Isaiah's larger efforts to harass King Ahaz (Isa. 8). The most developed narrative of a prophetic marriage and family belongs, however, to Hosea. On Yahweh's command, Hosea marries Gomer, who is described as an *'ēšet zěnûnîm*, a "promiscuous woman."[2] Gomer bears three children for Hosea, who gives them inauspicious names and orders them to condemn their mother. The prophet's marriage is interwoven in the text with an account of Yahweh's marriage to Israel. This is no happy marriage, as Israel pursues other lovers while Yahweh threatens her with violence, exposure, and perhaps murder, before promising to win back her love. In chapter 3, Hosea is again commanded to marry; this time his bride must be "a woman who has committed adultery." Whether this woman is Gomer or another remains unclear.

The now-infamous marriage texts of Hosea 1–3 are at once compelling and disturbing, especially in their constellation of power, sex, and aggression. Yahweh's violence toward the feminized Israel, in particular, is often shocking to the contemporary reader. While some readers have insisted on treating Hosea 1–3 as a love story, most recognize the marriage as exploitative, disturbing, shocking, or provocative. Domestic violence, pornography, even sadism are often brought up in the critical conversation, even more so when Hosea's marriage is set against Yahweh's marriage to Israel, a still more violent and disturbing relationship.[3] Given this potent mix of sex and violence, it is not surprising that Hosea 1–3 played a central role in the "prophetic pornography" debates of the 1980s and 1990s.[4] In addition to pornography, Hosea 1–3 has been read in many other ways: as performance art, as alienation effect, and as economic critique expressed through (or disguised as) rhetoric of the female body.[5] Still, the dominant read-ing strategy at present remains one of identifying and documenting the gendered violence of the text.

Given all this, what is left to say? Especially, perhaps, with respect to gender, which has formed the centerpiece of so many readings of Hosea? A great deal, I will suggest. In particular, I am interested in pushing beyond a critical response that testifies, documents, or bears witness to gendered terror and violence. There are already many readings of Hosea that emphasize domestic violence, femicide, and pornography. These readings, like much of a certain generation of feminist biblical criticism, exist primarily to document and to testify to certain orderings of gender, power, and representation in the text. And bearing witness is a vital critical project, especially with respect to texts that serve as a nexus of violence or hatred. Recent work in biblical studies on trauma theory and the witnessing of disaster has only underscored this point.[6]

However, I want to suggest that witnessing is not the only critical position possible with respect to texts of violence, suffering, and gendered terror. This is especially the case, I will argue, in texts in which (1) the horror of the text is par-ticularly pronounced, obvious, or unavoidable, and (2) the naming of this horror has already been carried out in critical scholarship. In the case of a text such as Hosea 1–3, simply naming the gendered violence is no longer a novel or inno-vative critical move. Instead, repeating the same arguments threatens to sap the debate, and indeed the critique itself, of its vibrancy and even its importance. As the critique becomes scholarly habit or even ritual, it loses the ability to offer new insight or to destabilize critical conversations.

As an alternate approach to Hosea, I will set the prophetic text against the model of the horror film. Horror, often considered a culturally and critically dubious genre, has proved a remarkably fruitful site for feminist cultural criti-cism.[7] This is especially true of subgenres such as the slasher, the possession film, and the rape-revenge film. These films offer alternate scripts for gender perfor-mance, alternate representations of the social gendering of the body, and alternate relations of identification between the work and its audience.

And this is not all. Hosea, I will suggest, *resembles a horror film*. This is true in both structure and content. More specifically, Hosea 1–3 resembles a horror film—and in particular, I will argue, a possession film—in the violence it imag-ines inflicting upon the female body and especially in the emphasis it places on bodily openness. Israel, who is imagined as a woman and given a female body, is subjected to outrageous violence. Her body is violated, sexually assaulted, and murdered, then brought back for more. Yahweh's pursuit of Israel and promise to "hedge her up with thorns" and murder her calls to mind Dario Argento's *Suspiria* and the barbed wire death scene, even as the repetition of gruesome violence suggests the interchangeable female victims of the classic slasher film. The latter parallel is also heightened by the seeming interchangeability of female bodies (of Gomer, of Israel, of the other woman) in the eyes of the male agent of violence. And Yahweh's opening words to Hosea in chapter 3, "Go, marry another woman," are, at the most basic level, a demand for a sequel— and what genre is more obliging of the sequel than horror, with its endless Freddy Kruegers and *Friday the 13th*s?

The parallel between Hosea and horror does not simply concern content; it is also structural. This is another reason that a horror reading opens the text in a way that straightforward readings of abuse or violence do not. Hosea 1–3 is organized around the opened female body. The female body, moreover, is central to a negotiation of *masculinity* in the text. In this way, the book of Hosea has the same internal logic as a specific genre of horror film, the possession film. This parallel chiefly occurs in the context of Hosea's obsessive interest in opening the female body, in making the female form into both a space (consider the land as body in the Hebrew Bible) and a conduit (the basic structure of prophecy). And it similarly resembles the possession film in the use of the opened female body to effect a masculine transformation.

In reading Hosea 1–3 as horror, I will draw in particular on the work of Carol Clover, which offers an excellent model for encountering and thinking through gender and horror. Clover's study *Men, Women, and Chain Saws* offers studies of a number of types of horror films, including the slasher, the possession film, and the rape-revenge film. Taking up this material, she constructs a sophisticated analysis of gender, embodiment, and the politics of identification.[8] Clover convincingly argues for the complexity of the representations of gender in horror, representations that too often are ignored or dismissed. Clover's work is invaluable not just for film studies, but also for understanding the biblical text. Reading it together with Hosea yields a significant critical payoff. First, naming the text as horror at once acknowledges the violence, terror, and trauma of the text and makes possible a critical move beyond a stance of witnessing or condemnation. Horror as a category opens the possibility of alternate critical readings. Second, reading Hosea as horror, with particular emphasis on the structural parallels to the subgenre of the possession film, allows us to think through masculinity in the text. Hosea 1–3 *seems* to present a text obsessed with female bodies—of Hosea's wife Gomer (in chapter 1), of Israel (in chapter 2), of the woman who has committed adultery (in chapter 3). The function, use, and abuse of these bodies is a textual concern. However, as in the possession film, the attention seemingly paid to the opened female body conceals an overarching concern with *masculinity*. The open female body provides a space for working through the dilemmas of masculinity and masculine embodiment. As in the possession films Clover analyzes, the female body in Hosea 1–3 is essential to the dilemma of embodied masculinity into which prophecy thrusts the male prophet.

In this chapter, I will chart the relations of masculinity, female bodies, violence, and horror in Hosea 1–3. I will begin with the question of gendered violence, drawing out the violence implicit in chapters 1 and 3 (Hosea's experiments in matrimony) and explicit in chapter 2 (Yahweh's marriage to Israel), indicating how they relate to each other. After briefly reviewing several common critical approaches to these texts, I will set forth in greater detail the argument for reading the texts as horror, and for applying the analytical categories Clover sets forth in her book. Drawing on Clover's treatment of the possession film, I will argue that the central problem is one of openness, and specifically of the opened female body. Openness is linked to pain and torture, but also to fertility, to sexuality, and, insofar as the open body presents a conduit, to the central drama of prophecy itself. As such, the open female body becomes an essential site for negotiating the problem of prophetic masculinity. Masculinity is at once wholly central to and largely excluded from the text of Hosea 1–3; it is through the application of Clover's work on horror that its significance to the text becomes fully apparent.

Reading Hosea 1–3 through Clover also opens the possibility of reading queerness in and around Hosea's body. I will suggest that displacing the question of masculinity away from the male body opens the possibility of imagining other configurations of sex, gender, and sexuality. There is something queer in using the female body as the privileged ground to negotiate masculinity. If masculinity can be explored on and through bodies other than male bodies, then other configurations of masculinity may be possible. Perhaps the male body can even be queer. This possibility comes, however, at a cost for the female body, as this chapter will also show. It becomes a ground for negotiating masculinity at cost to itself. Still, treating Hosea 1–3 as an account of opened female bodies and masculine anxieties is a crucial step to understanding the working of masculinity in Hosea.

On Hosea

The book of Hosea is the longest of the Minor Prophets. The text consists of two distinct sections, the marriage accounts of chapters 1–3 and the prophecies of 4–14. The first chapter of Hosea opens, in typical biblical fashion, with the word of God coming to Hosea. Yahweh's initial message, however, is somewhat less traditional: "Go, take for yourself a promiscuous woman and have promiscuous children, for the land is whoring away from Yahweh" (Hos. 1:2). The phrase used to describe Gomer, 'ēšet zĕnûnîm, or "wife/woman characterized by zĕnûnîm," is never fully explained, either within Hosea 1 or elsewhere in the biblical corpus. Zĕnûnîm, often translated "whoredom," "fornication," or "sexual impropriety," is an abstract noun from the root *znh*, which refers to sexual acts and promiscuity and which the standard biblical dictionaries all define, heavily, as "to commit fornication."[9] The root *znh* is nearly exclusively used to describe female characters and their sexual actions.[10] At a minimum, the fact the woman represents the unfaithful Israel in Hosea's symbolic marriage (Hosea, of course, represents Yahweh) suggests a strong whiff of sexual impropriety.

The specific wife that Hosea chooses to fulfill this command, Gomer, is likewise an enigma. Beyond her father's name, Diblaim, nothing is known of her—including what, if anything, "qualifies" her as a "promiscuous woman." Though Gomer is often assumed to be a whore or adulteress, the text is silent on this question.[11] Instead, we know only that she bears three children for Hosea, who names them Jezreel, No-Mercy (Hebrew *lōʾ ruḥāmâ*), and Not-My-People (Hebrew *lōʾ ʿammî*) (Hos. 1:3–9). Gomer's responses to Hosea, or to her status as a "woman of whoredom," are, unsurprisingly, omitted from the text.

Chapter 2 presents a second marriage, this one between Yahweh and Israel. Yahweh, speaking through Hosea, promises his children he will strip naked, harass, and torture their unfaithful mother (Hos. 2:4–15, according to the Hebrew numbering of verses[12]), before seducing her again and promising to "betroth [her] forever" (Hos. 2:21; see further 2:17–25). The violence to which Israel is subjected is disturbing, as is the reconciliation that follows, which more than one scholar has compared to a scene of domestic violence. Chapter 3 rounds out the marriage metaphor in Hosea. The chapter shifts back to third-person narrative prose, and Hosea is again instructed to "go, love a woman who is loved by another and who commits adultery" (Hos. 3:1). Hosea obliges. This woman is unnamed and may or may not be Gomer from chapter 1. The remainder of the book, chapter 4–14, contains a series of Hosea's prophecies; Gomer, the children, and the marriage never again appear. Instead, in densely metaphorical language, Hosea describes the coming judgment of Yahweh.

The Male Body

Understanding the complex negotiations of gender in Hosea 1–3 begins with the text's representations of male and female embodiment. I will start by considering the male body as it appears in chapters 1–3. Unfortunately, we do not have much to go on here. The body of Hosea is largely absent, appearing only briefly and in fragments. Its specific parts do not really appear in the text. We know that Hosea fathers children and avoids sexual contact and raisin cakes. (The latter are associated with sexuality elsewhere in the text, as in the Song of Songs [Song 2:5][13]). All other details of his body and its activities are left unsaid. This is especially unusual given the degree to which Hosea's prophetic work depends upon his body. His first prophetic tasks are performances—specifically, taking a wife and fathering children. But despite the necessity of the body for these actions, the male body is not really fleshed out. The pain and pleasure that these actions create in the prophet's body are likewise left unstated, though we do receive some suggestion through the metaphorical association of Hosea with Yahweh.

Nor is Yahweh's body present to a much greater degree. Instead, as elsewhere in the biblical text, his body is troublesome and mostly elusive. Yahweh's actions are described in the text, especially as they pertain to Israel's female body, but the specific body parts that perform these actions remain obscure. Instead, the realm of metaphor provides for a reassuring fuzziness to surround the question of Yahweh's body. There is also a neat gendered division of labor between characters who act (Hosea, Yahweh) and bodies that are acted upon (Gomer, Israel). Hosea acts to take a wife; God acts upon Israel. Men act, but without attention to their own materiality; women provide the bodies and bodily spaces that are acted in and upon.

Beyond Hosea and Yahweh, there is little attention paid to other male bodies in the text. Gomer does bear two male children, Jezreel and Not-My-People. However, they do not occupy male spaces in the text but rather, as children, fit into a broader "not-male" category. The other male figures in Hosea 1–3 are equally elusive. The woman in Hosea 3 (perhaps Gomer, perhaps another) who has loved other men, these men however, remain absent from the text. In chapter 2, it is Israel who has other lovers, the baʿals.[14] If the baʿals assume specific material and masculine forms, then this is not clear from the text. But even as they stir up Yahweh's jealousy and occasion his punishment of Israel, they remain absent, appearing only as mediated through speech and perhaps as votive images. Instead, the bodies that draw the text's interest and attention are emphatically its female ones. This does not mean that masculinity and masculine embodiment are not at stake, however. Instead, unpacking the textual representations of masculinity requires us to turn to the female body.

The Female Bodies of Hosea 1–3

Female bodies draw considerably more attention in Hosea 1–3, both in the biblical text itself and in the history of its interpretation. First is Gomer, in chapter 1. Gomer is selected for marriage based upon her association with zĕnûnîm, linked to the sexual openness of her body; her body likewise figures in the text for its reproductive function, as she bears three children for Hosea. In these scenes of birth, there is a typical division of labor: Gomer is described as conceiving and bearing the children; Hosea assigns their names. The woman in Hosea 3, perhaps Gomer, also assumes bodily form in the text primarily through her sexuality and her use of her body; according to the text she "is loved by another" and "commits adultery" (Hos. 3:1). Hosea buys her for a combination of silver, wine, and barley and then rehabilitates her primarily by refusing to touch her or engage with her in sexual activity. The bodies of Gomer and this woman appear in the text primarily as sexual objects whose actions are controlled by male power and discursive practices. Hosea 3:3 reads, "And I said to her, 'For many days, you will remain with me, and you shall not whore around, and you shall not be with another man, and neither will I be with you'"; the phrase "be with," though elliptical, implies sexual intercourse.

Where the female body truly appears, and suffers, is in Hosea 2, which describes the fate of the feminized Israel in great detail. While the rebuke of Gomer and the woman in Hosea 3 is relatively mild, the female-bodied Israel is subjected to a range of pains and humiliations. She is to be stripped naked, exposed, transformed into wilderness and desert, and murdered by thirst (Hos. 2:5). Yahweh promises,

> I will remove my wool and my flax, which were to cover her nakedness.[15]
>   Now I shall uncover her genitals[16] before the eyes of her lovers, and no
>   one shall rescue her. (Hos. 2:11)

In between these fantasies of vengeance, he imagines the body of his faithless wife in the arms of her lovers, the baʿals. The text alternates between constructing punishments and reconstructing forbidden, idolatrous or adulterous embraces. These two tendencies come together in Yahweh's fantasy of destruction:

> I will destroy her vines and her fig trees, of which she said,
>   "These are my wages, which my lovers gave me."
>   I will make them a thicket, beasts of the field will devour them.
> I will call her to account for the days of the baʿals, when she
>   burned[17] incense to them,
>   and she adorned herself with ring and necklace, and went
>   after her lovers, and forgot me. (Hos. 2:14–15)

Yahweh's words are primarily a vision of punishment. Both sides of the woman-as-land metaphor come into play as he promises to destroy Israel as a woman (she has lovers and celebrates festivals) and as a place (her primary attributes are vines and fig trees). There is also a certain obsessive reimagining of "the days of the baʿals," as Yahweh imagines her exchanging words and more with her lovers. At points, Yahweh almost seems to express more interest in Israel's relations with the baʿals than with himself.

In the final third of chapter 2, the fantasies of violence are abruptly replaced with promises of devotion and tenderness (though not without raising the suspicions of a number of readers).[18] The body, once punished for its sexual transgressions, is now eroticized. The desire to exercise control over it, however, remains the same. Though Yahweh claims he will *entice* Israel, her pleasure or indeed her consent are never mentioned. Instead, the emphasis in the text is on controlling the body, the land, and what they bring forth. The female body is both emphasized and portrayed as an object to be acted upon, as Yahweh promises:

> And it will be on that day—an oracle of Yahweh—she[19]
>   will say "my husband,"
>   And will no longer say to me "my ba'al."
> And I will remove the names of the ba'als from her mouth,
>   and they will no longer be remembered by their names.
>   (Hos. 2:18–19)

As Yahweh controls what the land brings forth, so too will he control the words and actions that the woman herself produces. And yet despite Yahweh's self-positioning—"my husband" ('*îšî*) but not "my ba'al" (*ba'lî*)—the passage is very much about asserting ownership of a woman and her body.[20] "Husband ('*îš*) is indeed ba'al—a word that may equally be translated "master." The erasure of the woman under the power of male control of the land is completed in the following verse, where Yahweh makes a covenant—not with the woman, who has been reduced entirely to passive object, but with the *animals* (Hos. 2:20). Though her betrothal to Yahweh follows in verse 21, Israel's secondary position vis-à-vis the animal world is no accident. Neither is her loss of a voice. In verse 18, the woman's speech is compelled by Yahweh ("She will not say . . ."); in the final lines, her voice is entirely replaced by the voices of the earth and heaven, as well as by Yahweh's/Hosea's *son*:

> And I will sow her for myself in the land,
>   and I will have mercy on No-Mercy, I will say to
>   Not-My-People, "You are my people!"
> And he will say, "My God!" (Hos. 2:25)

Even Israel's voice, which is heard earlier in the passage, is now absent, replaced by masculine vocality—the voice of her son. The metaphorical association of the female body and the land is likewise collapsed, with Israel reduced to a sowable field. The metaphor of the body as land has come full circle.

Thinking Horror with the Female Body: Torture and Openness

The male bodies of Hosea 1–3 are almost absent; the female bodies, for their part, are all too present. In thinking embodiment in this text, there are two features of the female body that are especially significant: the female body as tortured and the female body as opened. The suffering of Israel's body is obvious—she is stripped, exposed, repeatedly murdered. The openness of this body, however, requires some explanation. In the case of the female-bodied Israel, openness is both problem and punishment. The transgressions of Israel, which drive Yahweh to rage and violence, are fundamentally problems of openness. Israel is dangerously open to the ba'als, as both foreign influence and rival lovers. Playing the whore, the favored metaphor of the prophets to condemn idolatry or bad religious practice, likewise represents a problematics of openness—the access to the body is no longer under the proper control of the patriarchal author- ity. Even if we read the opening chapters of Hosea as an allegory about exploitative economic practices—a not uncommon interpretive move— the problem is still one of openness to foreign influences and economic liaisons. The boundaries of the body, personal or national, are threaten- ingly porous, unregulated, and accessible.

The punishments that Yahweh promises to bring upon this body also revolve around openness. Yahweh pledges to strip Israel naked (Hos. 2:11), to expose her genitals (2:12), to destroy her vines and fig trees (2:14)—all of these punishments centered on opening the body, and on exposing its most vulnerable margins to violence. The same is true of the promise, in the supposedly romantic final third of the text, to remove the names of the ba'als from her mouth (2:17). We might remember here, as well, the association of the mouth and genitals.[21] The destruc- tion of vines and fig trees functions doubly, both exposing the literal land and leaving Israel vulnerable and unprotected within this open expanse. The trap that Yahweh sets is the first step in a process of confinement, exposure, and torture that culminates in the forced opening of the body/land to Yahweh. Even the promise to "hedge up her way with thorns" and "block her road with a wall of stones," though it seems to suggest enclosure and confinement, also implies the forced opening of the body. The thorns anticipate the penetration of the body that is to come, while the hedging up and confinement are the immediate and necessary precursors to the actions of removing and uncovering in verses 11–12. And in the restoration and re-seduction scene in the final third of the chapter, the body is so opened to Yahweh and so thoroughly collapsed in the land that Israel loses even the possibility of voicing any objection. Instead, her voice is replaced by the voice of her son, the patriarchal line from father to son unbroken by the feminine or the maternal. While the masculine flourishes, the female body becomes a site of violence.

The double thematics of torture and openness are central to perceiving Hosea 1–3 as a horror text. In suggesting this parallel, I do not mean simply to suggest that Hosea belongs with the "high" or critically acclaimed horror of Hitchcock and De Palma and a handful of others. Hosea belongs, too—even more so—with "low" and other popular horror, in all its messy violence. The horror films that parallel Hosea, and that Carol Clover takes up in *Men, Women, and Chain Saws*, are films saturated with violence against women. Women are dismembered, tortured, chased by masked men, confronted with repeated and excessive violence and bodily violation. To name such violence is an obvious task. It is not particularly innovative or illuminating, however, to center all critical energy on arguing, for example, that the repeated murder of sexualized women in the slasher film is "problematic" or "misogynistic." This is both obvious and generally unproductive, in the sense that this reading does not "produce" anything, any insight or new way of thinking. Who are the intended readers of such an argument, who are deeply concerned about gender, interested in reading about horror, but have never stopped to consider that the repeated, brutal murders of female characters might be understood as problematic? And who, for that matter, are the readers of the Hebrew Bible who are deeply concerned about gender, interested in reading about Gomer and the feminized Israel, but have never stopped to consider that their representation and treatment might be problematic?

It is certainly true that for a significant period of time, biblical scholars and critics did *not*, in fact, pause to consider Gomer, or Israel as a woman, or women, really at all. But now that attention has begun to be paid consistently, it is time to consider other ways of reading, of engaging with and challenging texts. There is more that can be done with a text such as Hosea 1–3 than diagnosing its terrors. It is for this reason that I want to model a new approach to Hosea 1–3, intentionally informed by horror and by horror scholarship. And in building this reading of Hosea as horror, I want to turn now to Clover's work. Clover is adept at isolating the foundational structures of horror genres and at teasing out their complex attitudes toward gender, sex, and embodiment. Her work is especially engaged with, as she puts it, "those subgenres in which female figures and/or gender issues loom especially large: slasher films, occult or possession films, and rape-revenge films."[22] These are films that—like the Hebrew prophets—are saturated with violence against women. Women are dismembered, tortured, chased, possessed, menaced by chain saws, and impregnated by the devil. They are also films in which, as Clover demonstrates over and over again, masculinity is contested, problematized, and renegotiated in complicated—if often violent, unstable, or frightening—ways.

In adapting and applying Clover's analysis, I want to highlight three central contributions that her study of the horror contributes to a reading of masculinity and biblical prophecy:

1. Recognizing torture as more complex than simple misogyny;
2. Articulating a crisis of masculinity;
3. Staging a problematics of openness.

I will begin with torture.

1. Recognizing Torture as More Complex than Simple Misogyny

The genres of horror that Clover takes up are filled with violence, and this violence is primarily directed against the female body (as in the slasher film), or through it (as in the possession film). This does not, however, mean that their relations to sex, gender, and embodiment are simple, or that the films are simply misogynistic. Instead, one of the major contributions of *Men, Women, and Chain Saws* is the way in which it dismantles this facile assumption about horror, offering in its place a far more complex scene. In the introduction to the book, Clover acknowledges the potential for sadism and voyeurism in the viewing experience, but continues,

> I do not, however, believe that sadistic voyeurism is the first cause of horror. Nor do I believe that real-life women and feminist politics have been entirely well served by the astonishingly insistent claim that horror's satisfactions begin and end in sadism . . . horror's misogyny is a far more complicated matter than the "bloodlust" formula would have it, and I suspect that the critical insistence on that formula constitutes its own version of a politics of displacement.[23]

A few lines later, Clover adds, "the standard critique of horror as straightforward sadistic misogyny itself needs not only a critical but a political interrogation."[24] This statement, calling out the "standard critique of horror" with its uncomplicated and insufficient treatment of gender, is incredibly important, both for the films Clover discusses and for "texts of terror" more broadly. Too often, we slip into repeating what we already know in our reading of texts. This is especially the case, I would suggest, with texts that appall us. But instead of such a rehearsal of truisms, Clover calls for an interpretive practice that rethinks gender while interrogating the ideological underpinnings of the "standard critique."

This is a valuable and important direction for biblical reading as well. Like the films Clover discusses, the Hebrew prophetic texts are too often treated as "straightforward sadistic misogyny." As I have already suggested above, this "standard critique" introduces nothing new. It assumes a "faith in exposure," the idea that exposing violence is the best way to neutralize it.[25] The problem with prophetic violence, however, is not that it is unknown, not even that it has passed unproblematized. It is no surprise to find that there is a great deal of literature documenting Hosea as pornographer, pervert, and abuser. But what else might we find in Hosea? How else might we understand the politics of identification, the use of violence, the construction and dismantling of gender categories?

2. Articulating a Crisis of Masculinity

Beyond critiquing the facile dismissal of horror as misogyny, Clover's work is valuable for the critical attention it directs toward *masculinity* in the horror film. As Clover's analysis of multiple horror genres makes clear, masculinity is contested and unstable. In her study of the slasher film genre (such as *Friday the 13th, Halloween, Scream*, their endless sequels), Clover demonstrates that even when the central figure is female, the psychic drama is masculine.[26] Clover writes,

> That the slasher film speaks deeply and obsessively to male anxieties and desires seems clear—if nothing else from the maleness of the majority audience. And yet these are texts in which the categories masculine and feminine, traditionally embodied in male and female, are collapsed into one and the same character—a character who is anatomically female and one whose point of view the spectator is unambiguously invited, by the usual set of literary-structural and cinematic conventions, to share.[27]

In the slasher film, the drama of the female character is intimately linked to a negotiation of masculinity. The problem of masculinity becomes even clearer in Clover's reading of the possession film, which has special relevance for reading Hosea. The possession film is a genre that includes classics such as *The Exorcist* and *Witchboard* (both discussed in detail by Clover), as well as more recent specimens such as *The Exorcism of Emily Rose, The Last Exorcism*, and countless other movies in which an innocent victim—almost always female—is possessed by evil spirits, demons, the devil, or other nefarious forces. Like Hosea 1–3, these films appear to center on a suffering, open female body. The plot hinges upon the attempts, usually by a male protagonist or protagonists, to vanquish evil and to close the dangerous openness of the female body.

Such possession films resemble Hosea 1–3 not simply in the opened female body, but in the *use* of this body as a space to negotiate masculinity, and in particular the question of masculine openness. As Clover argues, while the possession film *seems* to be about the possessed young woman, her role is fundamentally secondary (if dramatic and frequently visually spectacular). The real concern of the text is with the transformation of the male character, who begins the story too suspicious, too closed off, too skeptical, and too traditionally masculine, and who must be "feminized" and opened by the text. Here a clear example is *The Exorcist*, directed by William Friedkin and based on a novel by William Peter Blatty.[28] At first, *The Exorcist* appears to be the story of Regan MacNeil, a twelve-year-old girl who is possessed by a demon. The most vivid and memorable images of the film are clearly of the possessed Regan, as she screams, writhes, and inflicts great damage on those around her. And yet, as Clover argues, Regan's spectacle is only secondary to the central drama of the story: the spiritual transformation of one of the priests involved in the exorcism, Father Karras. Karras's struggle to maintain faith is central to his interactions with Regan and her mother. In the final climactic showdown, it is he who takes the demon into his own body, destroying it along with himself.

Karras's story is mirrored by two additional priests. The film opens with Father Merrin in Iraq, encountering (on an archaeological dig) the demon that will eventually possess Regan; it is Merrin's scenes with Karras that likewise hold the greatest emotional intensity (if not the affects of horror and disgust). Similarly, the film ends with Father Dyer, another priest and close confidant to Karras, looking over the lonely street where Karras died. Dyer, moreover, plays the role of witness to Karras's death, administering last rites to the dying priest and thus marking the resolution of his spiritual crisis. The scene likewise provides a final moment of intimacy and emotional force. As Clover writes, "For all its spectacle value, Regan's story is finally significant only insofar as it affects the lives of others, above all the tormented spiritual life of Karras . . . The accessory nature of Regan's story could hardly be clearer; she is the evidence, proof, testimony that the faltering Karras has been yearning for."[29] Regan ultimately functions as a proxy for Karras's crisis. More broadly, the female body is instrumental in articulating an (otherwise unspeakable) crisis of masculinity.

3. Staging a Problematics of Openness

Clover's account of the possession film demonstrates a third problematic that is significant to Hosea 1–3 as well: openness. In the possession film, it is not simply that the female body stands in for the male psyche—a common enough substitution that we find at least as far back as Diotima's account of love in Plato's

Symposium.[30] Instead, and of specific relevance to Hosea, the possession film thematizes the open/opened body and its relationship to gender. In *The Exorcist*, to continue with the example, Regan stands in for Karras *with her body*, which is violently opened by demonic possession. It is not enough that Regan be possessed and tortured; her corporeality and experience of embodiment must be foregrounded. Regan's body provides what Clover terms the "palpable field" for Karras to negotiate his spirituality and his masculinity—literally so, in a key scene when words appear on Regan's abdomen. New forms of masculinity depend upon broken open women. This is the case as well in the Babylonian Enuma Elish, in which the god Marduk murders his mother, the monstrous sea goddess Tiamat, and then creates the world from her corpse. And this is likewise true in Hosea 1–3, which manifests, to use Clover's language, a "remapping of the masculine . . . [which] entails a kind of territorial displacement in the world of gender."[31] The opened female body of Israel (and, to a lesser degree, Gomer and the woman in chapter 3) points to a crisis in openness and masculinity in Hosea.

Openness itself, meanwhile, is also gendered; it is intentionally associated with the female body. The association of openness with the male body is considered a threat. This openness of the female body is, as Clover notes, an idea with a lengthy history; women have long been represented as threateningly "open," both physically and psychically.[32] This is true in the Hebrew Bible as well.

With these three contributions from Clover outlined, I want to consider how they relate to Hosea 1–3. Here, the first two points—the recognition of the complexity of violence and the articulation of a crisis of masculinity—are preconditions of the central argument, the problematics of openness as the key to gender, embodiment, and prophecy.

Recognizing Torture as more Complex than Simple Misogyny: The Violence of Hosea 1–3

The first three chapters of Hosea are clearly filled with violence. We have already traced out many of these forms of violence. The most explicit physical violence is reserved for the feminized Israel, who is threatened, physically violated, and buried in the earth. The metaphorical association of the land and the female body is exploited all too well here, as the land is at once tortured (transformed into a wilderness) and used as an instrument of violence against the woman (who is menaced with thorns and murdered with thirst). The close parallels between the first two-thirds of the chapter, which describe Israel's punishment, and the final third, which chronicles her re-seduction, imbue the latter scene of reconciliation with threat. In Hosea 1 and 3, the violence against the female body is not explicit. However, read through chapter 2, these chapters reveal their own role in a larger textual economy of violence. The representation of Gomer is not neutral. Neither is the account of the woman in chapter 3. Both texts instrumentalize the female body and reduce the woman to object.

As I have suggested above, however, simply identifying Hosea 1–3 as a site of gendered violence does not exhaust the range of meanings in the text, nor does it offer the only possible response. By now, my point should be clear: to say Hosea 1–3 is violent is perhaps necessary, but it is not sufficient, at least at the present moment, to address the text. And so pushing forward, I will argue that the gendered violence of Hosea 1–3 is significant not only as violence in its own right, but also for what it contributes to the (uneasy) construction of masculinity and the male body in the prophetic text.

Articulating a Crisis of Masculinity: Yahweh and his Prophets

Hosea is a text characterized by a crisis of masculinity. As I argue throughout in *Are We Not Men?* masculinity is frequently contested, unstable, or problematic for prophecy. This is true as well for Hosea. Though the opening chapters of the book revolve around heterosexual marriage, the marriages between Hosea and Gomer and between Yahweh and Israel do not shore up masculinity, but rather destabilize it. Marrying a promiscuous woman is hardly a conventional way of asserting masculine privilege, particularly at a time when the secure paternity of children is of utmost importance. The association of Gomer with whoredom calls Hosea's paternity of her children into question. As Susan Haddox writes, "In Hosea's female imagery, the presence of children vouches for the virility of the husband, but the possibility that they are not his threatens this element of his masculinity."[33] The very children who serve as fleshly signs of Hosea's prophecy destabilize his role as patriarch and provider.

Ken Stone has also taken up the instability of masculinity in Hosea, linking the prophet's masculinity to a crisis of divine masculinity. He directs special attention to Yahweh's complaints that Israel has failed to recognize the food he has provided (Hos. 2:7, 2:10–11), suggesting that this almost obsessive interest in the origins of "the grain, the wine, and the olive oil" conceals an anxiety over masculinity and the male obligation as provider. Israel credits baʿal, not Yahweh; thus as punishment, Yahweh will expose the land and leave Israel vulnerable and unprotected. This punishment is necessary because the misattribution threatens the male honor of the deity.[34] At the same time, this shame is also linked to a sneaking sense that Yahweh in fact does *not* exercise sole control over fertility and is not the exclusive provider. As Stone writes, "Hosea ironically leaves the Yhwh he constructs open to the charge of revealing through anxious assertion a sort of divine insecurity about Yhwh's ability to be (playing again here on Herzfeld's phrase) 'good at being a male god.'"[35] This reading raises the provocative possibility that the disturbances of masculinity in Hosea are not limited to the prophet himself. Instead, the crisis of masculinity proves contagious, spreading to Yahweh as well.

As Haddox and Stone make clear, there are numerous problems of masculinity in Hosea. What is not yet present in their analysis, however, is an attention to the role of the *body* in this crisis of masculinity. As in the horror film, the problem of masculinity is articulated as a problem of *openness*. And so it is openness to which I want now to turn.

Staging a Problematics of Openness: Open Bodies, Open Problems

The crisis of masculinity in Hosea 1–3 is linked specifically to the openness of the body. Openness recurs across the first three chapters of Hosea. The transgressions of Israel, which drive Yahweh to rage and violence, are fundamentally problems of openness. Israel is dangerously open to the baʿals, as both foreign influence and rival lovers. Playing the whore, the favored metaphor of the prophets to condemn idolatry or bad religious practice, likewise represents—and furthers—a problematics of openness; the access to the body is no longer under the proper control of the patriarchal authority. This opening of the female body threatens the patriarchal order in a number of ways. If the woman opens her body to other male lovers, the paternity of her children is not assured and the (normative) masculinity of her husband is called into question.[36] Even the raisin cakes of Hosea 3 are condemned, like the woman's adulterous practices, because they suggest the untoward opening of the body.

Gomer is likewise always already too "open" in the text. As an ʾēšet zĕnûnîm, her body is opened sexually, and it is her very sexual openness and accessibility, her association with zĕnûnîm, that motivates Hosea's taking her in marriage. Yet in marrying Gomer and conceiving children with her, Hosea opens himself and his body to her threatening openness. Hosea is also "opened" through the openness of *Israel's* body and sexuality in Hosea 2, because Hosea, as an Israelite man, is part of the collective body of Israel. The openness—first to foreign others, then to God—of the female body in chapter 2 is also a narrative about the openness of a community. This is also, of course, a narrative about the openness of the male bodies that constitute the Israelite corporate body, as Howard Eilberg-Schwartz has shown.[37]

This thematization of the open body evokes a number of themes that we have already discussed—violence, the violation of the female body, the ambivalence and even crisis of accompanying masculinity. Centrally, the open, violated female body, however transfixing it is in the text, is a site for working through *masculinity*. Torturing—more specifically, *opening*—the female body is a way of speaking about, and around, masculinity. To return to the language of Carol Clover, the female body provides a "palpable field" to negotiate masculinity. In *The Exorcist*, this metaphor becomes literal, as the girl Regan's abdomen is manipulated to spell out messages. This is a part of her demonic possession that, in Clover's reading, speaks the Catholic priest Karras's masculine crisis. In Hosea, the metaphor is literalized in another way, as Israel—literally, a field, or at least a land—is represented as a violently opened place/woman. Gomer, too, is opened, through childbirth and the implicit violence of the text and its traffic in, and response to, sexualized women. These female and feminized figures provide a ground for contesting masculinity and, especially, the problematics of openness with respect to prophetic masculinity.

How Does the Opened Female Body Speak about Prophetic Masculinity?

The text of Hosea betrays a deep anxiety about proper masculine performance, a performance that Yahweh and his prophet may fail at, deviate from, or even intentionally subvert. The crisis, however, does not simply concern masculinity as performance. Instead, it is intimately tied up in the body, and in the complex and contradictory relations of masculinity, prophecy, and embodiment.

Hosea is opened by the demands of prophecy. No longer able to act as an ordinary man, Hosea is opened to the word of Yahweh, which comes to him, fills him, and compels his actions. The coming of the word is described twice in the text: verse 1 reads: "The word of Yahweh, which came to Hosea, son of Beeri . . ."; verse 2: "At the beginning, when Yahweh began talking to Hosea . . ." There is little hint of an opening up here, except, just perhaps, in the doubling of the coming of Yahweh's words to Hosea. (Why must the word come twice? Does repetition imply resistance?) Here, a turn to intertextual parallels offers some clues. Elsewhere in the biblical text, the coming of the prophetic word is figured more clearly as the opening up of the body. Jeremiah describes the word as entering into his bones (Jer. 20:9); Ezekiel experiences eating a scroll with the divine word written on it, tasting of honey (Ezek. 3:1–3). And yet Hosea himself is also opened by his prophetic calling. But in the book of Hosea, this openness of the prophet is *displaced* onto the female body. The violently opened bodies of Gomer and especially of Israel represent the opening of the male subject effected by the prophetic calling.

Prophecy opens by making the prophet into a medium, an opening between God and people. While it is not strictly or even necessarily sexual, the openness that prophecy demands nevertheless calls into question the organization of masculinity for the prophet. The result appears to be a feminizing of the prophetic position—but to speak more precisely, this is not a feminization, but rather, as the comparison with Clover suggests, a transformation of the experience of masculinity that leads to the prophet's displacement from, or queering of, the category of normative masculinity. Hosea experiences an opening, a different sort of masculinity. But because male openness is paradoxical and largely unthinkable under the order of hegemonic biblical masculinity, it is displaced to the female body, which provides an alternate ground to think through and theorize prophetic openness and its consequences for prophetic masculinity.

Such openness also animates a possible queerness of the prophetic body. I have suggested that the strategies of displacement employed in Hos. 1–3 work to separate the question of masculinity from the object of the male body. That masculinity can be "thought" via the female body suggests a larger flexibility and lability concerning gender and sexual difference. This flexibility suggests, in turn, novel queer trajectories for the body of the prophet. If masculinity can be temporarily severed or displaced from the male body, what other forms may this male body assume? And for that matter, what other forms of masculinity may emerge while masculinity as such is under negotiation elsewhere, on the flesh of the female body? The prophet's male body-without-masculinity begins to look like a rather queer object. This is not to suggest that a move beyond or outside traditional or hegemonic forms of masculinity is queer, but rather that a body that is even temporarily severed from its gender and sexuality (the male prophetic body, the male body in the possession film) is a body opened to new potential.

This masculine openness comes, however, at a cost. As Clover writes of the possession film,

> I would suggest that the remapping of the masculine in the occult film entails a kind of territorial displacement in the world of gender.... Crudely put, for a space to be created in which men can weep without being labeled feminine, women must be relocated to a space where they will be made to wail uncontrollably; for men to be able to relinquish emotional rigidity, control, women must be relocated to a space in which they will undergo a flamboyant psychotic break, and so on.[38]

The possession film is not about spectacular, tortured, opened female bodies, but rather about the work of crafting a more "open" masculinity. Negotiating the possibility of alternate masculinity requires a radical displacement of femininity.

This displacement, moreover, relies on the excessive opening of the girl or woman's body, first by the evil that possesses her, then by the man or men who seek to "cure" her. For a space to be created in which Hosea can experience openness and nonnormative biblical masculinity, Gomer must be relocated to a space of whoredom, shame, and cultural exile. For Yahweh to set aside a hypermasculine rivalry with the baʿals,[39] Israel must undergo excessive physical suffering, psychological fragmentation, and an eventual merging into one with the land. Hosea uses the female body not just to work through anxieties about the land and the sources of its prosperous productivity, but also to negotiate the specific anxiety of prophecy as a forced opening of the male prophetic subject to Yahweh. This is a queer opening for the male prophet, but it comes at the expense of the female body. Or as Clover writes of the possession film, "the standard scheme puts, or at least seems to put, the female body on the line only in order to put the male psyche on the line."[40] In Hosea 1–3, the text opens and exposes the female body in order to explore the opening and exposure to Yahweh of the male prophetic body.

The opening up of the category of masculinity ultimately threatens the stability of the representation of the *male* body as well. The relationship of proxy—female body, male psyche—is intended to keep the two separate. There remains, however, the risk of contamination between terms. The relations of metaphor are not completely stable. *The Exorcist* offers a dramatic example of such a category breach. In the final moments of the exorcism, the demon leaves Regan's body and enters Karras. The transformation of the masculine body is no longer strictly symbolic and ideological. Instead, it has become literal—and, for Karras, deadly. There is no parallel scene of transformation in Hosea 1–3. Still, the very relationship of proxy—the female body is opened up so that the male body does not have to be—introduces the risk of a breach. If masculinity can be opened *symbolically*, there is the possibility that it can be opened *literally* as well. Though the book of Hosea does not explore this possibility further, it emerges at other moments in the prophetic literature, including in Jeremiah and Ezekiel (explored in chapters 3 and 4, below). Still, the queer potentiality of bodily transformation is already present, however, tenuously, in Hosea.

Coda: The Dream of a Therapeutic Ending

When I began this project, I had hopes of finding a different, better, less hateful Hosea hidden in the details of the text. As an earlier generation of feminist scholars worked to give voice to Gomer, so did I imagine giving voice to a kinder, gentler Hosea. Perhaps a better prophet was possible. Perhaps there was more to Hosea—and to Hosea's Yahweh—than violence, misogyny, rage. Over time, this dream of a better prophet transmuted into a dream of a better prophetic *masculinity*—a masculine ideal that would resist normative performances of biblical masculinity, performances with a weighty and damaging legacy.

In the time I have spent with the text, I have become convinced that the opening chapters of Hosea fracture the norms of biblical masculinity. Masculinity in Hosea is many things—unstable, rage-filled, impotent, acting with and acted upon by violence—but it is a different masculine norm than that of hegemonic masculinity. It is even possible to conceive of masculinity in Hosea as a queering of biblical masculinity. This does not mean, however, that it is not a masculinity built upon the torture of the female body. As such, masculinity in Hosea places the feminist critic of Hosea in somewhat of a bind. Insofar as the marriage narratives in Hosea offer alternate scripts for masculinity, they perform valuable work in dismantling oppressive categories. But insofar as this dismantling is built on the violently opened bodies of women, it is deeply disturbing.

It is here, too that the horror film offers a model for moving beyond this bind. Critical readings of horror, such as Clover's, offer a helpful model for differentiating between the work and the character. Clover convincingly argues for the feminist potential of the slasher film, for example, and yet it would be ridiculous—and a misconstrual of Clover's argument—to treat Freddy Krueger or Jason Voorhees as a feminist hero. Insofar as the slasher film reconfigures gender, it occurs on the level of the work itself, not in the form of the individual characters. Feminist utopias, like all utopias, make bad fictions; the critical potential of the text is not confined to the degree to which it manifests a theme. Conversely, it is the very excess of horror that destabilizes gender and opens a space in the text for queer reading.

Instead, what therapeutic conclusion there is comes in the securing of the category of the masculinity. While we may desire a more open, less misogynistic entry point into the prophets, in Hosea the figure of the woman is ultimately still instrumentalized as a tool for creating a different masculinity. The possession films that Clover discusses, for all the extravagant physicalized anguish of their heroines, end with the therapeutic or redemptive opening of their *male* characters. The central story is a male story, as the title of another of Clover's chapters, "Her Body, Himself," makes clear.[41] In the marriage texts of Hosea 1–3, there are similar gestures toward a redemptive conclusion, particularly in Yahweh's promises to speak gently to Israel and to win back her love in the second half of chapter 2. The coda of Hosea's domestic narrative likewise promises restoration for Israel. Hosea 2:1 reads, "The number of the children of Israel will be like the sand of the sea, which cannot be measured and cannot be counted. And instead of saying, 'You are not my people,' it will be said to them, 'Children of the living God.'" A therapeutic renaming of Hosea's children follows. Even chapter 3 ends with a promise of Davidic restoration.

Notably, each of these moments of restoration or redemption focuses on the feminine and its associated figures: Gomer, Israel, or their children. A transformed self-understanding by either Yahweh or Hosea is nowhere in evidence. If anything, if we take Yahweh's instructions in Hosea 3:1 to read "Go again, love a woman who is loved by another and who commits adultery," then Hosea emphatically does *not* learn or evolve as a character. Instead, we have displacement and disavowal, indicating anxiety over an open masculinity that cannot easily be dispersed or filled. Even the promises of restoration at the end of the marriage texts do not promise a whole or restored prophetic body, but rather a multiplication of prophetic descendants.

These moments of redemption are ultimately linked to a shoring up of the masculinity of prophecy. If the opened female body speaks (without speaking) the crisis of prophetic opening, then the moments of restoration—Israel buried, the children renamed, the woman of chapter 3 loved again—represent a restoration of the masculine order. The disruptive threat—of prophecy, to prophecy—is no longer. The margins of the body, temporarily opened, are again sealed. Yahweh promises Israel he will remove the baʿals from her mouth. Similarly, the prophetic body—the body of the prophet and the body in the prophetic text—is purged of its subversions, its margins rendered clean. Prophecy is again fixed. The masculine is again secure. The queer is again absent. And the body of Israel is reduced to dirt and securely buried in the earth.

3

The Hysteria of Jeremiah

GENDER AND VOICE IN THE CONFESSIONS

OUR BODIES HAVE voices; our voices are embodied. The voice issues forth from the body and relies on it to produce sound. And yet the voice is also separate from the body, and sometimes even positioned antagonistically against it. Mladen Dolar describes it as "the link which ties the signifier to the body," pointing to voice's ambiguous, interstitial status—between sound and meaning, between body and signifier, between self and other.[1]

If the voice is at once central to and separable from the body, the same is true of the relationship of the voice to prophecy. The voice, in and out of the body, is deeply important to prophecy. The voice crying out in the wilderness (Isa. 40:3) often functions as a synecdoche for the prophet. To be a prophet, this passage suggests, is to have a *voice*. And yet the prophetic voice, for all its power (and, as this chapter will take up subsequently, all of its failures) is not all that the prophet is. There may be a voice, and a wilderness from which the voice emanates, and yet in that wilderness the voice also comes forth from a body. Taking these complexities as a starting point, this chapter will use the voice to offer a new understanding of the prophetic body. The voice, I will suggest, offers a new way of orienting the troubled bodies and inspired speech of biblical prophecy. It also poses questions of gender to both body and sound in unusual and unexpected ways.

This is especially true in the case of Jeremiah's "Confessions," a collection of angry, anguished first-person complaints scattered through the first half of the book. These complaints repeatedly take up the theme of the voice and its many difficulties. Jeremiah's attention to speech and sound, combined with his repeated difficulties and failures, are so pronounced as to drive readers to exasperation and exhaustion. Even the most inveterate literary critics begin to question this troublesome prophet; thus Geoffrey Hartman asks, with at least a hint of frustration, "Why can't Jeremiah talk in a normal voice? What is the matter with him?"[2]

Why can't Jeremiah talk in a normal voice? There are many ways in which Jeremiah's voice is peculiar. He cries and shouts out in pain or anger. He repeats and revoices the words of others. Meaning threatens to collapse into a wash of sound and anguish. At other moments, he abandons what he has been saying in order to speak about speech itself, lamenting its difficulties. These features, which occur across the Confessions, are not simply secondary phenomena. Instead, Jeremiah's voice presents a meaningful break with cultural norms of sound and speech. Rather than communicating a specific meaning, the prophet's repeated crying out represents the overwhelming affective force of suffering. It also feminizes him. There are certain sounds and voices that are textually and culturally "heard" as feminine; Jeremiah's speech in the Confessions, I will argue, resembles and even employs these sounds. Voice functions as an extension of the body; it is also one site where the male prophetic body is subverted and transformed.

What is the matter with him? The prophet's use of sound does not simply reflect gender disturbance. Instead, Jeremiah's speech is structured as hysteria. This does not mean that Jeremiah "is" a hysteric, but rather that his use of sound and language resembles the voices of hysterics in both form and content. Rehearing Jeremiah's speech through the category of hysteria helps explain his peculiar uses of sound and the crossing over of voice and body in his prophecy. It also offers a new perspective from which to interrogate the gendered social role of the prophet. Reading prophecy through hysteria likewise illuminates larger social dynamics of revulsion and erotic attraction, as well as the complex interweaving of pain, memory, and the hysterical body. Sound, and hysterical sound in particular, also opens a space of queer possibility in the text, challenging the configurations of voice, body, and desire.

The argument of this chapter unfolds in two stages. Part I begins with the specific features of Jeremiah's voice in the Confessions, with particular attention to the crying voice. I will trace the way gender is destabilized through sound. Part II sets Jeremiah's voice against several key case studies of hysteria: Sigmund Freud and Joseph Breuer's *Studies in Hysteria* (1895), as well "Fragment of an Analysis of a Case of Hysteria" (the Dora case), published by Freud a few years later (1905).[3] As Freud and Breuer describe it, hysteria is a category intimately bound up with modernity and with the attendant modern conceptions of gender, authority, and pathology.[4] Rather than telling a "truth" about female experience or malady, the texts about hysteria expose the constructions of gender, power, voice, and body. And this exposure is telling with respect to Jeremiah. Voice—and especially the hysterical voice—offers another way of thinking through prophetic masculinity and embodiment.

Part I: Jeremiah's Confessions and the Crying Voice

The Book of Jeremiah is a book organized around imminent disaster. Called as a prophet from within his mother's womb—"Before I formed you in the womb, I knew you, and before you were born, I sanctified you; I appointed you a prophet to the nations" (Jer. 1:5)—Jeremiah prophesies the destruction of Judah and the fall of Jerusalem. This message of impending destruction is shot through with great personal suffering, both emotional and physical. "My insides! My insides! I writhe in pain!" (4:19) and "My heart is sick" (8:18), the prophet complains, and yet he continues to prophesy, antagonizing the Judean king and people and bringing agony upon himself. As Jeremiah himself admits, his words are reviled by his listeners, who plot repeatedly to take his life (11:19, 17:17–18, 18:19–23, 20:10) and cast him into prison (36:26, 28:1–13). He likewise has a fraught relationship with the king and with his prophetic contemporaries. The final chapters of the book narrate the prophet's forced exile into Egypt and the fall of Jerusalem.

This chapter centers on a particular subsection of texts from Jeremiah, the Confessions. These first-person texts occur, interspersed with other material, in chapters 11–20. (The individual Confessions are, following the division of texts set forth by A. R. Pete Diamond, Jer. 11:18–23, 12:1–6, 15:10–14, 15:15–21, 17:14–18, 18:18–23, 20:7–13, and 20:14–18.[5]) In them, Jeremiah speaks back against God and expresses the pain and personal suffering his prophetic vocation has brought him. Jeremiah describes prophecy as a seduction, a painful trick, and the cause of his many enemies' desire to seek his life. This handful of themes occurs repeatedly. Indeed, it is chiefly their content that distinguishes the Confessions, as there are no other indications given in the original text. Still, while the various Confessions are not marked or set off from the remainder of the original text in any way, their existence is widely accepted by scholars, largely on the basis of this thematic unity.

Little else, however, is agreed upon. Even what to call these texts is a site of scholarly contention, with the traditional name widely criticized but neverthe-less generally maintained. In fact, nearly every scholar who writes about the texts begins with a few requisite remarks about the inadequacy and anachronism of the name "Confessions," sometimes proposing an alternative as well.[6] While acknowl-edging the problems with the name "Confessions"—Jeremiah is hardly confess-ing; he is far from an Augustine or even a Rousseau—I will use it here, largely for reasons of simplicity. But I would also suggest that there is something telling in the misreading of the passages' contents as "Confessions." The complaining prophet, like the hysteric, says what should not be said, in ways that are difficult to hear. Identifying such texts as "Confessions" domesticates their strangeness and inte-grates them into a genre—though one rather different than what the texts them-selves contain. Perhaps we persist in calling Jeremiah's complaints "Confessions" because we would like Jeremiah to be a bit more of an Augustine: passionate, self-reflective, theologically committed.[7] Or perhaps the misnaming signals a crisis in interpretation, a struggle to hear what the Confessions really say.

In any case, what is really at stake in the Confessions is not what they are *called*, but what they contain. As a first example, consider Jeremiah 11:18–23:

> Yahweh made known to me and I knew,
>> then you showed me[8] their evil deeds.
> But I was like a gentle lamb led to the slaughter,
>> and I did not know that they plotted schemes against me:
> "Let us destroy the tree with its fruit,[9] and cut him off from the land of
>> the living, and his name will be remembered no longer."
> But Yahweh, righteous judge, the one who tests my kidneys and heart,
>> Let me see your vengeance upon them, for to you I have disclosed
>>> my case.
> For thus says Yahweh to the men of Anathoth, the ones who seek your
>> life, saying, "'Do not prophesy in the name of Yahweh, lest you die
>> by our hand!' Behold, I will punish them! Their young men will die
>> by the sword, and their sons and their daughters will die of famine,
>> And there will be no remnant for them when I bring evil upon the
>> men of Anathoth, the year of their punishment." (Jer. 11:18–23)

The text is strikingly fluid. The speaker, Jeremiah, assumes multiple voices (his own, Yahweh's, the voices of the men of Anathoth) without clear textual signals marking the shifts in speaker. When he speaks as himself, he addresses Yahweh intimately, often with scathing complaints. Between grievances, he also voices his confidence (or perhaps *over*confidence, given the degree to which his difficulties recur in subsequent Confessions) that he will be delivered from his enemies. The desire to observe the men of Anathoth's punishment, meanwhile, suggests a certain sadism, especially when set against the references to knowledge, fertility, and the tenuous status of the prophet's own body. Knowledge is likewise articulated in relation to both violence and desire. In the final lines, Jeremiah becomes almost frenzied in imagining replacing his own suffering with the suffering of his enemies. Swords, famine, unspecified evil—what the vision lacks in singular focus, it compensates for in general excess.

These themes are repeated in another of the Confessions, Jeremiah 17:14–18:

> Heal me, Yahweh, and I will be healed,
>> deliver me and I will be delivered,
>>> for I praise you.
> Look, they say to me,
>> "Where is the word of Yahweh? Let it come!"
> But I did not hasten away from being a shepherd after you, but
>> I did not desire the calamitous day.[10]

> You know what comes forth from my lips, and it has been in
> front of your face.
> Do not be a terror to me;
> you are my refuge on the day of distress.
> Let my pursuers be shamed, but do not let me suffer shame.
> Let them be dismayed, but do not let me be dismayed.
> Bring upon them the day of distress, and shatter them with a
> double breaking.

Like the first Confession considered above, this text brings together trust, fear, and passionate appeals with insistent references to past speech and past promises. Terror is mixed with brash confidence. The body of the prophet is wounded or sick, in need of healing (Jer. 17:14), but also opened to Yahweh, both figuratively and bodily (17:16), and threatened with violence (17:16–18). In the final lines, the injury to the prophet's body in verse 14 is reimagined as the shaming and shattering of the bodies of his enemies. Pain again becomes pleasure in the suffering of others. This rapid shift in affective content, as well as the fluidity of subjects, repeats the form of Jeremiah 11:18–23, and indeed the other Confessions. In these texts, knowledge, embodiment, pain, and pleasure collide.

Between the repeated expressions of violence, anger, and desire, there is another theme that emerges in both of these texts, and indeed across the Confessions: the voice. The voice is essential to the Confessions. Prophecy depends upon the voice, and yet Jeremiah complains repeatedly of the difficulty of speaking as a prophet. His body likewise enters into the text more fully—if problematically—through voice, which at once provides an extension of the body and a means of describing it. Understanding the voice, then, is key to understanding the Confessions. This understanding encompasses a more thorough perception of the body and its difficulties in these texts.

The Cry and the Crying Body

Sound and voice play an essential role in the Confessions. Frequently, this role is disruptive, as the aural runs up against or threatens the clear transmission of meaning. This is already clear in the two passages from the Confessions considered above. In the first (Jer. 11:18–23), Jeremiah's appeal to Yahweh, his repeated accounts of threats, and the cries of enemies (starving, stabbed, and beset by raiders) vie uneasily, to chaotic effect. There is a similar layering of sounds in Jeremiah 17:14–18. In that passage, sound transgresses the boundaries of past and future, creating a temporal blurring. In the textual present (17:14), the prophet begs for healing from Yahweh, while also repeating the past words of his accusers against him (17:15). Future sound also enters in, as Jeremiah demands a day of distress and shattering against his enemies (17:18); the word for destruction, *šibbārôn*, is also a noisy one, associated with the sound of moaning in Ezekiel 21:5. In addition to using sound to unsettle time and figure future destruction, the text also links voice to knowledge. Jeremiah chides Yahweh, "You know what comes forth from my lips, and it has been in front of your face" (Jer. 17:16). This complaint positions voice as central to the divine-prophet relationship, while also suggesting that sound constructs meaning in the body.

The use of sound is not limited to these passages. The Confessions as a whole are a noisy text, filled with cries and whispers, sounds that overlap and drown out each other. Elsewhere, I have written about the "soundscape" of Jeremiah, arguing that sound is essential to the construction of meaning in the book.[11] This extends, as well, to the Confessions. I do not wish to repeat that argument here; instead, I want to consider in detail the ways in which the cry and the crying body at once constitute, subvert, and transform the prophet Jeremiah. Crying out is essential to the Confessions. I intend this phrase "crying out" in multiple senses: the voice crying in pain or suffering, the voice raised in outcry, the voice "crying out" to perform a specific speech act, the cry that exceeds words and even meanings.

All of these forms of crying out occur within the Confessions. They do not, however, necessarily occur at the pleasure of the prophet. Instead, Jeremiah describes vocality—like prophecy—as something thrust upon him unwillingly. *The prophet does not have full control over his voice.* At times, speech is explicitly figured as a compulsion, as in Jeremiah 20:8, which begins, "Whenever I speak, I cry; I call out Violence and Ruin!"[12] Jeremiah does not choose his words, or express control over them. Instead, when he opens his mouth to speak, the words force themselves out, independent of his will. This specific utterance is sometimes treated as legal, intercessional, or technical language.[13] While this may be the case, I want to stress the compulsion that accompanies the speech act. There is also the question of its affect. "Objection!" may be uttered in a courtroom with a wide range of forces and affects, for example, as an endless procession of legal procedurals has made undeniably clear. Hartman takes Jeremiah's outcry as "prophetic speech . . . in some sense discontinuous with normal speech," noting, the "word or a voice overwhelms the prophet. One might almost say that the word is the violence of which he complains."[14] Though Hartman is primarily concerned with genre analysis, this description captures nicely the sense of *compulsion* in the passage. Jeremiah is compelled to speak; when he opens his mouth, certain words are brought forth from it.

Thus the act of crying out comes upon the prophet against his will. The cry takes over his body while causing great suffering. Confronted with the cries of violence that force their way out of his mouth, Jeremiah continues,

> I said, "I will not remember it, and I will no longer speak in his name."
>   But it was like a fire consuming my heart,[15] shut up in my bones,
> I grew exhausted from containing it, and was not able to do so (Jer. 20:9).

Pain is forced upon the body through language; the compulsion to speak becomes a form of violence. Elsewhere in the Confessions, Jeremiah cries out curses on his birth (15:10, cf. 20:14–18):

> Woe is me, my mother, that you bore me, a man of contention and
>   a man of strife to the whole land.
>   I have not lent and they have not borrowed from me; yet all of
>   them curse me.[16] (Jer. 15:10)

The curse brings together an expression of suffering with a highly formalized speech act. Jeremiah's anguish is clear, even as the specifics of his words recede behind the act of cursing and expressing pain. The pain that others inflict upon him is likewise figured as voice: "yet all of them curse me." This mixture of vocality and anguish recurs across the text.

Nor is the crying in the text limited to Jeremiah. His friends and family cry out for his life: "For even your brothers and your father's house, even they deal treacherously with you, Even they are in full cry after you"[17] (Jer. 12:6; cf. 11:21). A cry rises up from the home of the prophet's enemies: "Let a cry be heard from their homes, when you bring a raiding party upon them suddenly, For they have dug a pit[18] to capture me, and they have hidden a trap for my feet" (18:22). At other points, the threatening voices are reduced to a whispering: "For I heard the whispering of the crowd, 'Terror all around! Let us inform against him!'" (20:10). These other voices echo in and through Jeremiah's own.

Jeremiah is obsessed with the speech of others, and with speech itself. And yet the voice does not only feature in suffering: there is also pleasure. In 15:16, he describes eating the words of Yahweh:

> Your words were found and I ate them.
>   Your words became a joy to me and a delight to my heart,
>   For I am called by your name, Yahweh of Hosts.

The word brings both pleasure and suffering. It enters into the body, delighting it. The Confession continues in 15:17–18:

> I did not sit in the circle of merrymakers and rejoice.
>> Because of your hand I have sat alone, for you have filled me with wrath.
>> Why is my pain unceasing? Why is my wound incurable, refusing to be healed?
>> Ah! You have become like a dried-up well,[19] water that cannot be relied upon.

The previously pleasing divine word takes over and contaminates the body, first as wrath, then as pain. At the end of verse 18, the word bursts forth, reconfigured as a complaint against Yahweh. In comparing Yahweh to a dry well, Jeremiah contrasts the moistness of the wound—and with it, the irreducible materiality of the body—with the inflexible divine word. The prophet's body has become both medium and message. Indeed, Jeremiah's use of voice begins to destabilize the representation of his body, and with it his performance of gender.

Does Jeremiah Cry Like a Woman?

Jeremiah has none of the stoic restraint of Hosea, instructed to marry a whoring woman (Hos. 1, 3), or of Ezekiel, ordered to perform all manner of humiliating acts (Ezek. 4–5). Neither does he possess the robust enthusiasm of Isaiah, who confidently accepts his calling as prophet (Isa. 6). But while Jeremiah is not an enthusiastic prophet, he is far from a silent one. Instead, as we have seen, he speaks frequently, but to confused and confusing effect. In part this is because the prophet's sounds are not always his own, but rather the result of compulsion. It is also because his speech is marked by pain. The affect of his Confessions even threatens to overwhelm their content.

The degree of pain expressed by Jeremiah and localized on his body is unusual for a male speaker in the biblical text, matched only by the suffering of Job (though that text is not a prophetic one). Instead, the voicing of suffering is typically associated with female speakers. Female vocality is deemed appropriate for grief and lamentation.[20] Women serve as professional mourners and at times of crisis are called upon to mourn for the people (Jer. 9:16–19 [9:17–20 English]).[21] The most famous voice in the book of Jeremiah is the voice of a woman weeping—"Rachel weeping for her children" (31:15). Female voices are also associated with pain, as when the woman in labor is used to represent the greatest possible physical pain and fear (6:24, 49:24, 50:43). This pain is communicated, moreover, in sound (e.g., 4:31), as the woman cries out in pain and terror. To vocalize pain and suffering is to use voice *as a woman*.

Jeremiah is not exempt from these norms. His voice, however, does not follow typical masculine patterns. Instead, he uses sound and voice in ways typically coded as feminine. The Confessions break with the masculine economy of
speech. Jeremiah frequently and insistently voices pain—often his own, but also
the pain of others. He mourns and commands others to mourn. He experiences
prophecy in and through his body, evoking the repeated (if not fully stable)
association between femininity and embodiment. And the content of his utterances, especially those in the Confessions, most strikingly resembles other forms
of biblical speech explicitly marked as feminine, such as the words of Daughter
Zion in Lamentations. Taking up the question of gender and sound in classical
literature, Anne Carson writes, "Female sound is bad to hear both because the
quality of a woman's voice is objectionable and because women say what should
not be said."[22] Though Carson is primarily describing ancient Greece, her assessment speaks to the Hebrew Bible as well. Feminine forms of sound are disruptive and destabilizing, both because of the identity of their speakers and because
of the occasions on which female voices are typically heard. Thus in the biblical
text, the threat of female vocality is addressed in part by splitting female voices
between sound and content. In the case of Rachel weeping (or the voice of the
bride), the content of female speech is elided by the text, leaving only sound
itself. Elsewhere, as in the story of Miriam exiled from the camp for speaking
against Moses (Num. 12), it is the content of female speech that is threatening
and that demands punishment.

Carson's description also illuminates Jeremiah's use of voice. Jeremiah has difficulty with his voice; Jeremiah's voice is "bad to hear." This is both because of
what he says (his complaints, judgments, expressions of suffering) and because
of the ways in which he says it (crying, weeping, confused referents, a seemingly feminine use of sound). The gendering of the prophet's voice is unstable.
Hartman's question, "Why can't Jeremiah talk in a normal voice?," means also
"Why must Jeremiah cry in such a feminine way?" The prophetic voice is no longer a normative masculine voice; the ordering of sound, gender, and body (for
voice is itself an extension of body) has been disrupted.[23]

Indeed, Jeremiah's propensity for feminine forms of sound has been observed
by other scholars. In particular, Barbara Bakke Kaiser has argued that the feminine features of prophetic discourse are best understood through the model of
the prophet/poet as "female impersonator." Taking up Jeremiah 4:19–26, 4:31,
and 10:19–21, Kaiser argues that Jeremiah is "compelled to become the woman
bearing her first child, the pollutant female socially and ritually isolated, and
the mother bereft of her children."[24] In complicating Jeremiah's relationship to
masculinity, her reading helpfully troubles the text, opening the possibility for
alternate imaginaries.[25] And yet Kaiser herself does not follow through on the
potentials her argument raises. Instead, she chooses to soften its subversive thrust,

reassuring the reader, "The portrayal of Jeremiah as a 'female impersonator' is, of course, a metaphor suggesting that the prophet seriously and deliberately adopts the female persona."[26]

I direct attention to this statement because it demonstrates both the promise and the limits of Kaiser's approach. In treating gender impersonation as metaphor, Kaiser forecloses the possibility of any real unsettling of gender in the text. Her language of "persona" and "impersonation" assume a stable actor—here, the male prophet—behind a female "mask." This interpretation likewise treats the (female) body as a metaphorical space that the prophet may temporarily choose to occupy. In the case of the Confessions, however, the body that appears most prominently is the male body of the prophet himself. The text repeatedly makes us aware of his body, particularly as he complains of its pains and incurable wounds (Jer. 15:18). This effect is reinforced by additional references to the body—as repository of truth (11:20), as receptacle for the divine word (15:16), as impregnable fortress (15:20), as object of social violence (11:19, 12:6, 17:17–18, and so on). It is likewise underscored by the textual association of suffering with childbirth, frequently expressed with reference to screaming out in pain. If bodily pain is conventionally represented by reference to the pain of the woman giving birth, then why is Jeremiah so concerned with the painful transformation of his own body? As intriguing as Kaiser's reading is, it is not enough, especially confronted with the cries of the Confessions. Against the model of "impersonation," I will pursue a different direction in negotiating Jeremiah's feminine uses of sound: hysteria.

Part II: Prophecy and Hysteria

It is not enough to identify the forms of sound in the Confessions as associated with feminine sound. In addition, *prophecy is structured as hysteria*. This is not to say that prophecy *is* hysteria, but rather that hysteria offers meaningful parallels that illuminate Jeremiah's use of sound. In particular, I will take up two: *the speech of the hysteric* as a parallel to Jeremiah's speech and *the scene of treatment* as a parallel to the scene of prophecy. Previously, I have considered that Jeremiah uses sound in ways textually coded as feminine; now, I want to sharpen that argument to claim that Jeremiah's use of sound is better understood through a specific category of sound, one typically associated with the feminine. I refer, of course, to hysteria.

One note before proceeding: hysteria is centrally a female affliction. This association is present in both the name of the disorder (*hystera* is the Greek word for uterus) and in the often-repeated (if not fully accurate) story that the Greeks believed hysteria's cause to be the womb's wandering through the body.[27] The case studies in Freud and Breuer's *Studies in Hysteria* are all of women; there is a single mention of the "male hysteric" in Breuer's discussion of the theoretical issues.[28] And yet male hysteria is not unknown. Freud's first lecture was on male hysteria; he likewise described himself as hysterical.[29] Flaubert, Mallarmé, and Baudelaire all identified themselves, at various moments, as male hysterics.[30] Of male hysteria, Daniel Boyarin writes,

> If being gendered "male" in our culture is having power and speech—phallus and logos—the silenced and powerless subject is female, whatever her anatomical construction. "Hysteria" itself—a female malady, as feminist historians have properly registered—provides an elegant demonstration of this thesis, precisely because hysteria was not exclusive to anatomical women but to women and certain racially marked men.[31]

Boyarin's larger argument concerns the twisting relationships of Zionism, European ethnic nationalism, and masculinity. And yet he also articulates a connection between hysteria and masculinity that is not limited simply to a recent historical moment. Hysteria is a crisis of power, even as male hysteria reflects the crossing over of gender with other marked categories, such as race or ethnicity. In the case of Jeremiah, the prophet's powerlessness is not racial, but rather the double effect of being subjugated to Yahweh and being forced to prophesy the destruction of his own world.[32] The prophet is threatened, marginalized, excluded from power. And like certain other subjects placed in this position—women, primarily, but also a few men—he responds with hysteria. This becomes clearer with attention to the specifically hysterical features of the prophet's speech.

The Speech of the Hysteric

In reading Jeremiah's Confessions as hysteria, I will follow the descriptions set forth by Freud and Breuer in *Studies in Hysteria* and elaborated by Freud in "Fragment of an Analysis of a Case of Hysteria" (henceforth "Fragment"). I will make particular reference to the case studies of "Anna O." and "Frau Emmy von N." from the former text, along with "Dora" from the latter. My reading will also place greater weight on the descriptions of hysteria and its symptoms—including those offered by the hysterics themselves—than on the more abstract analytical material that Freud and Breuer append. In turning to these texts, I am not suggesting that the Confessions demand diagnosis. Neither am I interested in a practice of "hysterical" reading that pushes Jeremiah into an already strained category of "hysterical narrative" or "women's writing," any more than I intend to read the prophet as a "female impersonator."[33] Instead, I wish to trace the hysterical features of Jeremiah's voice as a way of entering into the question of gender and sound, and how the prophet's use of sound destabilizes and unsettles the gendering of his body.

Crucially, hysteria is a disturbance that makes itself known in sound. The early hysterical patients cry, murmur, expound in foreign languages, click their tongues, or cannot speak at all. In "Fragment," one of Dora's prime symptoms is a loss of voice; she is likewise plagued by a recurring cough that functions perversely as a sort of speech.[34] Anna O., the first hysteric in *Studies in Hysteria*, loses the ability to speak her native language, German. In her study of gender and sound, Carson suggests a continuity between the voices of twentieth-century hysterics and the disruptive, threatening feminine voices of classical Greece.[35] There is an analogous continuity between these forms of speech and Jeremiah's Confessions. In both cases, hysterical speech forces attention on the body; it directs attention as well to the ambiguities and moments of weakness in ordinary language. Reading the Confessions alongside hysterical discourse emphasizes the complicated relation of desire and resistance between Jeremiah's cries and the larger aural and ideological forces of the text.

The stability of Jeremiah's identity in the Confessions is already disrupted. What remains is to understand how and why this disruption occurs, and what role the feminizing of sound plays on the masculine prophetic body and subject. In arguing that Jeremiah's voice is structured as hysteria, I will trace three tendencies: crying out, incoherent virtuosity, and somatic compliance.

Crying Out

As I have already indicated in some detail, Jeremiah's Confessions are filled with crying. This crying is in the voice of the prophet; frequently, however, it seems forced upon him. Such crying out, especially in pain, is also a key feature of hysterical discourse. Freud and Breuer repeatedly describe their patients as compelled to speak or make noise. Importantly, this production of sound is not willingly undertaken by the speaker. Instead, it seems to force itself to be uttered. In these utterances, the pain that the hysterical patients experience comes through clearly. Early in his treatment of Frau Emmy von N., Freud notes,

> What she says is completely coherent and clear evidence of an unusual degree of education and intelligence. This makes it all the more disconcerting that every few minutes she should suddenly break off, contort her face into an expression of horror and revulsion, stretch out her hand towards me with her fingers splayed and crooked, and in an altered, fearful voice call out the words: "Keep still – don't say anything – don't touch me!"[36]

Though Emmy is "coherent" and "unusual[ly] ... intelligen[t]", her speech is frequently on the edge of collapse. Outcries of terror threaten to overwhelm all other structures of meaning. She confides in Freud, "I'm frightened, so frightened, I think I'm going to die."[37] A few days later, she confesses to him again, "I am frightened to death, oh, I can hardly bear to tell you, I hate myself."[38] Like Jeremiah appealing to Yahweh, Emmy seems compelled to seek a listener, even as she doubts whether a different way of being is possible. When Emmy speaks in Freud's text, it is almost always to express her fear; Freud also notes that she frequently utters "a peculiar clicking noise, which I am unable to reproduce."[39] I will return to this noise, and Freud's difficulties with it, in discussing somatic compliance below; for now I wish only to point out that such clicking represents the pure, abstracted form of the cry of pain. Here, there are no words at all, only pure sound. Freud adds, in an odd little note, "On hearing it, colleagues of mine who knew something about hunting compared the final notes with the mating cry of the capercaillie."[40] The outcry has become animal.

Nor is Emmy the only hysteric to cry out in pain. Instead, the sound of anguish—without, however, rising to the level of the sentence—is a common hysterical feature. Breuer, who treated Anna O., describes similar outcries:

> Throughout the entire course of the illness until this point the patient was overcome by somnolence in the afternoons, which at sunset turned into a deeper sleep. . . . After an hour or so of the sopor, she would become restless and toss to and fro, crying again and again, "Torment, torment," all the while keeping her eyes closed.[41]

Like Emmy, Anna cries out in terror, as indicated by both the content of her words and the structure of her outcry. This is a torment that disturbs her rest, even as it cannot be vocalized without additional words. Her utterance is, moreover, very much like Jeremiah's, as the prophet cries out repeatedly, "Terror all around!" (Jer. 20:10; cf. 17:17). This pain and fear assume various forms, whether human enemies for Jeremiah, vague terror for Anna, or repulsive dead animals for Emmy. But the fundamental structure remains the same. For the hysterical patients, as for the prophet, terror is truly all around—little wonder, then, that each is compelled to cry out.

Incoherence and Virtuosity

Even when it is not consumed with crying, hysterical speech is difficult speech. For all the excessive vocalizations that fill both Jeremiah's Confessions and the records of hysterical patients, both sound and meaning are produced only through difficulty. Freud notes, at multiple points, Emmy's clicking noises, as well as her stutter. Dora has a troublesome cough.[42] At the point when the hysteric succeeds in forming words, hysterical speech is constantly on the edge of slipping into incoherence. Breuer describes Anna as plagued by "a deep functional disorganization of speech," such that "she could find almost no words at all, and would painfully piece them together out of four or five different languages, which made her almost incomprehensible."[43] And yet this incoherence is matched by a lucidity, even a virtuosity. Anna cannot speak; Anna speaks in five languages. The primary impression throughout the case study is not one incoherence but of intelligence and awareness. She communicates her complaints effectively, often quite lucidly, and is credited with creating that cornerstone of psychoanalysis, "the talking cure."[44] Breuer is clearly impressed by her, noting her "rich poetic and imaginative gifts," though also her stubbornness, which "made her *quite closed to suggestion*."[45]

It is not only Anna who has a gift for language. As recorded in the *Studies*, the hysterics are remarkably effective at describing their own experiences. Indeed, it is the patient's own reflections that often contain the key to the therapeutic treatment, though this process is often paradoxical. Thus Freud writes, "I always sit up and pay attention when I hear a patient speak so disparagingly of an idea that has occurred to him. It is, in fact, a sign of successful defense that pathogenic ideas which re-emerge seem of such little significance."[46] What Freud is describing here is a speech act that succeeds in its very failure—a communication by means of denial. This is the flipside of the sort of dazzling self-awareness Anna O., for example, displays. Meaning and denial are bound up in the artful use of language.

This paradoxical description of the struggle to speak, paired with a peculiar and seductive virtuosity, again evokes the Confessions. Even with his unstable voice, his shifting complaints and forms of sound production, and his general obstinacy, there is a beauty in Jeremiah's words. This does not emerge, however, without confusion. By way of brief example, I want to revisit the Confession with which this chapter opened. Stripped of verse divisions, line breaks, and most of the clarifying punctuation (all of which add a degree of certainty and stability not present in the original text), the text reads,

> I was like a gentle lamb led to the slaughter and I did not know that they plotted schemes against me. Let us destroy the tree with its fruit and cut him off from the land of the living and his name will be remembered no longer. But Yahweh righteous judge the one who tests my kidneys and heart let me see your vengeance upon them for to you I have disclosed my case. For thus says Yahweh to the men of Anathoth the ones who seek your

life saying do not prophesy in the name of Yahweh lest you die by our hand behold I will punish them their young men will die by the sword and their sons and their daughters will die of famine . . . (Jer. 11:19–22)[47]

Throughout the passage, the speaker shifts, often without textual signals. "Let us destroy the tree with its fruit" is the beginning of a threat against Jeremiah, but it is not marked as indirect discourse or the words of others. At other points, the text seems intentionally misleading, as when "For thus says Yahweh" precedes "do not prophesy in the name of Yahweh," a speech act that is not Yahweh's at all, but belongs to the men of Anathoth.[48] Punishment follows, but who is to do this punishing? The text's meaning is unstable and partially concealed; the reader, like the psychoanalyst, is called in to do the work of interpretation. And yet the text, like Anna O., also asserts its own demands upon the reader; it does not simply wait passively for the work of interpretation to be done to it.

Somatic Compliance

Stubbornness and trouble speaking are not adequate to justify identifying the prophet's speech as hysterical. There is also an essential parallel in hysteria's connections between sound and body. Hysterical speech as a discourse is not limited to the voice, but also implicates and contaminates the body. Freud describes this process in his account of Emmy von N.:

> She speaks as if it were arduous, in a quiet voice that is occasionally interrupted to the point of stuttering by spastic breaks in her speech. When she speaks she keeps her fingers, which exhibit a ceaseless agitation resembling athetosis, tightly interlaced. Numerous tic-like twitches in her face and neck muscles, some of which, in particular the right sterno-cleido-mastoid, protrude quite prominently. In addition, she frequently interrupts herself in order to produce a peculiar clicking noise, which I am unable to reproduce.[49]

As with Anna O., Emmy's difficulty speaking is an audible marker of her hysteria. As she struggles to speak, her body, twitching, speaks for her (though against her will). Even the "peculiar clicking noise" represents a bodily substitution for the ordered production of words that characterizes proper speech. This bodily sound is interruptive and unregulated. Little surprise that Freud, the guardian of the discursive order, notes his inability to reproduce it. The sound cannot be reproduced or recorded—yet this does not prevent him from naturalizing and sexualizing it (by comparing it to the mating cry of the capercaillie).

In hysteria, that which is shameful or otherwise cannot be spoken aloud is displaced onto the body, which then "speaks" through symptoms. This is a process that Freud terms "somatic compliance." Dolar describes it as a "strange loop, the tie between inner and outer, the short circuit between the external contingency and the intimate."[50] Jeremiah's Confessions display such a short circuit, which occurs primarily through pain. Jeremiah can only intermittently voice his protest against prophecy (his complaints are frequently truncated in favor of boilerplate statements about Yahweh's greatness, as in Jer. 15:18–19 or 20:10–11, 12–13). His wounds, however, testify to his ongoing suffering. In 15:18, he demands, "Why is my pain unceasing? Why is my wound incurable, refusing to be healed?" The unhealed wound "speaks" like the hysterical symptom. Elsewhere in the Confessions, Jeremiah refers to his heart, his kidneys, and his bones in order to map out an internal topography of anguish, with fire in his heart and bones, compelling him to cry out (20:8–9). His account of his symptoms displays both an attempt at silencing and the return of what is unspeakable through its transposition to the body. Jeremiah's fiery bones speak what is unspeakable. Like Emmy von N. or the capercaillie, Jeremiah cannot contain himself.

Somatic compliance hinges on, in Carson's words, "the use of signs to transcribe upon the outside of the body a meaning from inside the body which does not pass through the control point of *logos*."[51] Under this definition, Jeremiah's cries, as well as his wounds, present a similar structure of displaced speech. When Jeremiah cries out, his sounds function like bodily symptoms insofar as they circumvent this "control point of *logos*." We might note, as well, that Jeremiah's outcries subvert the dominant theology by refusing to accept the deity's actions. Here again, Jeremiah parallels the hysterics. Like the prophet, the hysteric cries out in pain, a sudden interruption as disturbing as the bodily symptom. The cry of terror (consider as well Jeremiah's "terror all around!") is another form of symptom, an interruption in the ordinary regulated form of discourse and an intrusion of pain and affect. And within both the soundscape of Jeremiah's Confessions and the discursive regime of psychoanalysis, it is destabilizing, threatening, and insistently embodied.

Hysteria and the Scene of Treatment

It is not only the *content* of hysterical speech that offers a structural parallel to Jeremiah's Confessions. So too, I will suggest, do the treatments to which this hysteria is subjected. This section will shift from a literary close reading of the key features of hysteria and prophetic discourse to a broader comparison of the scene of hysterical treatment and the scene of prophecy. In particular, I want to highlight two competing discourses surrounding hysteria: revulsion and eroticism. Here too we find Jeremiah's Confessions structured as hysteria.

Revulsion

Hysteria can produce revulsion in those who witness it or who engage with the hysteric. This revulsion has parallels to prophecy, and especially to the Confessions. Jeremiah is the object of much dislike. He frequently complains that his life is in peril; his kinsmen and others seek to inflict violence and even to kill him. This feature reappears elsewhere in the book as well; Jeremiah 37 and 38 describe Jeremiah's imprisonment and near death; the book ends with the prophet taken away to exile in Egypt. As I have already mentioned, Jeremiah speaks frequently of terror (*māgôr*); in 20:10, he cries,

> For I heard the whispering of the crowd, "Terror all around!
> Let us inform against him!" Each of my close friends watches for me to stumble.
> "Maybe he will be deceived and we will prevail, and take our vengeance upon him!"

Many readings, following the text's own lead, portray the prophet as anguished, suffering, oppressed. But is this the only way to understand Jeremiah? Are there, perhaps, reasons for his constant social alienation? Is Jeremiah a reliable narrator of his own experience?

That Jeremiah is terrorized and even victimized does not preclude the possibility that he is also deeply unpleasant, or is perceived as such. Such is the case with Dora, perhaps Freud's most famous hysterical patient, but far from his favorite.[52] Instead, the father of psychoanalysis finds Dora unpleasant, even a bit repulsive. After Dora breaks off treatment—an event that Freud deems premature, and that engenders no small degree of obsession on his part—he later refuses to take her back as a patient.[53] Nor does Dora fare much better after Freud's case study. In "A Footnote to Freud's 'Fragment of an Analysis of a Case of Hysteria,'" Felix Deutsch traces what is known of Dora following her termination of analytic treatment, concluding, "Her death . . . seemed a blessing to those who were close to her. She had been, as my informant phrased it, 'one of the most repulsive hysterics' he had ever met."[54] Though he carefully attributes the judgment to an "informant," Deutsch offers strong hints that he shares it. Indeed, acknowledging and redressing this maligning of Dora has been a recurring theme of subsequent feminist work on hysteria and psychoanalysis.[55] Freud's revulsion, it seems, is still being rectified.

A repulsive hysteric and a lamenting prophet: in significant ways, the case of Dora doubles that of Jeremiah. Both Dora and Jeremiah protest, repeatedly, and on the same themes (Dora, for example, complains that no one will listen;[56] Jeremiah raises the same complaint against Yahweh). This failure of listening is especially upsetting because both Dora and Jeremiah find themselves in impossible situations. In the case of Dora, as Steven Marcus writes,

> Her situation was a desperate one. The three adults to whom she was closest, whom she loved the most in the world, were apparently conspiring—separately, in tandem, or in concert—to deny her the reality of her experience. They were conspiring to deny Dora her reality and reality itself. This betrayal hinged upon matters that might easily unhinge the mind of a young person; the three adults were not betraying Dora's love and trust alone, they were betraying the structure of the actual world.[57]

Dora is in a terrible position, the very organization of her world collapsing. The threats against Jeremiah are, meanwhile, well documented in the biblical text. Placing Jeremiah and Dora together forces us to recognize the play of social forces and the subtle manipulations of our sympathies. Jeremiah's repeated and almost frenzied protests in the Confessions grow out of a situation as desperate as Dora's. Jeremiah is betrayed from all sides, by the men of Anathoth who seek to kill him and by the deity who has placed him in the position of prophecy. This structure is amplified by the fact that Jeremiah must fail at reaching the people in order for the prophecy to succeed. Jeremiah suffers doubly: he must prophesy against his people, and he must bear the burden of knowing his prophecy will not succeed. Mary Mills calls this the "tragic logic" of Jeremiah, writing that the prophet's "fraught personal state forms an exact copy of the coming fragmentation and collapse of his community."[58] The logic of the book, both historical and theological, means that the prophet must fail.

In this failure, too, the prophet resembles the hysteric. Jeremiah's position, no less than Dora's, is a desperate and even impossible one. The more he speaks—whether in protest to God or in prophecy to the people around him—the less likely he is to be *heard*. The deck is stacked; neither prophet nor hysteric can be understood. Instead, speech and voice become a marker of this failure, even as they engender revulsion in their listeners. Jeremiah and Dora are listened to only to be denied, rejected, or silenced.

Erotic Attraction

Freud's and Dora's mutual dislike is especially striking given how it breaks with patterns in psychoanalysis. Against the discourse of revulsion, there is a countercurrent, one of eroticism and attraction. In *Studies in Hysteria*, Freud writes,

> I could not imagine myself able to become absorbed in the psychical mechanism of a hysteria in someone who seemed to me base or repellent,

and who would not on closer acquaintance be able to arouse human sympathy, whereas I can of course carry out the treatment of someone suffering from tabes or rheumatism independently of whether or not they appeal to me personally.[59]

The scene of hysterical treatment entails a certain attraction. Freud frequently comments on the intelligence of his hysterical patients, and sometimes their beauty as well. This becomes especially relevant when we return to Breuer and Anna O. Breuer notes that Anna is a woman "of considerable intelligence, remarkably acute powers of reasoning, and a clear-sighted intuitive sense," and his admiration for her comes through clearly in the case study.[60] Perhaps Breuer admired his patient too much altogether—according to a famous story from the annals of psychoanalysis, treatment ended abruptly when Anna O. experienced a hysterical pregnancy with Breuer's child. Unprepared for this level of countertransference, Breuer broke off treatment and fled with his wife.[61]

This account of Breuer and Anna O., though oft-repeated, has not gone unchallenged; recent scholarly work has suggested, convincingly, that Anna's pregnancy was itself a later embellishment of the scholarly record.[62] This story may even have been invented by Freud.[63] But whether it occurred or not, it points to a larger tendency toward eroticism and seduction in the scene of hysteria. The hysteric is increasingly drawn into a fraught, eroticized relationship with the analyst; neither is the analyst immune to the hysteric's pull. Freud is simultaneously attracted and a bit repelled by his hysterical patients, writing to Fliess that they remind him of sorceresses.[64] And, as should be evident, this eroticism is not innocent of the power dynamics of the scene. It is the analyst who holds the power, a power that reinforces the larger interplay of gender and power (Freud the older man, the medical expert; Dora the young woman, betrayed by the adults she has trusted, including the father that Freud views so favorably).[65]

This tension between seduction and repulsion occurs in Jeremiah as well. Jeremiah 20:7, the opening of one of the Confessions, reads,

> You seduced me, Yahweh, and I was seduced, you overpowered me and
>   you prevailed.
> I became a continual laughingstock; everyone has mocked me.

Prophecy is a seduction and a revulsion all at once. Jeremiah describes Yahweh's action with *pittîtanî*, "you seduced me"; the verb has also been translated as "enticed," "persuaded," and "deceived." While I think "seduced" is the best translation—largely for the reasons set forth by Ken Stone[66]—I also want to note that this constellation of meanings in many ways resembles the language used to describe the scene of psychoanalysis. Was Anna O. seduced, enticed, or persuaded? Or have we been deceived, perhaps by Freud, or perhaps by our own desires?

Stone's reading of Jeremiah 20:7–13 especially captures the charged eroticism of the passage. In a careful reading, he dismantles the arguments for taking the passage as either deception or rape, noting that "it is not at all clear that 'rape' is the most appropriate descriptor for a sexual experience that involves not only power but also, for example, trust. We seem to have something closer to sadomasochism."[67] He proceeds to read the passage through the lens of male homoeroticism and s/m, with Jeremiah in the role of "aggressive bottom."[68] The erotic masochism that Stone traces in this text is more difficult to trace in the other Confessions; the sexual language in particular is strongest here. However, the broader dynamics occur across the Confessions. Reading the text as a masochistic seduction, meanwhile, forces us to acknowledge the passage's eroticism while also again encountering the prophet as embodied. There is a kind of queer desire here, a novel reconfiguration of the body. The reading situates this body and its sounds in a larger economy of pleasure, suggesting yet another mode of "crying out." Seduced and overpowered, Jeremiah's cries and complaints seduce and repel his audience.

What the masochistic reading perhaps glosses over is the *vulnerability* of the prophet's body, as well as the pain he experiences. Unlike a participant in the contemporary BDSM community, Jeremiah does not enter in with full consent. He has no safe word. Commissioned from the womb, his body is not wholly his own. And his body, including its pains, is bound up with his relation to the people. This relation, however, is a relationship predicated on suffering. The question is whether the suffering prophet—or the suffering hysteric—is a destabilizing, radical figure, or whether the text simply reflects the larger dynamics of power. Still, I would suggest that Stone's masochistic reading fits into a larger analytical framing of hysteria and gender. Freud, after all, associated masochism with the feminine.[69] And Karmen MacKendrick writes, "s/m seems to fit with a cultural feminist sexuality in at least this respect: it diverts energy and desire away from the goal oriented genitality so often labeled masculine."[70] In this way masochism offers an alternate formulation of what I have been describing as hysteria: the prophet's language and body as resisting or refusing dominant norms of gender, sexuality, and speech.

This refusal comes at a cost to the prophet. In this way, too, Jeremiah resembles Dora. The prophet and the hysteric are each positioned in an economy of seduction; each, however, resists its demands and norms. The speech of the hysteric is at once revolting and compelling; the listener vacillates uneasily between the two positions, as Freud shows. The same is true of the prophet Jeremiah. And in both cases, hysteria and prophecy, the revulsion/seduction dichotomy even extends from speech to the body itself. The body of the prophet/hysteric becomes a body to be seduced. "You seduced me, you overpowered me, and you prevailed," Jeremiah protests to Yahweh. Might not Dora say the same to Freud? And does not Freud, in reconstructing and narrating the "case" of Dora, say the same thing back to Dora?

Is Hysteria Radical? Is Gender Destabilized?

In reading Jeremiah as hysterical, I have traced both the internal features of Jeremiah's speech—crying, incoherent virtuosity, somatic compliance—and the larger scene of hysterical treatment—dynamics of revulsion and erotic attraction. Both lines of inquiry suggest that Jeremiah's voice is meaningfully structured as hysteria. The final issue related to hysteria that I wish to consider is whether this hysteria represents a radical departure from the norms of gender and embodiment in the text. In asking this question, I am concerned, primarily, with resistance. Male hysteria is sometimes interpreted as a mode of resistance against dominant norms of masculinity; Jan Goldstein, for example, makes such an argument about nineteenth-century male French writers and their strategic uses of hysteria. Invoking Baudelaire, Flaubert, and Mallarmé, Goldstein argues that hysterical self-identification by men serves as a critical response to the constraints of masculinity.[71] In this reading, the male hysteric draws on the medical discourse of hysteria to legitimize himself, even as he rejects the repressive power of that same discourse. To identify as a (male) hysteric is thus to participate in a critique of masculine identity and the narrowness of its constraints. Goldstein's interpretation raises the possibility of reading Jeremiah's hysteria as a critique of masculinity. The very refusal of Jeremiah to conform to ordinary masculine registers of sound suggests, in Goldstein's words, "a conceptual space for the subversion of gender stereotypes."[72]

While I agree that hysteria represents one way of destabilizing masculinity in Jeremiah, I would push back against the notion of subversion, which suggests an intentional action. There is an important difference between the poet and the prophet, one that concerns, as well, the question of hysteria. To be a poet or writer, at least in the mode of Baudelaire, Flaubert, or Mallarmé, assumes some level of choice on the part of the author. To be sure, writing is a difficult, painful business (as writers so frequently remind us). There is nevertheless a degree of choice in pursuing writing as a recognizable, (potentially) viable career in a known social sphere. As represented by the Hebrew prophets, however, prophecy brings with it no such sense of choice. The call comes upon the prophet, as when Yahweh's words appear to Jeremiah. This question of volition is particularly important with respect to hysteria. As Goldstein acknowledges, the most damaging critique of male hysteria as critical stance is what Elaine Showalter terms "critical cross-dressing."[73] If hysteria is an affectation or even a willing choice made by the male poet—or male prophet—then its radical stance is diminished. Male hysteria as a form of "female impersonation" fails to address the underlying problems of impersonation as an interpretive model.

It is also possible, however, to read hysteria as a form of resistance without taking it as intentional (masculine) critique. Feminist theorists have made similar arguments with respect to female hysteria; thus Hélène Cixous, for example, advocates for the female hysteric as a figure of resistance. Of Dora, she writes,

> Dora seemed to me to be the one who resists the system, the one who cannot stand that the family and society are founded on the body of women, on bodies despised, rejected, bodies that are humiliating once they have been used. And this girl—like all hysterics, deprived of the possibility of saying directly what she perceived, of speaking face-to-face or on the telephone as father B. or father K. or Freud, et cetera do—still had the strength to make it known.[74]

For Cixous, Dora is a feminist heroine, speaking truth to power, resisting the oppressive masculine economy, and following the path of her own desire. ("The source of Dora's strength is, in spite of everything, her desire.")[75]

There is a persuasive argument to be made for the strategic use of male hysteria to subvert gender in certain modern European contexts.[76] There are also striking parallels between Jeremiah and the classic female hysterics, including Dora, who may even be "the one who resists the system." To an even greater degree than Dora or Freud's and Breuer's other patients, Jeremiah vocalizes specific complaints against "the system"; he clearly views himself as its victim. His protests against Yahweh's actions in particular likewise reject the dominant structures of power, especially when contrasted with the response of a prophet like Isaiah or Ezekiel. In employing feminine forms of sound and foregrounding the pains (and pleasures?) of the body, Jeremiah seems to subvert the dominant representations of masculinity. There is even, perhaps, a queer pleasure in the prophet's seduction, though I do not wish to subsume the specific protests of the hysteric against the injustices of power into a generalized narrative of masochism.

Nor must Jeremiah's experience be one of pleasure for it to be queer. In reading Hosea, I have suggested that disconnecting the problem of masculinity from the male body opens the possibility of a queer reimagining of this body. In the case of Jeremiah, the prophet's use of sound defies the normative association of male voices and bodies. In doing so, it suggests the possibility of a queer use of sound, even if the only vocalizations possible are of pain and hysteria. The queerest use of voice may be to express not pleasure but pain. Sara Ahmed has written about the importance of maintaining a space for queer unhappiness, a point I will return to in chapter 5.[77] For now, it is enough to remember that Jeremiah's voice may be queer in its outcries, whether they are pain, pleasure, resistance, or something else.

The subversive or resistant power of hysteria is not, however, guaranteed. This is the case even with Dora, who proves a contentious, if central, figure in feminist debates over hysteria. Cixous's portrayal of Dora as a force of desire and resistance has been countered by Catherine Clément, whose reading of the case is gathered together with Cixous's in *The Newly Born Woman*. Clément argues that hysteria, in the final analysis, supports the dominant structures of power. Hysteria, she writes, "mimics, it metaphorizes destruction, but the family reconstitutes itself around it. As when you throw a stone in the water, the water ripples but becomes smooth again."[78] In Clément's analysis, hysteria may be a form of protest, but the hysteric's outbursts ultimately only sustain the system. Indeed, dominant structures of power benefit from localized resistance. This is true as well of the norms of gender. In Clément's reading, hysteria presents a form of social deviance that ultimately reinforces the system—" it makes them [those with power] comfortable," in Clément's words.[79]

Indeed, it is Clément's reading that ultimately speaks more closely to the experience of Jeremiah. As I have already suggested, with reference to Mills's reading of the tragic logic of Jeremiah, the prophet is doomed to fail. This failure extends, as well, to the possibility of a radical subversion of gender by means of prophecy. Jeremiah may speak with a feminine voice, Jeremiah may function as a hysteric, but Jeremiah does not fundamentally transform the economy of masculinity, any more than he alters the future of Judah. His masculinity may be queer, but masculinity as a larger category remains stable. There is no radical hysteric, no deliverance by means of Anna O. here. There is no queer prophet as hero. Jeremiah goes on to die in exile in Egypt. His prophecy fails. Subversion fails. The feminized voice fails. The system keeps working.

Coda: The Little Circus Keeps Working

The Newly Born Woman leaves the debate over the radical status of hysteria unsettled. In its wake, however, scholars have largely sided with Clément, against hysteria as a radical act of subversion and resistance. Cixous's descriptions of Dora and of hysteria are compelling, insofar as they offer the possibility of resistance. And yet Dora seems silenced, erased, made victim. This debate is relevant to the figure of Jeremiah in at least two ways. First, it captures the pull between triumphant resistance and resignation to suffering. Second, it highlights the relationship between dominant structures of power and localized resistance, a struggle as relevant to prophecy as to other moments when the hysterical voice is heard. Hysteria illuminates the sounds of prophecy.

I want to end my reflections on the hysteria of Jeremiah by considering an exchange between Clément and Cixous:

[Clément]: Listen, you love Dora, but to me she never seemed a revolutionary character.

[Cixous]: I don't give a damn about Dora; I don't fetishize her. She is the name of a certain force, which makes the little circus not work anymore.[80]

I would like to believe, with Cixous, that Dora represents a certain and undeniable force, and with this, that Jeremiah's gender transgressions in sound and body "make the little circus not work anymore." I would like to read the text as a radical queering of desire, the emergence of a new form of prophecy. And yet I cannot find proof of such transgression in the text. *You love Jeremiah, but to me he never seemed a revolutionary character.* Nothing changes as a result of his complaint, not even his own experience of prophecy or the prophetic body. His protests effect nothing. He remains pained and persecuted. If he enters into a kind of queer subjectivity, it is not undertaken willingly. The book ends with his willing exile, embracing the destruction of his nation. Jeremiah does not succeed as a prophet, indeed, he is fated to fail. Why should we assume that he succeeds at deconstructing gender? Or even at making his feminized voice heard? Is Dora "a certain force," or simply a suffering woman? And how much more so Jeremiah?

Jeremiah speaks and cries with a hysterical voice. As with hysteria, this use of voice at once implicates the body and disturbs it. Hysteria insistently blurs the distinctions between sound and body. The hysterical body speaks; the voice extends (and, at points, challenges) the body. Thus the disturbances of Jeremiah's voice are disturbances, as well, of his body, and if the prophet's hysterical sounds are queer, then so too is his body. The prophetic body is queered by the prophetic voice. Hysteria destabilizes more than sound—it challenges the body and its performance of masculinity.

However, hearing Jeremiah's voice as hysterical does not transform the Confessions into a radical text of liberation and resistance, any more than hearing Jeremiah's voice as feminine represents the emergence of an "authentic feminine" in the prophets. In both cases, the prophet's uses of sound, voice, and body are prestructured by the norms of gender and genre. Reading Jeremiah's voice through the categories of gendered sound and hysterical sound does not lead to a genderless (or transgender, or postgender, utopia).

This does not mean, however, that such a reading is without value. Instead, it forces us to confront the complex relations between gendered body, gendered voice, and the use of the feminine. The prophet's obsession with crying out is linked not simply to suffering and outrage, but to specifically feminine sounds of lamentation and embodied pain. The model of hysteria illuminates Jeremiah's struggles to speak, his playfulness with language that quickly becomes anger at the impossibility of communication. Hysteria also illuminates the use of the body to "speak" what cannot be said, a somatic compliance that becomes primarily expressed through wounding and pain. The scene of hysterical treatment likewise reveals the competing pulls of revulsion and seduction in the scene of prophecy. And, finally, reading prophecy through hysteria helps us to perceive our own desires as readers, the hope that Jeremiah will represent a figure of resistance, not simply another instance of suffering. But more often, in prophecy, the little circus keeps working, however much the prophet may scream.

The Unmanning of Ezekiel

THE PROPHET'S BODY VOLUPTUOUS AND SHATTERED
IN EZEKIEL 1–5

OF THE MANY readers of the Hebrew prophets, William Blake is one of the few
to imagine them as guests at a dinner party. In one of the sections of *The Marriage
of Heaven and Hell* entitled "A Memorable Fancy," he describes his fantastical
meal with the prophets, whom he confronts with a series of questions. Blake raises
the problem of inspiration, as well as of authority—how can a prophet persuade
the audience the message is a "true" prophecy and not a false one? But beyond
these general concerns, he is interested in the peculiar actions of his guests:

> I also asked Isaiah what made him go naked and barefoot three years? He
> answerd, the same that made our friend Diogenes, the Grecian.

> I then asked Ezekiel. why he eat dung, & lay so long on his right & left
> side? he answerd. the desire of raising other men into a perception of the
> infinite this the North American tribes practise, & is he honest who resists
> his genius or conscience only for the sake of present ease or gratification?[1]

Blake's dinner party may be a "memorable fancy," but the scenes he takes up
are very much a part of the Hebrew Bible. While Isaiah spends three years naked
(Isa. 20), Ezekiel's actions are even more dramatic. In the opening chapters of
the book, Ezekiel witnesses an incredible theophany (Ezek. 1–2), is struck dumb
by Yahweh (3), and then begins his work as a prophet with a number of bizarre
somatic performances (4–5), known as the "sign acts."[2]

Yahweh's first command to his performing prophet involves building a model
city. He instructs,

> And you, mortal, take a brick and lay it before you and draw a city upon it,
> Jerusalem. Lay siege to it; build siegeworks against it; set camps against it;
> place battering rams[3] all around. And you, take an iron griddle and place it

as an iron wall between you and the city. Set your face against it and let it be besieged. This is a sign for the house of Israel. (Ezek. 4:1–3)

During this siege of the model Jerusalem, Ezekiel passes his time lying bound on his side, for first 390 and then forty days (Ezek. 4:4–8). He also, despite being bound with cords, raises his arm to prophesy against his tiny city (4:7). He makes bread from a repulsive combination of foodstuffs, then eats only twenty shekels (about eight ounces) of it a day, plus a small amount of water (4:9–13).[4] This bread, moreover, is baked over cow dung—Yahweh at first orders Ezekiel to use human excrement, but he objects on grounds of purity. This is the only time the prophet complains, or indeed says anything. In chapter 5, the acts continue, as Yahweh commands Ezekiel to shave his head and beard with a sword. With the remaining hair,

A third[5] you shall set on fire in the city when the days of the siege are completed, a third you shall take and strike with the sword all around, and a third you shall scatter to the wind and I will unsheathe the sword after them. (Ezek. 5:1–2)

This harsh, symbolically charged haircut is the last of the sign acts, and concludes the episode. Ezekiel turns from actions to language for most of the remainder of the book.

In the "Memorable Fancy," the prophets have no shortage of explanations for their seemingly peculiar actions. Isaiah appeals to the model of Diogenes (conveniently positioning Hebrew prophecy in the intellectual and cultural genealogy of the Greeks), while Ezekiel invokes the "perception of the infinite," with the "North American tribes" tossed in for good measure. He further attributes the true core of prophecy to "the Poetic Genius (as you now call it)." For Blake, the actions of the prophets only *seem* bizarre or illogical; in fact, they reveal a broader intentionality (and one that can come forth at a single auspicious dinner party).

Blake's fanciful solution is among the more creative, but it is far from the only explanation of the prophets' actions. Other readers have turned to ecstasy or trance states, performances, or even symptoms of pathology (Ezekiel in particular has been diagnosed as a schizophrenic).[6] Still other readers, unable to reconcile the sign acts with a broader understanding of prophecy, insist that the "actions" must be understood as metaphorical only. This is because, in the words of Moses Maimonides, "God is too exalted than that He should turn His prophets into a laughingstock and a mockery for fools by ordering them to carry out crazy actions."[7]

This range of readings offers a number of perspectives on the sign acts. And yet in these readings, the *body*, the very thing that performs the sign acts, is largely neglected. Like Blake, we are too quick to jump from the body lying on the ground to the field of possible meanings and interpretations that surround this body. (Unless, following Maimonides, we deny that there is a "body" behind these acts at all). This chapter will offer a different approach, focusing closely on the body of Ezekiel without resolving its difficulties through recourse to extrabodily forms of understanding. I will employ two strategies in understanding Ezekiel. First, I will offer a close reading of the bodies described in the opening chapters that sets up the complex construction of embodiment and gender in the text. Second, I will position Ezekiel's embodiment against another (unconventional) text about bodies, displacement, performance, and pathology (as well as gender, divinity, and prophecy): Daniel Paul Schreber's *Memoirs of My Nervous Illness*. Schreber's text is an essential intertext because it restores the body to the foremost position in prophecy while also pushing questions of gender, disaster, and masculinity. It is also, in its self-presentation, a prophetic text, describing the divine commissioning—and divine abuse—of one man's body.

Daniel Paul Schreber was born in 1842, the child of German child-rearing expert Moritz Schreber.[8] A respected judge, he suffered a nervous illness in 1884, but recovered the following year and resumed his judicial career. In 1893, he was struck by a second nervous illness and institutionalized. Upon regaining his freedom in 1902, he published *Denkwürdigkeiten eines Nervenkranken*, known in English as *Memoirs of My Nervous Illness* (1903).[9] These memoirs are no typical narrative of illness and recovery. Instead, they read as an account of discovery, offering a carefully articulated explanation of his new understanding of the world. Schreber describes a malevolent, nonomniscient god, made of nerves, and a world in great crisis. This crisis, moreover, is centered upon Schreber's own body, which must be "unmanned" in order to save the universe. Unmanning (German *Entmannung*) is a central process in the *Memoirs* and involves the forced transformation of the prophet's body into the form of a woman.[10]

In Schreber's memoirs, the body becomes both an object of divine violence (particularly sexual violence) and an instrument of critique. Schreber's "unmanning" signals the passivity of the body of the prophet as well as its resistance to culturally dominant norms of masculinity. Schreber and Ezekiel share an experience of prophecy as undertaken in crisis and located in the body. Both men are called as prophets within a space of disaster, and both struggle with language and the possibility of communication itself. Moreover, in both cases, the body—tortured and abject—assumes prophetic importance. Sexualized, charged with meaning, and reduced to suffering flesh, the body enacts the dilemmas of prophetic masculinity. Approaching Ezekiel through Schreber does what a close reading or a historical analysis alone cannot: it forces us to confront the demands of masculinity and embodiment for the male prophet.

In reading Ezekiel through and against Schreber, this chapter will explore two possibilities: the prophetic body as critique of dominant forms of masculinity and the prophetic body as pleasurable emergence of an alternate masculinity. Both Schreber and Ezekiel place great emphasis on the pain and suffering of prophecy, which affect language and body alike. A reading attuned to gender reveals that both texts situate their respective prophets in passive, masochistic, and penetrated relations to a male divine figure, creating a failed prophetic masculinity. To be a prophet is to fail to be a man. And yet, Schreber's text in particular raises the possibility of the prophetic body not as emasculated victim, but as the source of a new understanding of masculinity, one that refuses traditional understandings of power and penetration in favor of something pleasurable, strange, and wholly new. Reading Schreber with Ezekiel makes it possible to trace this alternate, unmanned (and perhaps queer) masculinity in the biblical text. Though Ezekiel never fully follows Schreber—for a number of reasons, which this chapter will address—reading the two texts together reveals both the critique and the utopian fantasy in the penetrated, masochistic, and glorious prophetic body.

Ezekiel's Body

Before setting the body of Ezekiel against the body of Schreber, I want to sketch out the ways in which the biblical prophet's body is constructed in the text. The opening chapters of the book give few explicit details about the body of the prophet. And yet as the text unfolds, this same body assumes a high degree of importance. The body comes to prominence in the text in four ways:

1. Ezekiel's body in relation to the body of Yahweh;
2. Ezekiel's body as penetrated by the divine scroll;
3. Ezekiel's body in relation to the bodies of the people;
4. Ezekiel's body as ecstatic submissive.

I will consider each in turn.

1. Ezekiel's Body in Relation to the Body of Yahweh

As the book opens, Ezekiel ben Buzi, a priest (or possibly son of a priest), is living among the exiled Judean elite on the banks of the Chebar (Ezek. 1:1) when Yahweh appears from the north, conveyed in a fiery chariot and accompanied by a bizarre, terrifying entourage. The date of this spectacular event is set by the text at 593 BCE, a few years before the final fall of Jerusalem. Initially, the prophet is defined only by his father's name (Buzi), his geographical and temporal location (in the Babylonian exile), and his social position (as priest). There is no explicit mention of his body, although it is implied in the references to seeing and hearing the coming of Yahweh ("I saw divine visions," 1:1; "As I looked . . . ," 1:4; "I heard the sound . . . ," 1:24). We become aware of the prophet's body peripherally, through descriptions of perception. And then, suddenly, undeniably, it becomes present: "When I saw, I fell on my face, and I heard the voice of one speaking" (1:28). No sooner has Yahweh appeared than Ezekiel collapses before him.

From the first rumble of the approaching chariot to the tumble into the dust, the body of the prophet is constructed in relation to the divine bodies that enter and increasingly dominate the scene. First, within a rush of wind and a confusion of cloud and fire, Ezekiel perceives four "living creatures" (*ḥayyôt*) with a human form, wings, and four faces drawing the chariot. These creatures actively blur the boundaries of human and animal, animate and inanimate, placing under scrutiny the otherwise taken-for-granted boundaries of the human body. It is the divine body within the chariot, however, that has the greatest consequences for understanding Ezekiel's body. Yahweh's body, set in contrast to Ezekiel's body, is revealed as spectacular and perfect.

At first, the prophet struggles to explain what he sees:

> Upon the likeness of the throne, a likeness of something like the appearance of a man. And I saw something like the dazzle of *ḥashmal*,[11] something like the appearance of fire surrounding it all about, upward from what appeared to be his loins. And downward from what appeared to be his loins, I saw something like the appearance of fire, and he was surrounded by brightness. Like the rainbow in a cloud on a rainy day, such was the appearance of the splendor all around. This was the appearance of the likeness of the glory of Yahweh. (Ezek. 1:26b–27)

Ezekiel's speech is filled with evasions, substitutions, and linguistic hedging. Yahweh's form is at once virile and beautiful, sparkling with fire and rainbows, perfect in its masculinity.[12] Ezekiel's attention is attracted in particular to this perfect body's specific marker of masculinity—the divine penis. The prophet is simultaneously fascinated by the divine loins and unable to bring himself to gaze directly upon them. This interest in Yahweh's genitals is central to constructing the body in relation to sexuality.[13] The gaze is a sexualized act, as both biblical texts (Gen. 9) and psychoanalytic ones make clear.[14] At the moment Ezekiel's gaze shifts to the loins, the human form of the body is replaced with fire, a neat displacement that only heightens the genital fascination. This combination of desire to look and refusal to see also calls to mind Freud's argument concerning fetishism, and the reaction of the child to observing the "castrated" genitals of the mother.[15] As in the formation of the fetish, Ezekiel's gaze upon the forbidden genitals engenders a crisis. The scene is organized around the desire *to look*, even as this desire is overwhelmed by the danger that such an action threatens. Even if we assume that the prophet's desire is to gaze upon the *body* of Yahweh and not his genitals specifically, the physical markers of masculinity, and thus the basic sexualized dynamic, remain central to the scene. And the pain, weakness, and openness of the prophet's body to the divine word are placed in contrast to this dazzling male form. Ezekiel's body, first simply prostrate (Ezek. 1:28), later bound, immobile, and slowly starving (chapters 4–5), lies in sharp contradistinction to the dazzling, hypermasculine divine body.

2. Ezekiel's Body as Penetrated by the Divine Scroll

The opening scene, in which Yahweh appears to Ezekiel, represents the prophet's body as weak (it falls), open to stimuli (it receives and responds to sensation), and comparatively unattractive (it does not sparkle like fire or glow like a rainbow; its genitals are less impressive than Yahweh's). In the interview with Yahweh that follows, the power relations between the bodies of God and prophet become more pronounced as the divine word enters Ezekiel's body. The prophet is symbolically and literally penetrated:

> I looked and a hand was stretched out to me, and in it was a written scroll. He spread it before me; it was written on the front and the back, and written on it were lamentations and mourning and woe. He said to me, "Mortal, eat this scroll[16] and go speak to the house of Israel." So I opened my mouth and he gave me this scroll to eat. He said to me, "Mortal, let your belly eat and let your stomach be filled with this scroll that I have given you." I ate it, and in my mouth it was sweet as honey. (Ezek. 2:9–3:3)

Prophecy comes to Ezekiel from outside; his only active action is one of swallowing, taking the prophetic word into his body. The action is clearly physicalized in the text. When Jeremiah speaks of the divine word as sweet (Jer. 15:16), it is possible to understand his words metaphorically. For Ezekiel, however, the act is insistently physical. The word is literally eaten, not simply symbolically incorporated into the body. It even has a taste—sweetness. Like the sign acts that are to come, this scene with the scroll shows that prophecy is understood as deeply embodied and as dependent upon the body.

The scene is also sexualized; more than one scholar has noticed its resemblance to fellatio.[17] Honey is likewise associated with sexuality (Song 4:11).

Similarly, oral penetration is closely linked with questions of power, with Ezekiel placed in the position of swallowing the divine scroll. Here, as S. Tamar Kamionkowski notes, the text uses more passive verbs than the analogous passage in Jeremiah; thus grammatically and thematically, "Ezekiel is a passive recipient and not an agent in his own destiny."[18] For Kamionkowski, this act of consumption is linked to a series of other incidents, including his dumbness (Ezek. 3:26) and his visionary transport (2:2, 3:12), in which "Ezekiel is a passive male whose physical body is always controlled by another."[19] Ezekiel's body is not active, but acted *upon* by other male agents. The only action of the prophet is to open himself to prophecy. Ezekiel swallows the scroll and his body and subjectivity are, in turn, opened from within. The body of the prophet is a body opened and pained.

3. Ezekiel's Body in Relation to the Bodies of the People

The vulnerability and openness of the prophet's body is reinforced through the contrast between Ezekiel and the Israelite people to whom he is sent. The bodies of the Israelites are described as hard, impenetrable, threatening to the other. Immediately before the scroll appears to Ezekiel, Yahweh instructs him,

> He said to me, "Mortal, I am sending you to the house of Israel, to the rebellious ones[20] who have rebelled against me; they and their fathers have transgressed against me to this very day. And[21] you will say to them, thus says the Lord Yahweh. They—whether they listen or not, for they are a rebellious house—will know that a prophet has been in their midst. And you, mortal, do not be afraid of them and do not be afraid of their words, for nettles[22] and thorns are with you, and you sit upon scorpions. Do not be afraid of their words, do not be daunted by their faces, for they are a rebellious house." (Ezek. 2:3–6)

Ezekiel's body may be open to Yahweh and his word; the bodies of the Israelites, however, are not. They are, instead, a "rebellious house"; their rebellion is a refusal to be opened to Yahweh.

Instead of vulnerability and discontinuity, the people are characterized with images of pain, rebellion, and resistance to penetration by the prophet's words. Neither is Ezekiel's body prepared to encounter these people; he must be armed with nettles and thorns and placed upon scorpions. The weaponization of the prophetic body suggests its fundamental insufficiency. Notably, Ezekiel's body is not transformed, but simply equipped with the accouterments—drawn from the natural world—to penetrate the bodies of others. Ezekiel's own vulnerability, meanwhile, is not addressed, either by the text or by Yahweh's actions. Just as Ezekiel fails to achieve the glory of divine masculinity, so does he fail to conform to the forms of human embodiment represented by the Israelites. Confronted with the rebellious Israelites, he is given the weapons to penetrate their midst—but not to transform or shield his own open body.

After Ezekiel swallows the scroll, materially incorporating the divine word of commissioning, Yahweh offers a second description of the Israelites, this time with specific reference to their bodies. He warns his newly commissioned prophet that the Israelites each possess a "hard forehead and stubborn heart" (ḥizqê-mēṣaḥ ûqᵉšê-lēḇ, Ezek. 3:7); in consequence, he tells Ezekiel, "I will make your face as hard as theirs, and your forehead as brazen as theirs. I will make your forehead like adamant, harder than flint" (3:8–9). The hardness and impenetrability of the Israelite bodies remain, even as they are extended, belatedly, to the prophet himself.[23] In the case of the collective body of Israelites, these descriptions are pejorative—they are described as stiff-necked or hard-headed when they resist Yahweh. However, on the level of the individual body, hardness and resistance are valorized as essential traits of the male body.[24] Ezekiel's body must be made hard; male bodies must be hard (though for Ezekiel, at least, this bodily impenetrability is fleeting at best, perhaps because it begins with openness, an openness to the divine word).

Meanwhile, the promised transformation of Ezekiel's body—"I will make your forehead like adamant, harder than flint"—never seems to occur in the text. Instead of strength, Ezekiel finds only silence, as he sits, dumbstruck, for seven days. Unlike the hardened bodies and hearts of the people, Ezekiel remains opened, silent, passive.

4. Ezekiel's Body as Ecstatic Submissive

The glorious body of Yahweh, the penetration by the divine scroll, and the resistant bodies of the house of Israel all conspire to create an image of Ezekiel's body as soft, weak, vulnerable, opened, and acted upon. In the sign acts that follow in chapters 4–5, this representation is pushed further still. Ezekiel is the actor in the sign acts, performing a series of actions including lying on his side, prophesying against the brick, eating survival rations, and cutting and destroying his hair. Yet Ezekiel does not act independently, but rather on the command of Yahweh. There is a basic continuity between the passive, receptive body of Ezekiel 1–3 and the active body of Ezekiel 4–5: even when he acts, he acts masochistically.[25] To act, for Ezekiel, is to submit.

In the previous chapter, I considered Ken Stone's argument that Jeremiah is best understood through the category of masochism. If Jeremiah is a feisty masochist (or, in Stone's formulation, an "aggressive bottom"),[26] Ezekiel is an enthusiastic one, never protesting against Yahweh's commands. The only exception is his objection to cooking over human excrement, an action that would invalidate his priestly bodily purity. Even this seeming moment of resistance is part of a larger dynamic of preserving the priest-prophet's body to be acted upon by divine desires.

There is even the suggestion of a certain economy of pleasure in the scene. Jan Tarlin describes the sign acts as follows:

> Yahweh forces Ezekiel to undergo the fall of the southern kingdom in his own body. The all-sufficient priestly body is subjected to famine, shorn of its hair, and reduced to muteness and paralysis. This degradation of the self, like its displacement, is part and parcel of the prophet's ecstatic submission to Yahweh, a submission and an ecstasy that, given the unmistakably male characterization of Yahweh in the book of Ezekiel, can only be described as homoerotic masochism.[27]

For Tarlin, Ezekiel's masochistic submission is part of a reconfiguration of the economy of masculinity in the text. Tarlin argues that Ezekiel represents a novel, shattered, non-phallic masculinity, analogous to that of Erwin in Rainer Werner Fassbinder's film *In a Year of 13 Moons*. Fassbinder's film tells the story of Elvira (formerly Erwin), a man who had his genitals removed and became a woman in an attempt to win over another (primarily heterosexual) man. There is nothing simple about gender, sexuality, or desire here; Erwin/Elvira is, in Tarlin's description, a "new creature . . . a visitor from a utopia beyond the western dominant fiction" of masculinity.[28] I will return to Tarlin's arguments, as well as to the suggestion of the prophet as constructing an alternate masculinity. For now, I want to draw attention to Ezekiel's fundamentally masochistic and submissive position.

Finally, I cannot leave the subject of masochism without considering its relationship to pleasure (a theme that will become important, as well, in reading Schreber's memoirs). As Tarlin suggests, Ezekiel's is a body pushed to extremity and pain, but also implicated in pleasure, and more precisely, the pleasure of masochism. As Karmen MacKendrick writes, "To understand the perverse pleasures of restraint and restrained (ritualized, ceremonial, and especially *stylized*) violence (including the pleasure of pain), we must remember what Foucault has told us: that it is always the body that is at issue, especially in pleasure."[29] This is especially true of Ezekiel. But to draw out the complexities of pleasure, extremity, and passivity, I want to set Ezekiel's body against another body, that of Daniel Paul Schreber.

Schreber and His *Memoirs*

Schreber's memoirs offer an account of a world on the brink of disaster, with his own body serving as ground zero of the conflict. The Court Examiner assigned to Schreber's case offers an admirably concise summary of Schreber's belief system. His report reads,

> [Schreber] is called to redeem the world and to bring back to mankind the lost state of Blessedness. He maintains he has been given this task by direct divine inspiration, similar to that taught by the prophets; he maintains that nerves in a state of excitation, as his have been for a long time, have the property of attracting God, but it is a question of things which are either not at all expressible in human language or only with greatest difficulty, because he maintains they lie outside all human experience and have been revealed only to him. The most essential part of his mission of redemption is that it is necessary for him first of all to be *transformed into a woman*.[30]

Schreber's own text begins, after several prefaces, with nerves: "The human soul is contained in the nerves of the body," Schreber writes, adding a page later that "God to start with is only nerve, not body, and akin therefore to the human soul."[31] Schreber's god is nonomniscient and imperfect, constantly threatened by the attraction of the divine nerves to their human counterparts, as well as to what Schreber terms "soul-voluptuousness."[32] After an unknown party attempts "soul murder" on Schreber,[33] the divine nerves develop a powerful attraction to Schreber's body. They seek, moreover, to "unman" it; this *Entmannung*, or "unmanning," is necessary to forestall cosmic disaster.[34] The experience of unmanning is described as both incredibly painful and intensely pleasurable.

The publication of Schreber's memoirs inspired a number of critical responses, some psychological or psychoanalytic, some literary, and others concerned with history, ideology, or power. Freud's case study "Psychoanalytic Notes on an Autobiographical Account of a Case of Paranoia (*Dementia Paranoides*)," published a few years after Schreber's memoir, is perhaps the most famous, and is an important source of Freud's theory of homosexuality. However, it is more useful in tracking the development of Freud's own thought than in understanding Schreber's situation (Freud, after all, never met the patient, despite developing an extensive artifice of theory around him).[35] But in spite of its flaws, Freud's case study inaugurated Schreber's memoirs as a significant text for modern psychoanalysis, philosophy, and critical theory, with Freud, Lacan, Canetti, and Deleuze and Guattari numbering among Schreber's many readers.[36]

While I draw on this rich interpretive history, I am not interested in diagnosing, historicizing, or treating Schreber as a philosophical object or text. In using the memoirs as a literary and theoretical text to read the book of Ezekiel, I take Schreber as a prophetic figure, rather than as a model patient, a historical symptom, or an effect of power. Here I follow the work of Lucy Bregman, who has argued that Schreber's memoirs are best understood through the category of religion. Bregman writes,

> Schreber's Memoirs was a religious text before it became a case history, and the ground gained by Otto and Eliade in marking out a space for religious language ought to be solid and broad enough to allow Schreber to stand on it, too. Few of Schreber's interpreters and none of his turn-of-the-century contemporaries doubted that he was mad, insane, mentally ill, or whatever other term their conceptual schemes supplied. In other words, he was quite as crazy as he was religious. But I think both these perspectives on his Memoirs should be taken seriously.[37]

As Bregman suggests, the memoirs are productively read as an intentional text, with a coherent—if radically unfamiliar—ideological and religious system. In this system, the body is foregrounded as a site of conflict. Schreber's ideas about embodiment, masculinity, outrageous suffering, and unexpected pleasure, moreover, offer an opening into a text no less painfully charged—the book of Ezekiel.

Schreber and Ezekiel: Three Parallels

There are a number of striking parallels between the experiences of Ezekiel and of Daniel Paul Schreber. I will delineate three of the most important below.

Parallel 1: Prophecy and Pain

Like Ezekiel, Schreber understands himself as divinely called in times of trouble—of world-changing disaster, even—to prophesy to a recalcitrant and resistant people. And like Ezekiel, Schreber experiences his body as thrust into a world of pain. His prophetic vocation brings with it seemingly endless anguish and torture. He suffers a number of forced and painful transformations of his body, which he dubs "miracles."[38] He describes his torment by his doctors, by the staff in the institution, by a legal system that refuses him his freedom. More than anything else, the memoirs express Schreber's great suffering and his attempt to communicate it. At one point, he laments,

When I think of my sacrifices through loss of an honorable professional position, a happy marriage practically dissolved, deprived of all the pleasures of life, subjected to bodily pain, mental torture, and terrors of a hitherto unknown kind, the picture emerges of a martyrdom which all in all I can only compare with the crucifixion of Jesus Christ.[39]

This statement's messianic aspirations come hundreds of pages in to his account of suffering.

Unlike Schreber, who cannot seem to stop speaking—and writing—about his anguish, Ezekiel never articulates his suffering. (In this, he also differs from Jeremiah, who frequently complains about his physical and emotional anguish over prophecy.) However, Ezekiel, no less than Schreber, is deeply marked by the experience of pain, which is clearly visible in the sign acts. Mary Mills describes the body of the prophet as positioned in a universe of pain.[40] God demands that Ezekiel perform acts that are painful, even torturous. To lie unmoving for more than a year, to eat food baked on excrement, to enact with one's body the destruction of the world (Ezek. 4–5)—these are not so much attention-getting tricks as scenes of agony. Thus Ezekiel holding up his arm against the tiny city is not simply an action of farce, but the cause of great physical discomfort. This becomes clear when we set Ezekiel's stillness and repetitive actions against Elaine Scarry's work on pain. In *The Body in Pain*, Scarry writes,

> Standing rigidly for eleven hours produces as violent muscle and spine pain as can injury from elaborate equipment and apparatus, though any of us outside this situation, used to adjusting our body positions every few moments before even mild discomfort is felt, may not immediately recognize this. . . . Only when a person throws his head back and swallows three times does he begin to apprehend what is involved in one hundred and three or three hundred and three swallows, what atrocities one's own body, muscle, and bone structure can inflict on oneself.[41]

In seeking to write the experience of pain, Scarry draws on a range of contemporary documents, including Amnesty International accounts by survivors of torture. And yet her account speaks to Ezekiel as well. Stillness can be a form of torture as surely as movement. There is a similar pain in Ezekiel's more than a year of lying motionless. The body, immobile, brings itself torture. As Scarry writes, "what atrocities one's own body, muscle, and bone structure can inflict on oneself."[42]

The other sign acts, too, implicate the prophet Ezekiel's body in a universe of pain and abjection. Ezekiel's food, so carefully prepared, is part of a slow process of starvation. This starvation, moreover, occurs in an overarching context of disgust. The mixture of grains in Ezekiel's bread symbolizes the impurity and degeneration of the starvation rations in a besieged city.[43] The use of excrement as cooking fuel further increases the sense of disgust. Julia Kristeva has argued that feces and other marginalia of the body—hair, nails, blood—are "abject" and are reviled because they remind us of our own mortality.[44] To cook over feces is to introduce the margins of the body, and thus the possibility of death, into the scene of eating and nourishment. This basic structure of disgust remains even after Yahweh permits the prophet to substitute cow dung for human excrement. From the beginning, Ezekiel's prophecy is intimately bound up with disgust and death, which are enacted on the body through the basic act of consumption.

The pain in Ezekiel is shocking both because it seems unhelpful and unnecessary for the prophetic message, and because it is caused by ordinary, unremarkable objects used in remarkable ways. In *The Body in Pain*, Scarry writes about how pain brings about the "dissolution of the world."[45] She argues that one of the most powerful, and terrifying, strategies used by torturers is to transform ordinary objects into weapons. A chair, a light bulb, a bathtub, even the sound of a door locking—these ordinary things are used by the torturer to inflict pain upon the prisoner. Furthermore, the very ordinariness of these objects means that their violent use is an inversion of the order of things. In Scarry's words, this inversion is part of "a process which not only converts but announces the conversion of every conceivable aspect of the event and the environment into an agent of pain."[46] This is precisely what happens to Ezekiel. Ordinary objects such as ropes, a brick, and foodstuffs are turned into weapons against the body. Ezekiel shares with Schreber the experience of prophecy as torturous pain. But how is this pain to be spoken of? This question leads us to the second parallel.

Parallel 2: Suffering and the Crisis of Language

For both Schreber and Ezekiel, the pain of prophecy is bound up in a crisis of language. The problem is not simply what has happened, but how to communicate it. This is a problem common to the experience of pain; for instance, Scarry's study emphasizes the oppositional relationship between pain and language. "There is no language for pain," Scarry writes, but only "fragmentary means of verbalization."[47] The difficulty of communication is made worse by the fact that pain occurs on the level of the individual and represents an intimate experience that is difficult or impossible to share with others. This produces a complex relationship between pain and trust in the other: because "physical pain has no voice," "to have pain is to have *certainty*; to hear about pain is to have *doubt*."[48]

Given this complex relationship between pain, doubt, and interpersonal communication, it is not surprising to find that dumbness and other difficulties with speech characterize prophecy in disaster. As he recounts in his memoir, Schreber has difficulty in communicating both his experiences and his new understanding of the world. In the introduction to his manuscript, he describes its purpose as "to give an at least partly comprehensible exposition of supernatural matters, knowledge of which has been revealed to me."[49] His opening commitment to explain "supernatural matters" is immediately followed, however, by hedging:

> I cannot of course count upon being *fully* understood because things are dealt with which cannot be expressed in human language; they exceed human understanding. Nor can I maintain that *everything* is irrefutably certain even for me: much remains only presumption and probability. After all, I too am only a human being and therefore limited by the confines of human understanding.[50]

The text that follows is likewise almost overwhelmed with explanatory asides, apologies to the reader, and reassurances. Beyond this persistent and apologetic self-positioning, the text manifests a deep—and deeply strange—relation to language. Much of Schreber's explanation is dedicated to the language of the divine nerves, of birds, and of God himself. And like Ezekiel, Schreber himself is struck dumb. When he regains his voice, it is not to speak, but rather to experience what he names, with one of many neologisms, the "bellowing miracle," the forced production of nonlinguistic sound. Language is thus shattered in the space of the disaster.

The dumbness of the prophet Ezekiel (Ezek. 3:15, 25–26; see also 24:25–27, 33:21–22) is likewise a clear sign of the crisis of language. Ezekiel's sign acts, as we have seen, fail rather badly as communicative acts. There is no indication that they serve to persuade anyone of anything; the immediate audience is both already in exile and preemptively denied the possibility of understanding. Likewise, even as metaphors or textual events, the sign acts remain oddly ineffective. As David Stacey writes, "Ezekiel's actions may arrest attention, but few of them can be said to communicate meaning more easily than words."[51] Ezekiel's binding, fasting, and hair burning, while striking, are not effective as signs. His body is emphatically not the spectacle of suffering that forms the centerpiece of martyrdom. Nor is the suffering of this body necessarily implicated in a larger economy of pleasure, as in sadism or masochism. Instead, as with Kafka's hunger artist, the meaning of the performance eludes the observers and is incommunicable by the performer.[52] Schreber, too, is plagued by the incommunicability of his experience. In the

Memoirs, he manipulates language and contorts meaning to explain the divine violation of his body. And yet, as with Ezekiel, the situation does not resolve into intelligibility. Instead, the experience exceeds and defies language.

Parallel 3: Disaster and Masculinity

There is a still broader parallel: the experience of disaster, and its consequences for gender. The book of Ezekiel and *Memoirs of my Nervous Illness* are both written within the space of disaster. As detailed in the memoirs, the unthinkable has already happened: what Schreber terms the "Order of the World" has been ruptured, Schreber himself has been "unmanned," and everything has been impossibly changed.[53] There is no longer the possibility of averting the crisis; it is already upon us. This textual location within the time of the disaster sets the text apart from forms of future-oriented prophecy that leave open the possibility, however slim, of averting the crisis.

Ezekiel, too, is living in disaster. The opening lines of the book position the prophet in the space of the disaster—this time, not the cosmic rending of the order of the world, but the historical disaster of the Exile. As Daniel Smith-Christopher reminds us, the exile is not merely a setting or a historical backdrop. Instead, the context is intimately felt and lived as an experience of extreme suffering. He argues that any reading of Ezekiel must acknowledge the context of historical trauma. Not just the prophet, but the entire book of Ezekiel, represents, for Smith-Christopher, the "voices of traumatized communities"—communities that have experienced violence, forced migration, humiliation of all sorts, and even "state-sponsored terrorism."[54] This experience of disaster, moreover, is highly significant to Ezekiel's own experience, including his experience of embodiment and gender. In a second study of Ezekiel, this one entitled "Ezekiel in Abu Ghraib," Smith-Christopher elaborates on the relationship between historical trauma and gender:

> Ezekiel is a refugee; his rhetoric cannot be read as the normative observations of an "average ancient Israelite," and thus a reflection of normal gender relations and imagery. Rather, Ezekiel's rhetoric is the language of suffering—and the rhetoric of suffering and anger is not "normal." . . . [I]mages of violence, bloodshed, vengeance, and terror are not concoctions of Ezekiel's normative theological reflection, but the realities within which he is living![55]

Here, Smith-Christopher links the national and personal experience of disaster to a specific (violent) reconfiguration of the norms of gender. Exile is traumatic in many ways, among them for the forced dismantling of social relations and social categories. This is particularly true of Ezekiel, living through forced migration, culminating in the destruction of the Temple and the permanent loss of his livelihood as priest.

Smith-Christopher is not the only reader to link Ezekiel's experience of trauma to his experience of gender. Kamionkowski makes a similar point, tracing two possible responses to the crisis of gender: hypervirility (as in Yahweh's violent assertion of his masculinity in Ezek. 16) and emasculation (as in the case of Ezekiel himself, particularly in his dumbness, his immobility, and his passive penetration by the divine word). In tracing Ezekiel's passivity, Kamionkowski even makes a brief reference to Schreber, whom she argues exemplifies emasculation as a response to crisis.[56] Though her interest in Schreber passes quickly, she notes the close relationship between persecution, emasculation, and divine mandate, a constellation that unites both texts.

Schreber and Ezekiel are each confronted by a profound threat to masculinity. Emasculation and hypermasculinity are two possible responses to this crisis. And yet these are not the only possible responses. Instead, Schreber's own account of his experience, centered on what he terms "unmanning," offers a complex response to gender crisis that cannot be reduced to general categories.

Unmanning Ezekiel

Schreber and Ezekiel share in pain, in the difficulty of language, and in the overarching experience of disaster. These parallels hold significance for gender, as both men experience a fundamental disruption in gender norms. For Schreber, this breakdown of gender is centered on the body. What Schreber terms his "unmanning" is not simply metaphor, but rather describes a physical transformation. He experiences the sex of his own body as in flux, including the sensation of female breasts and buttocks and the "retraction of the male organ."[57] This reconfiguration of the breasts and genitals is matched by an increased sense of what he terms "voluptuousness," a feeling he treats as feminine and that increases his capacity to experience sexual pleasure, even as it renders him sexually irresistible to the divine nerves.

Schreber's unmanning is central to many of the critical readings of his memoir. It provides the crucial hook for Freud's theory of homosexuality and for Deleuze and Guattari's notion of "becoming woman," as well as their model of "schizoanalysis," for example. Schreber likewise anticipates Eilberg-Schwartz's argument in *God's Phallus* that the monotheistic norms of the Bible are deeply problematic for, and perhaps incompatible with, heterosexual masculinity. Eilberg-Schwartz writes,

[Schreber] was able to think the unthinkable and thus expresses what traditional theology has always been afraid to face. When a man confronts
a male God, he is put into the female position so as to be intimate with
God. . . . The defining traits of what it meant to be a man were called into
question. In the literature of ancient Judaism, this threat to masculinity
proceeds in ways parallel to Schreber's: sometimes through violence that
threatens castration, even death, at other times in more subtle forms of
gender reversal.[58]

For Eilberg-Schwartz, Schreber exemplifies the ways in which the male believer's relationship with God places him in a passive, nonmasculine position. In particular, Schreber's memoirs critique the impossible subject position of the male religious subject in biblical and postbiblical religion.

Bringing Eilberg-Schwartz's reading together with the provocative parallels between Schreber and Ezekiel, it is tempting to see the biblical prophet as a proto-Schreber, "put into the female position so as to be intimate with God" and, in the process, stripped of his masculinity. Ezekiel is penetrated by the divine word, his body is insufficient, and we can even trace pleasure in his passive, masochistic position. The primary difference is that while Schreber writes down his critique (in the form of the memoirs), Ezekiel's response to the dilemmas of prophetic masculinity remains unwritten and unspoken. It appears only elliptically through his excessive, ineffective embodied actions. In effect, Schreber writes what Ezekiel cannot himself communicate.

Plenitude, Utopia, and Masculinity beyond Phallocentrism

Schreber's unmanning dramatizes the ways in which the passivity of prophecy alters the experience of masculinity, producing a trenchant critique of the relations of gender to religious subjectivity. And yet Schreber's memoir is far from the only source to sketch out the difficulty of the relationship of the male believer to the male God in the biblical and postbiblical traditions. Eilberg-Schwartz argues that the Rabbis find themselves in a similar position; Stephen Moore makes a parallel argument about the dilemmas of Christian male exegetes of the Song of Songs.[59] To be sure, Schreber, unlike these other sources, emphasizes the prophetic, but the problems of prophecy can and have been articulated without reference to divine nerves, unmanning, or "soul-voluptuousness." What need, then, for Schreber?

I will suggest that Schreber offers an essential model for thinking the move beyond normative masculinity in Ezekiel. While the critique of masculine religious subjectivity is an important component of Schreber's memoirs—and has provided a fertile site of engagement for contemporary theory—it is not the only function of unmanning in the text. Schreber complains a great deal about his unmanning, but it is not all work and no play. As the memoir recounts, he also finds power, pleasure, and new forms of knowledge. This aspect of Schreber plays an important role for Deleuze and Guattari, who return to the German judge repeatedly, both explicitly and elliptically, in both volumes of *Capitalism and Schizophrenia*. Within the first paragraph of *Anti-Oedipus*, Schreber and his body make an appearance: "Judge Schreber has sunbeams in his anus. A solar anus."[60] Throughout this text, the "schizophrenic out for a walk,"[61] is a key figure for the critique of psychoanalysis and the cultivation of an alternative, schizoanalysis. And who better exemplifies this figure than Schreber, who keeps his delusions but earns his freedom? Schreber likewise figures in *Capitalism and Schizophrenia*'s notions of "becoming woman"[62] and of the "body without organs,"[63] both of which Schreber experiences as literal transformations of his body. Indeed, tracing Schreber's body as it reappears across Deleuze and Guattari's work means following an itinerary of desire and, not infrequently, pleasure.

This pleasure, moreover, is directly linked to Schreber's body. Schreber describes the "soul-voluptuousness" he experiences—a pleasure more sensual, or perhaps sexual, than spiritual. At moments in the *Memoirs*, he seems uncertain as to whether his experience is one of pain or of pleasure—it is the intensity of affect that comes through most clearly, rather than the content assigned to it. This experience of pleasure and affective intensity is also bound up with a reconfiguration of the masculine. Jonathan Kemp argues that Schreber enacts "a DeleuzoGuattarian becoming-minoritarian/woman/queer which shatters the neat and stable confines of the concept 'man.'" The notion of becoming that is so fundamental to Deleuze and Guattari is catastrophic for the Enlightenment conception of the subject, and in particular for those subjects nestled neatly in the category of "man." Instead of such a stable and self-contained subject, Deleuze and Guattari offer a "flux of radical jouissance, a surface shot through with holes into which and out of which sensations flow, deterritorialising masculine subjectivity and locating the penetrated/penetrable (male) body as a condition of reterritorialised male subjectivity."[64] This is a radical reconfiguration of the body and subjectivity alike, transforming both masculinity and male embodiment. It suggests a queering of both masculinity (as category) and body (as object).

Nor does the reading of Schreber as shattered masculine subjectivity end with Deleuze and Guattari. Jill Marsden directs attention to the "tactility, multiplicity, and emergent creativity" of Schreber's system.[65] Noting the association of "blessedness" with femininity and the voluptuous attraction of the divine rays to Schreber's feminized body, she argues for treating his body as a lesbian system. She writes,

> The souls who seek this pleasure in Schreber's nervous system are already implicitly feminized, and by extension, so is the God who comprises them. If homosexuality is an issue at all, then arguably it is an autoerotic *lesbian* economy that is here being engineered . . . it is thus by no means certain that becoming woman symbolizes a deficient masculinity or passive homosexuality. Indeed, where is castration to be found within Schreber's glorious "unmanning"—a process of corporealization which is only ever addressed in terms of *growth, abundance, and plenitude?*[66]

Marsden suggests that Schreber's feminized body represents a self-contained lesbian network. Instead of anxiously pursuing castration, she takes seriously the possibility of other genitalities and configurations of pleasure. Her reading offers a new perspective on Schreber while also reconfiguring the connotations of the female body. Read this way, Schreber's body functions not so much as a critique of the patriarchal theological system, but as a destabilizing alternative to it—a move outside oppressive masculinity, into *"growth, abundance, and plenitude."* The body that emerges is not a failed masculine body, but something else entirely, a "self-organizing system, illegible from the perspective of extrinsic binary determination."[67] Schreber's *Memoirs* describes a new body for the prophet, a body rich in pleasure and exterior to the constrained category of masculinity that precedes the crisis of his nervous illness. The body itself is more than a critique—it is a productive materiality that shatters categories and augurs new pleasures. In this sense, Schreber is best understood not simply with cyberpsychology and posthumanism, but also with a turn to feminist theory. Marsden further associates Schreber with Luce Irigaray's "sex which is not one," arguing that Schreber's body is both (1) incomprehensible from a normative Freudian perspective (recall Freud's serious difficulties with understanding both Schreber and women) and (2) multiple, pleasurable, and open in the ways in that Irigaray describes female sexuality.[68]

Marsden's reading is particularly useful because it suggests another way to look at Schreber—and, by extension, Ezekiel—beyond a rigid masculinity negotiated between men. Marsden's Schreber, read through Deleuze and Irigaray, becomes a generative, emergent pleasure machine, exterior to the norms of masculinity. This exteriority is not a failure, but rather the possibility of doing something different with the male body. Schreber, his body unmanned, voluptuous, and multiple, has become the sex that is not one. This is a plurality of pleasures and polymorphous perversities, exterior to the norms of masculinity. Is such an understanding possible with Ezekiel? Tarlin concludes that the prophet, violently torn between masochistic self-abasement and sadistic violence against women, is positioned outside of normal masculine subjectivity. He writes,

> His male subjectivity in ruins, but still in the throes of a transcendental male homoerotic relationship, feminized but not female, Ezekiel, like Fassbinder's Erwin, is a visitor from the utopia beyond male and female. The return onto male subjectivity of the violence that males usually inflict onto females has, for Ezekiel, created a new form of subjectivity: a person with a penis who has renounced any claim to possessing the phallus. This subjectivity bears and lives the violence that gives rise to the primal human subject in solidarity with other selves rather than inflicting or projecting it upon them. This new subjectivity that voluntarily incorporates symbolic castration in a masculine body is not recognizable to western eyes as either male or female.[69]

Tarlin's key insight is to recognize Ezekiel as positioned outside of the normative boundaries of biblical masculinity. Ezekiel represents "a new form of subjectivity: a person with a penis who has renounced any claim to possessing the phallus."[70] Instead of refusing the category of the masculine, Ezekiel experiences transformation within it, suggesting the possibility of discontinuity, vulnerability, and openness. This is an opening of the body and the self alike that goes beyond homoerotic ecstasy into a new queer imagining of body, sex, and prophecy, as well as their mutual relations. The prophetic body, masochistic or otherwise, offers another possibility of a different masculinity—a queer masculinity—although it never emerges fully in the text. The book of Ezekiel not only documents the impossible position of the embodied male prophet but also leaves open the suggestion that this impossibility contains, within it, other possible masculinities.

Read in conjunction with Schreber (and with Deleuze and Guattari, as well as Marsden and Kemp), it is possible in Ezekiel to see the traces of an alternate organization of masculinity, a form of male subjectivity that is not organized around the phallus, to use the psychoanalytic language that both Marsden and Tarlin employ. That this does not emerge more clearly in the text is the result of the text's own diversionary strategy: the displacement of the prophetic body onto the Temple in the final chapters of the book.

Ezekiel and the Strategic Use of Displacement

Like *Memoirs of My Nervous Illness*, the book of Ezekiel is an account of transformation. His transformation is not, however, of the human body, but rather of space. The final nine chapters of the book are devoted to an elaborate vision of the rebuilt Temple and its environs, its dimensions, construction, and the priests who will serve within it. In a vision that mirrors the theophany at the book's beginning, Ezekiel is transported to the new Temple:

> The hand of Yahweh was upon me, and he brought me there. He brought me in divine visions to the land of Israel and set me upon a very high mountain, and upon was a building like a city to the south. (Ezek. 40:1b–2)

He is guided by a man "whose appearance was like that of bronze, with a linen cord and a measuring rod in his hand" (Ezek. 40:3)—a combination of technical and metallurgical details again reminiscent of the vision of God's chariot in Ezekiel 1. The vision of the new Temple gradually expands to include the entire land, and the final chapter lists the tribes of Israel and their location in the land. The final line of the book gives a name to the city: "and the name of the city from now on shall be: *Yahweh is there*" (48:35).

The fantasy of the rebuilt Temple imagines a healing for the trauma of exile. At the same time, it transposes the imagery of the opening theophany from the chariot to the Temple itself, where Yahweh returns to dwell in chapter 43. As Albert Cook points out, the time of disaster is replaced with a utopian imagining of space.[71] The final chapters and the opening chapters, taken together, form both an inclusio and a reversal.

The resolution of the problems of the body (Ezekiel's body, Yahweh's gazed-upon body, as well as the bodies engaged in abominations in the Temple in chapter 8, the violated bodies of chapters 16 and 23, the raised bodies of chapter 37) is thus the restoration of the Temple. In 40–48, the Temple body is the repository of utopian fantasy, replacing the specific body of the prophet with an abstract and collective "body." This shift in focus to the Temple does many things: it brings an end to the agonies of Exile, it furnishes Yahweh with a new and glorious home, it sets forth a proper ordering of space for the many returned Israelite peoples. The restoration of the Temple in the final chapters of Ezekiel likewise resembles Schreber's experience of bodily transformation. As with Schreber, the transformed vision represents a new world after the disaster, a world healed. And the transformation also marks a renewed relationship with the deity that at once preserves the passivity of the prophet (Ezekiel is first transported, then led around the Temple by a divine emissary; Schreber remains in voluptuous contact with the divine rays) and moves beyond pain.

But what of the crisis of masculinity? The Temple is frequently understood as a body,[72] just as the space of the city is frequently anthropomorphized, often as a woman.[73] In Ezekiel's final vision, the Temple returns as reimagined body.

However, this body is emphatically *not* a female or feminized body. As Christl Maier writes,

> In the concluding vision of the new temple (Ezekiel 40–48), every trace of Jerusalem's female character as well as her name has been deleted. The space of the city is greatly diminished and separated from the temple precinct (Ezek. 45:1–6) in order to express the discontinuity between the new temple and the defiled preexilic city.[74]

The reimagined space of the new city and the new Temple are predicated on the removal of the feminization of space. Bennett Simon echoes Maier's argument, writing, "The temple vision is almost totally devoid of feminine elements."[75] Instead, as Simon notes, the form of the Temple is traditionally, normatively masculine and shores up hegemonic representations of masculinity. Imagining a new Israelite history and a new Israelite Temple body requires, it seems, erasing every trace of the nonnormative masculinity staged on a previous symbolic body, the body of the prophet Ezekiel. The prophet's body is replaced by an architectural body whose gender stability opposes the shattered remnants of Ezekiel's own masculinity.

The turn to the Temple, moreover, represents a divergence from the Schreber pattern, as well as a move away from radical reconfigurations of any kind. What begins as critique is ultimately reintegrated into the dominant system. Roland Boer has argued that, while the early chapters of Ezekiel are ecstatic, anarchic, and carnivalesque, the anarchic and utopian impulses in the text are ultimately unsustainable;[76] I would link this argument to the fate of masculine embodiment in particular. By concluding with the restoration of the Temple, the book of Ezekiel ends up reinstating order, not subverting it. The traditional system of categories, represented by the Temple and the law, are reestablished. This is represented textually by the measuring of the Temple, which the text takes care to repeat, emphasizing its authority. Everything wrong is righted again; everything old is new again. In Boer's terms, subversive and marginal practice (including Ezekiel's subversive practice of prophecy and marginal experience of embodiment), are subsumed into the dominant hegemonic ideals.

Boer's analysis of Ezekiel speaks to the problems of masculinity and embodiment as well. The text, in substituting a restored Temple body for an open and abject male human body, stabilizes the dominant ideology of the text. Thus the transformation of religious and city space in Ezekiel does not fully resolve the problem of the prophetic body, as Schreber's unmanning does. In ending with Ezekiel's visionary transport to the rebuilt Temple, the book neatly leaves behind the messy question of prophetic embodiment, of the suffering and linguistic crisis and fraught masculinity that figure so prominently in the opening chapters of the book. This quick move to set aside the problem of the body of the prophet is likewise what makes the conclusion of the book of Ezekiel, in the final analysis, unsatisfying. The text ends with a lovely architectural vision that also fails to respond to or resolve the dilemmas of embodiment in the opening pages of the book. Unlike Schreber, Ezekiel has no utopian experience of transformation, no radical self-reimagining. The move beyond critique into productive creativity is ultimately stunted, with the radical potentialities of the body replaced by the stasis of rebuilt architectural space carefully evacuated of gender and sexuality alike. There is no pleasure in unmanning to be found here, no radical reconfiguration of the male body or the category of masculinity, only a city that shares Yahweh's name.

Coda: From a Memorable Fancy to a Fanciful Body

William Blake's "memorable fancy" opens the possibility of questioning the body of the prophet Ezekiel. And yet Blake's own interests lie less in the body itself than in the problem of inspiration, as well as in the complex webs of ideas and influence that link the biblical prophet to other times and places, even to Blake himself. In order to take the body of Ezekiel seriously, it is not enough simply to read Blake. Instead, the contours of prophetic embodiment come to presence in relation to other bodies. And of great importance to this comparative project is the unmanned body of Daniel Paul Schreber, a body of plenitude and pleasure beyond phallic masculinity. Truly a memorable fancy!

In his account of his bodily unmanning, Schreber is able to describe and experience an alternate mode of masculine embodiment. His memoirs likewise propose an alternative to the patriarchal order and a form of masculinity that does not depend on active domination of the other—an economy of desire that, despite Schreber's emphasis on unmanning, is not organized around lack. Ezekiel has no such recourse and can imagine no such utopian transformation. Perhaps it is the critical, scientific, and discursive resources of modernity that make it possible for Schreber to imagine an alternative organization of embodiment, sexuality, and sexual pleasure, a newly configured male prophetic body at the boundaries of the human. Or perhaps Schreber only puts in words what Ezekiel already suggests with his silence. In any case, for Ezekiel, the transgressive, transformative impulse emerges only in glimpses before being displaced onto a reimagining of the body of the Temple—a fantastic vision that displaces the human body as body. The rebuilt Temple at the end of the book of Ezekiel substitutes (though imperfectly) for the unmanned body that emerges in Schreber's memoirs. Both are fantasies that pose an alternative to the intractable, anguished position of the male prophetic body in disaster.

Even as the book of Ezekiel documents the impossible position of the embodied male prophet, it is ultimately unable to articulate an ordering of desire beyond activity-passivity or a prophetic embodiment not predicated on violence and torture. Using Schreber to approach Ezekiel allows us both to understand the particular agony of male prophetic subjectivity and to imagine the possibility, however slim, of a different organization of bodies and pleasures. We can read prophetic masculinity not simply as critique, but also as potentiality, as destabilizing, pleasurable plentitude and emergent system. Schreber's body destabilizes normative masculinity and the religious relations built upon it—not just for Schreber, but also for Ezekiel. Reading the texts together exposes the fragile, painful male body that lies on the banks of the Chebar. It also forces us to confront prophetic masculinity, in all its messy embodiment. Ezekiel, no less than Schreber, demands it.

5

The Queer Prophetic Body

MARTIN LUTHER FAMOUSLY complained that the Hebrew prophets "have a queer way of talking, like people who, instead of proceeding in an orderly manner, ramble off from one thing to the next, so that you cannot make head or tail of them."[1] For Luther, there is something abnormal and even off-putting in the failure of prophetic speech to conform to order, something about its persistent peculiarity and antilinearity. Prophetic speech is displeasingly strange. This description—originally set forth in a discussion of Habakkuk—resurfaces in Gerhard von Rad's *Old Testament Theology*, as part of a larger argument about prophecy and the communication of meaning. It is also in this latter text—or, more precisely, in its English translation—that Luther's judgment of *strangeness* acquires its association with *queerness*.

Luther's focus is on the difficulties of comprehensibility, not of heterosexuality; von Rad is concerned with prophecy and orality. And yet we have, nevertheless, a "queer way of talking." This phrase is itself a (rather queer) translation of Luther's phrase "eine seltsame Weise zu reden," more typically expressed as an "odd" or "funny" or even "strange" way of talking. There is also a complex chain of transmission that produces this queerness. The quote from Luther appears (in English) in a footnote to the English translation of von Rad's text; von Rad's translator, D. M. G. Stalker, thanks a colleague "for this rendering" of Luther's words.[2] There is thus no single point of origin for the queerness of prophetic speech. Instead, as with Ezekiel swallowing the scroll (Ezek. 3:1–3), queerness emerges in the passage of the word (or text) between men.

The prophets have a queer way of talking—a felicitous phrase, and one that anticipates several of my own arguments about prophetic speech and voice.[3] But it is not only the prophets' "way of talking" that is queer. There is also a queerness that accompanies prophetic bodies. In the Hebrew Bible, prophecy is difficult, destabilizing, and even threatening. Prophecy disrupts the ordinary organizations of gender and embodiment; it renders the body unstable, painful, irregular, and threatening. Masculinity in particular is challenged and subverted by the transformations that prophecy brings to the body. Even more than a queer manner of speaking, *the prophets have a queer way of being embodied.*

In the preceding chapters, I have pursued this argument for the queerness of the prophetic body through multiple biblical texts, beginning with Moses and then shifting to the literary prophets. Certain passages have received particular attention—a scattering of texts describing Moses' body (Exod. 2–4, 12, 34:29–35; Num. 12; Deut. 34), Hosea's marriage (Hos. 1–3), Jeremiah's Confessions (scattered in Jer. 12–20), and Ezekiel's calling and sign acts (Ezek. 1–5). These texts offer excessive, norm-defying models of prophetic embodiment; they also destabilize the ideology of gender and the experience of the sexed body in the biblical text.

In arguing for the instability of masculinity and the male prophetic body, one theme that has surfaced repeatedly is the queerness of prophetic embodiment. The prophetic body's queerness has been evident at many points in the text—in Moses's peculiar body and peculiar intimacies with Yahweh, in Hosea's skittishness around heterosexual marriage; in Jeremiah's voice and Ezekiel's prostrate body. Building on the readings set forth in these earlier chapters, this chapter proposes a unified understanding of the prophetic body as queer. The prophetic body is queer in its forms, its embodiments, its desires. It resists heteronormativity and other norms; at times, this resistance seems forced upon the prophet.

This chapter traces the multiple trajectories of queerness that arise from, or are attracted to, the prophetic body. Many, but not all, of these trajectories draw together multiple prophetic bodies, though there is no single ideal type—instead, we might think, following Wittgenstein, of a family resemblance (or perhaps, with more recent trends in queer theory, of relations of kinship). Thus the work of the term "queer" in relation to the prophetic body is double—it both unites disparate prophetic bodies and provides a way of maintaining these bodies' differences. In identifying the prophetic body as queer, I am intentionally exploiting the openness and multiplicity that inheres in the term. This usage directs attention toward certain affects, tendencies, intensities, and assemblages as they cohere in and around the prophetic body.

I explore the queer prophetic body in two stages. Part I brings together the multiple, sometimes divergent queer trajectories and features of prophetic embodiment from the preceding chapters. These include the disturbance of the body, the use of women to negotiate questions of masculinity and subjectivity, the structures of hysteria and unmanning, and the problematics of fluidity. Some of these elements are immediately obvious as clearly queer; others reveal their queerness only after effort. Taken together, however, they enflesh a queer prophetic body. This body often presents a scene of pain and extremity, often entangled with misogyny as well. At moments, it seems primarily an assembly of symptoms—frequently but not always psychoanalytic ones; at other times, it seems to gesture toward the possibility of other ways of being, without recourse to pathology.

Part II of the chapter sets these findings against two additional (and previously unconsidered) prophetic bodies: Jonah and Miriam. These two prophets offer a limit case to test the claims about the queerness of the prophetic body. The book of Jonah seems to neglect sex, gender, and even the body; I will suggest, however, that a reading attuned to queer embodiment reveals these themes as a key element of Jonah's prophetic narrative. The case of Miriam, meanwhile, brings unstable masculinity into contact with another sort of prophet: a *woman*. As such, Miriam is at once a limit case for the norms of prophecy and a challenge to them. Taking seriously the example of this female prophet provides insight into the masculine norms of prophecy, as well as the possibility—and hazards— of transgressing them. The concluding analysis employs the disturbances of the body and the added examples of Jonah and Miriam to give full form to the queernesses of the prophetic body. I consider both the pleasures, critical and otherwise, such a body brings, as well as the costs it exacts.

My aim here is twofold: first, to refine some specific paradigms for thinking about prophetic embodiment, and second, to gesture toward the multiplicity of forms of the prophetic body. Rather than foreclosing possible readings and possible prophetic bodies, I encourage them to proliferate. My argument multiplies connections, disruptions, and queer forms of embodiment in the prophetic text. It assembles the prophetic bodies already discussed with new bodies, new theoretical perspectives, and a new forming of the "queer prophetic body." Jeremiah's body may have been known already in the womb to Yahweh (Jer. 1:5); we, however, must work to assemble knowledge of the prophetic bodies. It is a difficult thing to be a prophet; it is a difficult thing to have a body—and it is a difficult, though also deeply rewarding, task to know the prophetic body.

Part I: Some Queer Trajectories of Prophetic Embodiment

Drawing together the threads of previous chapters, it is now simple enough to say: the prophetic body is a queer body. Of course, it is delightfully simple to pronounce things queer, more difficult by far to define what such an identification means. As I have discussed in the Introduction, *queer* has many meanings in queer theory, spanning identity politics, nonheteronormative sexualities, and the troubling of normativities of all kinds (including those beyond the sexual). To call the prophetic body queer is not to slap a label on it or to pin it to an intersectional identity grid.[4] Instead, the work of *queer* with respect to the prophetic is double, offering two trajectories of movement between center and periphery.

The first, unifying movement of naming the prophetic body as queer is to draw together various disparate features of prophetic embodiment to show that they come together in an object we might call the queer prophetic body. This bears some relation to queer projects of identity, although, as I have already suggested, I am not interested in ascribing a particular sexual identity or sexuality to prophetic bodies. This project is not one of finding and recovering lost queer ancestors or textual specters. To borrow from Lee Edelman's reading of Ebenezer Scrooge in *No Future*, "I make no pretense of revealing an 'identity' encoded in the text."[5] Instead, in describing the prophetic body as queer, I wish to direct attention to certain features of this body, as well as their interpretive and political consequences.

The second, opposing movement of naming the prophetic body as queer invokes the disorienting, antifoundational side of queer theory. In calling the prophetic body queer, I wish to push back against the rigid categories and boundaries constructed by biblical text and the practice of interpretation alike. As an alternative, the body as troubled, wounded, transformed, and above all *queer* opens the possibility for embodiment as flux and assemblage. Queer suggests both resistance and refusal; it also hints at a reconfiguration of bodies and pleasures that is not bound to a logic of lack. I will return to this model in the final part of this chapter.

Avoiding strong identity claims has also led me to use the language of "queer trajectories" of the prophetic body. The trajectory splits the difference between identity and intensity; it suggests not a fixed notion of the self but rather a process of movement. Trajectory is also linked to the notion of orientation; while the former concerns movement, the latter emphasizes direction. The two concepts come together as objects are positioned in relation to each other, in space as well as over time. Of orientation, Ahmed writes, "Orientations involve different way of registering the proximity of objects and others."[6] The prophetic body, I have suggested, registers certain objects and others differently. Identifying the prophetic body in this way renders the particularities of its embodiment not secondary quirks, but central. Prophetic bodies offer other ways of being oriented; it is these ways of being oriented that this chapter will explore.

The Necessity of Disturbance

As this book has repeatedly suggested, prophets experience all kinds of difficulties with their bodies. These difficulties may begin at birth and persist until death, as in the case of Moses. Or they may come and go, representing a specific interval of time or signifying the bodily transformations effected by the prophetic call (as in the purified lips of Isaiah in Isa. 6). On a most basic level, these moments show the importance of the body. The trappings of the flesh are not distractions from the "true work" of prophecy, work carried out in words. Similarly, bodily suffering on the part of the prophets is not simply epiphenomenal. Instead, the body is fundamental to the transmission of the prophetic message, and to the very practice of prophecy. And this body must be disturbed—sometimes displaced, sometimes disabled, sometimes transformed—for prophecy to succeed.

It is tempting to push this observation and to conclude that it is in the moments of bodily extremity that prophecy is most fully and successfully enacted. In the case of a prophet like Ezekiel, this certainly seems to be the case. Suffering, tortured, unmanned—these are the moments when Ezekiel seems most fully to inhabit his prophetic self. But while prophecy disturbs the body, the result is not always bodily extremity. Jeremiah's extreme vocalizations are interwoven with other, more typical—or even mundane—uses of voice; his Confessions even seem at times at odds with his prophecy. Other prophetic entanglements with the body remain more ordinary, as in Jeremiah's humble sign acts or dalliances with a loincloth (Jer. 13), or Isaiah's undernarrated three-year foray into nakedness (Isa. 20). At still other points, the disturbance of the prophetic body is figured as akin to disability, pushing the body outside of the normative forms of embodiment into an alternate category. I have developed this argument most fully with respect to Moses in chapter 1; we might consider, as well, the ways in which Ezekiel's dumbness or the suffering of the servant described in Second Isaiah also figure as bodily disabilities, with consequences for gender and masculinity.

The difficulties of the body, in addition to the crucial role they play in the performance of prophecy, are also valuable as alternative points of entry into the text. Taking the body—and particularly, the body in its difficulties, peculiarities, and strangenesses—as a starting point makes possible a new kind of hermeneutic engagement. The prophetic body has its own orientations, orientations often identifiable as queer. It unsettles our familiar reading practices, forcing us (like a prophet, lying bound on his side, gazing up?) to encounter the known in a new way. In this way, the prophetic body does work that parallels the work of queer theory. The unsettling of foundations and foundational claims is a central task of queer theory—one already undertaken by the prophetic body. The "queerness" of the prophetic body thus describes, among other things, the queer work this body does. As Jan Tarlin writes of one of the most queerly embodied prophets, "Ezekiel forces its present-day readers to confront everything that is most difficult and disturbing about how human desire shapes our spiritual and political worlds."[7] The body, disturbed and disturbing, ushers in the possibility of other forms of transformation.

Hysteria

I have argued (in chapter 3) that prophecy is structured as hysteria. This claim, while enacted most fully by Jeremiah's hysterical discourse in the Confessions, resonates across the prophetic books. In fact, hysteria as a structure of prophecy offers a useful perspective for understanding even texts that do not seem, on the surface, hysterical. Hysteria is queer in multiple ways. As I have discussed in detail in chapter 3, hysteria is strongly associated with women. And yet men may also— either strategically or unwillingly—enter into the space of hysterical speech. In the case of Jeremiah's Confessions, the prophet's voice is precariously balanced between lucidity and chaos. At points, meaning is displayed onto the body, a process known as "somatic compliance" to psychoanalysis and as "fire in the bones" to Jeremiah himself. Jeremiah likewise proves a simultaneously repulsive and attractive object to those around him, reflecting the larger dynamics of the scene of treatment. Hysteria queers ordinary vectors of relation, even as it infiltrates and transforms the space of linguistic meaning.

While the specific details above come from Jeremiah, they pertain, as well, to prophecy more generally. Somatic compliance—the bodily symptom that speaks—is a particularly clear formulation of the general blurring of the boundaries of language and body in prophecy, in which the body is overtaken by, and forced to speak, the words of another. There is likewise something queer in the *ambiguity* of the voice at the heart of hysteria and "ordinary" prophecy alike. Indeed, as Michel Poizat notes, the voices that are most erotic, and most compelling, are often those that do not seem to correspond to a particular sex.[8] The voice thus serves as the vanguard of a queer reimagining of the body.

Reading prophecy as hysteria also raises the difficult question of liberation—a question often posed to queer bodies and queer theory. Here, the figure of Dora, the young woman at the heart of "Fragment of an Analysis of a Case of Hysteria," embodies a problem that vexes prophetic texts and their readers as well.[9] Is Dora a hero or a victim? Does she, as Hélène Cixous suggests, interfere with the working of psychoanalysis and patriarchy? Does Dora make the little circus stop working? (And if so, at what cost to herself?) These are questions, of course, not just for Dora, but for Jeremiah and the other prophets, and indeed for any reading practice that promises liberation. Who is empowered by a reading, and at what cost? Does hysteria benefit the prophet in any way? Does the prophet make the little circus stop working? Hysteria may subvert the dominant system, but it also engenders anguish. There is pain in the breaking it entails. This suffering is clear at the moments in *Studies in Hysteria* when Freud and Breuer allow their hysterical patients to speak; it comes through, as well, in the moments when Dora's own voice enters her case study. It is likewise all too easy to trace when reading with Daniel Paul Schreber, whose memoir contains, along with radical bodily transformation, a great deal of bodily pain. And it is clear as well in the prophetic texts, perhaps nowhere more so than in Jeremiah's cries. Moses, too, cries out, even identifying his suffering with that of women (Num. 11).

These vocal disturbances of gender suggest, in turn, a pain slipping through other margins in the text, as in Ezekiel and Hosea's silences. Prophecy is a burden, Cook writes.[10] Even more so, prophecy is a shattering, a suffering that cannot be excised from whatever liberating transformation or redemption the text promises. The queerness of the prophetic body is accompanied by its entry into a world of pain. Thus taking hysteria seriously offers another way of addressing the painful disturbance of the body that prophecy effects.

Thinking with Women

As the issue of hysteria suggests, the negotiation of masculinity and the prophetic body has a complex relationship to women. The texts often make use of women and their bodies. In the case of Moses, the prophet is frequently surrounded by women, especially in the early parts of his narrative. As his story progresses, women are increasingly shoved to the margins, culminating in the punishment of Miriam in Numbers 12. In the prophetic books, meanwhile, real women are few and far between—Hosea has a wife (Hos. 1–3), Isaiah is acquainted with a female prophet who bears him a child (Isa. 8:3), Ezekiel is married during the early portions of his prophecy (Ezek. 24: 15–19). Jeremiah remains unwed. Relations *between* women, meanwhile, are almost wholly absent, unless we count the few reported instances of speech between women (Ezekiel criticizes female prophets [Ezek. 13:17] and Jeremiah decries the women worshipping the Queen of Heaven [Jer. 7:18]), which come under censure in the text. Metaphorical women and their bodies, however, loom large. The spectacle of violence against the unfaithful wife is a crucial feature of the religious economy of the text. The maternal passages in Second Isaiah and elsewhere, meanwhile, are central to the construction of a certain identity for the deity. These moments, and many others, are all a part of a larger textual economy of "thinking with women."[11]

The figure of the female body proves tremendously useful for the prophets in negotiating the difficulties of male embodiment. Even as women are abandoned, tortured, opened, silenced, and occasionally killed, they remain an object of interest for the prophetic texts. Nowhere is this more evident than in Hosea, where the bodies of Gomer and of the gynomorphized Israel are essential to the question of male prophetic embodiment. Hosea's anxieties of masculinity are at once displaced onto, and negotiated through, the tortured and spectacularly opened female bodies. The fear of masculine openness—a fear that is at once somatic, symbolic, and social—is worked through by the opening of the feminine. The female body does similar, if not identical, work in the narratives of Moses. For Moses, even brief verbal flirtation with the feminine (Num. 11) offers a movement beyond the norms of ordinary embodied masculinity.

This practice of "thinking with women," while perhaps endlessly productive, also brings with it a cost. It is notable that when Jeremiah speaks like a woman, he screams and cries in pain; like the female hysterics that Freud treats, his pain cannot be understood within the masculine economy of discourse. "Thinking with women" is excellent work for masculinity; less so for women themselves. Consider another example from the biblical text, where Yahweh himself models the practice of "thinking with women":

> The word of Yahweh came to me: "Mortal, behold, I am taking from you the delight of your eyes with one blow, but you shall not lament or weep, nor shall your tears come. Groan, but not aloud; do not make any mourning for the dead. Put on your headdress, put your shoes on your feet, do not cover your face, do not eat the food of mourning." I spoke to the people in the morning, and my wife died in the evening. In the morning I did as I was commanded. The people said to me, "Won't you tell us what these things mean for us? Why are you acting like this?" (Ezek. 24:15–19)

The death of Ezekiel's wife may be a highly effective object lesson—except for the wife herself. She, unfortunately, must die for the lesson to succeed; as such, she does not really stand to benefit from it.

This use of women leads to an additional and important issue in considering the queer trajectory: the potential for queer analysis to become or remain complicit in misogyny. To name the prophetic body as queer does not absolve the prophets of all crimes against women. Queer bodies can participate in misogyny as much as straight bodies can. Indeed, the hypermasculinized space of male deity and male prophet can engender its own particular forms of misogyny. With the feminine absented, what is to stop the text from becoming, in Roland Boer's memorable phrase, "a prophetic sausage-fest"?[12] (Indeed, it seems that some prophets, and perhaps some interpreters, would prefer this to be the case.[13]) The space of queer masculinity may coexist with misogyny, in text and reading alike. Prophetic embodiment, even queer prophetic embodiment, demands feminist vigilance, so that naming the prophetic bodies as queer does not mean, in effect, erasing the often violent exploitation of women and female bodies that sustains the prophetic body.

Unmanning

It is not only the female body that is used and transformed in the text. The narratives of the prophets also destabilize the norms of the male prophetic body, challenging gender and embodiment alike. Drawing on the memoir of Daniel Paul Schreber (itself a quite queer text), I have described this process as the "unmanning" of the prophetic body (chapter 4). In his memoir, Schreber describes his body as penetrated and ultimately transformed by the electrosexual rays of a modern, sometimes malevolent deity. It is only through the transformation of Schreber's body into the body of a woman that the world can be delivered. Unmanning has consequences far beyond the body.

Though the particulars of Schreber's description are bound up in his specific experience of modernity, the notion of unmanning speaks to the prophetic body in the Hebrew Bible as well. Nowhere is this more obvious than in the book of Ezekiel, where the abjection and extreme suffering of the sign acts are also part of a radical transformation of the very category of the masculine. Indeed, Ezekiel's transgressions of the norms of the masculine body cannot be sustained, and eventually are displaced in favor of the reimagined space of the Temple. Place effaces and replaces body. This suggests the power the body asserts over the text, as well as the danger it poses. In the case of Hosea and Gomer, the displacement of the anxieties of masculinity onto the female body is an intentional strategy, aimed at managing masculine anxiety. In the case of Ezekiel and the Temple, things are a bit different. Here, the displacement is done *to* the masculine body, not so much to control its anxiety but to curtail its destructive power. The model of unmanning is also useful for understanding the various forms of disturbances across the prophetic bodies of the text. In Jeremiah, for example, unmanning occurs primarily through voice.

The "unmanned" body that Schreber describes is a dynamic, emergent assemblage. In the context of Schreber's memoir, unmanning does not simply mean the shattering of normative masculine subjectivity (though it encompasses that as well). Instead, it also describes the entry of the body into an autoerotic economy of pleasure and plenitude. This body is not best understood through the static categories of identity. Instead, its transformations and emergent potentials are most significant. Just as the process of unmanning suggests a movement from a fixed state to something new (and at once frightening and attractive), so too does unmanning direct attention to the transformative possibilities that inhere in the prophetic body. In this way, the concept of unmanning does similar work to that of hysteria. To say *prophecy is structured as hysteria* is to describe certain relations of gender, power, and voice; similarly, to say *prophecy is structured as unmanning* is to highlight shifting constellations of gender, body, pleasure, and suffering. This is another queer trajectory of prophetic embodiment: the (queer) prophetic body as hysterical and unmanned.

Fluidity and Openness

Are We Not Men? has also directed attention to the fluidities found in and around the bodies of prophets and the potential for a theory of fluids to upset the norms of embodied masculinity. In reading the "bridegroom of blood" narrative (Exod. 4:24–26), I have argued that fluidity offers a means of moving past the sealed-off, violent, and oppressive norms of masculinity by presenting the possibility of an open and in flux male body. "Fluidity" has at least two meanings in this analysis— first, literal (water, blood, and so on fill the text) and second, strategic and symbolic (fluidity provides a useful figure for describing bodily flux and openness). On this latter point, it may be helpful to recall that "fluidity" is not limited to liquids but can also describe, for example, air.[14] In this way, "fluidity" is another way of naming the openness that Hosea displaces onto the female body and that Schreber and Ezekiel experience as "unmanning."

There is significant fluidity to be found elsewhere among the Hebrew prophets. Jeremiah is afflicted with incurable wounds (Jer. 30:12). Hosea's body is "opened" through his marriage to, and sexual relations with, an "open" woman, Gomer. Ezekiel performs his actions on the banks of the Chebar. And Moses' body is repeatedly brought in contact with fluids: in birth and watery deliverance (Exod. 2:3–6), in meeting Zipporah at the well (2:15–18); in turning the Nile to blood (7:19–20); in crossing the Sea of Reeds (14:21–27); in twice striking the rock to release water (Num. 20:11). Emphasizing these moments as moments of fluidity makes it possible to perceive the connection between seemingly disparate incidents. Fluidity is not incidental, but rather a recurrent feature in the prophetic texts' project of gender and embodiment. Moreover, fluidity has the potential to destabilize the established order and to queer the ordinary configurations of masculinity and embodiment.

Fluid trajectories produce novel understandings of prophetic masculinity and the prophetic body. Organizing masculinity around openness in place of phallicism and closed-off borders offers a new way to imagine the male body, and with it, embodied prophecy.[15] If masculinity is destabilized or subverted in the prophetic texts, it is not through the willful action of the feminine. This is because the feminine features of these texts are wholly constituted by and for the masculine. Even a male deity with a womb and a maternal instinct is, fundamentally, a masculine fantasy of an appropriated female body. And because the female body is not sufficient to critique this masculine economy, something else is required. Fluidity fills this gap by offering a helpful way of thinking through both the disturbance and the transformative potential of the masculine prophetic body. The male prophetic body as *fluid* opposes the normative ideal of the male body as self-contained, closed off, and without defect. Instead, it suggests a body in flux, a body whose boundaries are not fully set. A body that presents a queer potentiality, open to queer trajectories. An alternate masculinity may be possible.

The Queerness of the Prophetic Body

Pace Moses and Deuteronomy 34, there is no single prophetic body that sums up all others. Instead, the bodies of the prophets manifest certain stylizations of embodiment, certain affects, and certain tendencies. There are, however, significant parallels among prophets and bodies. Prophecy destabilizes masculinity; prophecy queers the body. Importantly, the queerness of this prophetic body is not a rigid identity, but rather a trajectory or orientation. The disturbance of the body, hysteria, thinking with women, unmanning, fluidity, and fluid bodies—none of these occurs to the same degree in every text; there are important differences between bodies and prophets. Still, taken together they suggest a queer prophetic body. The body is reconfigured and realigned—re*oriented*, to use Ahmed's term. Whether willingly (Isaiah, Ezekiel, Hosea) or under duress (Jeremiah and, as we will soon see, Jonah), the prophetic body is given a queer orientation in the world.

I have also introduced several figures of queer possibility and transformation. The displacement of masculine anxiety onto the female body—thinking with women—is violent; it also suggests a curious extending of the body beyond the boundaries of a single individual. In the Confessions of Jeremiah, the body of the prophet is a body in pain, but also in defiance. I have proposed that this body and voice resemble the body and voice of the hysteric, displaying a curious crossing over of sound, flesh, and meaning. The unmanned body of Daniel Paul Schreber, meanwhile, offers an analog to the body of Ezekiel in the opening chapters of his book. This body offers a radical reconfiguration of pleasure and pain, presenting an autoerotic economy of what Schreber terms "soul voluptuousness." In the case of Ezekiel, such voluptuousness is ultimately impossible, and the prophetic body is replaced with the architectural body of the Temple.

In offering these readings, my aim has been to give some sense of the sheer breadth of the term "queer," and to show how these multiple meanings figure across the prophetic bodies and prophetic texts. The queer prophetic body is not one body—it is multiple, in bodies, meanings, and significations. If we are to think of the "prophetic body" as a unified concept, then it is essential to remember that this unity is one of assemblage and affinity, not of a single ideal type. The prophetic body is produced and repeatedly reimagined.

Part II: Multiplicities: Bodies, Prophets, Queernesses

The bodies of prophets are not like other bodies; they are also not always like *each other*. It is contrary to the spirit of queer theory, and of queer bodies, to insist too vigorously on a single model of prophetic embodiment. And it is true that not all of the prophets' bodies in the Hebrew Bible behave in the same way. Nevertheless, I have proposed that framing the prophetic body as a queer body offers meaningful insight into the intertwining of masculinity, embodiment, and prophecy across the biblical text. I want now to consider the potentially queer trajectories of two additional prophets, Jonah and Miriam. Both Jonah and Miriam are marginal figures, though in different ways. While Jonah is in many ways a typical prophet, the book of Jonah is often taken to offer a satirical, parodic, or subversive reworking of the conventions of the prophetic narrative. Where Hosea has marital difficulties, Jonah has fish problems. What can we say of the masculinity of a man who spends a quarter of his time sequestered in a fish?

Miriam is marginal in another way: her gender. She is not simply a prophet but also a woman. Her example forces us to reconsider the entanglements of gender and prophecy. Jonah and Miriam alike assert pressure on the category of the prophetic body. Their difficulties with embodiment, as well as difficult transformations, point to the challenges of prophetic embodiment, as well as such questions as fluidity, unmanning, and transformation.

Jonah

Jonah is a prophet of refusal. Commanded by Yahweh to prophesy against Nineveh, he heads in the opposite direction toward Tarshish (Jon. 1:1–3). Yahweh raises a massive storm, which abates only when the sailors cast Jonah overboard, and he passes three days inside a fish (1:11–2:1 [1:17 Engl.]). After this interlude, he fulfills his duty and heads to Nineveh, but is outraged when the people repent and are spared by Yahweh (3–4). The final chapter involves Jonah's unsuccessful attempt to witness Nineveh's destruction—instead, it is only the plant that shades Jonah that is destroyed (4).

Neither gender nor embodiment is explicitly addressed or thematized in the Jonah narrative. Still, these four chapters present a highly masculinized space. When not fish-bound, Jonah passes his time exclusively in the company of men. The story is almost entirely without women (though they are implicitly included among the residents of Nineveh). The most obvious gender issue of note, at least for the Hebrew reader, concerns the fish, which fluctuates grammatically between the masculine *dāg* and the feminine *dāgāh* (both mean "fish"). Similarly, perhaps the most feminine space in the text is the belly of the fish, which, in a reading that goes back at least to Pseudo-Chrysostom, can be taken to suggest a uterine space.[16] Supporting this reading, Jonah himself refers to the *beṭen* ("belly," "womb") from which he has been delivered (Jon. 2:3 [2:2 Eng.]), a word also used for the place occupied by the fetus in Isaiah 44:2 and 24.[17] Thus in this scene of confinement, we might perceive a novel way of thinking with (and in) the female body. The structures of displacement I have traced in Hosea reach a new intensity here, with the female human body replaced by the piscine.

Jonah's body also plays a notable role in the text. Unlike Moses or Ezekiel, his physical form is not marked with the signs of prophecy. Instead, the body itself becomes a sign. In Jonah 1, this is effected when the sailors cast Jonah overboard. It is only through this act—enacted using Jonah's body—that the sailors come to recognize the true power of Yahweh. The body must be subjected to violence for this realization to occur. This suggests, in turn, that Jonah is perhaps not so different from Ezekiel and the other queer prophets after all. Not shattered but submerged, the body becomes the sign of the prophetic word. Jonah's body is also at issue in the final incident in his brief book, the showdown over the plant (*qîqāyôn*). Jonah sits on a hill to watch the destruction of Nineveh; Yahweh causes a plant to grow over him, providing shade, but then withers it (Jon. 4:6–7). This, in turn, angers Jonah, as the destruction of the plant leaves his body without shelter. Just as the plants in Genesis 3 provide a primitive sort of garment, so does the stripping away of the plant in Jonah 4 leave the body naked. Jonah is exposed to the elements; he is likewise exposed to Yahweh, whose gaze is perhaps figured in the scorching heat of the sun that so distresses Jonah. This scene—which, like the events in Jonah 1, hinges upon the prophet's body—activates the larger problematics of bodily exposure across the biblical text. Jeremiah complains that his body is exposed to Yahweh, rendered vulnerable by the word. And, of course, gazing upon the body is an act of power, as Howard Eilberg-Schwartz has shown.[18] Read in this context, the destruction of the plant is not simply the destruction of a plant, or even an assertion of divine power over and against Jonah's ineffectiveness, but also an act of exposure that is deeply implicated in the textual politics of the male body.[19]

There is also a concern with fluidity in the book of Jonah. Chapter 1 ends with the prophet in the sea, where he is swallowed by a large fish. Above, I have suggested that fluidity offers one an alternative metaphorics of masculinity and the male body as unbounded, labile, and open to the other. This adds a certain significance to the fact that Jonah ends up not simply *in the sea* but rather *inside a fish*. From this perspective, the fish is not simply a resident of the deep (and thus a convenient place to stash a prophet) but a boundary, separating the body of the prophet from the waters and from fluidity more generally. The body of the fish is centrally *that which keeps Jonah separate from fluidity*. It is notable that after his time in the fish, Jonah no longer objects to prophesying. While this may be the simple effect of coercion (fishy internment is hardly pleasant), it also suggests an association between fluidity and openness to new forms of being. This may reflect the association of water with rebirth; it likewise opens a channel for thinking a fluid prophetic masculinity. It is the time in the watery deep (Jonah uses the word *tehôm*) that opens Jonah to prophecy.

Finally, with Jonah, I want to consider the issue of refusal. Jonah refuses to do what God commands; when he at last accepts his prophetic mission, he does so reluctantly and not fully properly (Yahweh must instruct him on what to say; Jonah breaks with his instructions and begins to prophesy against Nineveh after only a single day's walk into the city, and so on).[20] Even when he succeeds in persuading Nineveh to repent, Jonah refuses to accept this success. Instead, he remains filled with angry refusal. Jonah, it seems, is a rather bad prophet— or perhaps, a rather queer one. Refusal, after all, has a lengthy queer history.[21] In *The Promise of Happiness*, Ahmed describes how the refusal of certain orien- tations and trajectories, including the refusal of happiness, can become a queer act. Because "happiness *participates* in making things good," to refuse to be happy is to refuse to participate in much more than a feeling.[22] Certain bodies and subject positions, the queer among them, struggle with what Ahmed terms the "happiness duty."[23] Like the subjects Ahmed discusses—"feminist killjoys," "melancholic migrants," "unhappy queers"—Jonah *refuses to be happy*. Even when he succeeds, he interprets his success as a failure—the people of Nineveh succeed at repentance, Nineveh fails at being destroyed.

Indeed, perhaps Jonah's queer art of prophetic failure is telling about prophecy more broadly. Ahmed writes, "If certain people come first—we might say those who are already in place (such as parents, hosts, or citizens)—then their happiness comes first. For those who are positioned as coming after, *happiness means follow- ing somebody else's goods*."[24] The people of Nineveh are willing to follow Yahweh's goods; Jonah, however, is not. He chooses, instead, queer refusal. To be a prophet is to fail at the happiness duty. This failure—which is also resistance—is itself a queer action. To succeed as a prophet is to fail at the norms of embodiment; to achieve a prophetic body is to be acted upon, opened, unmanned. The demands of prophecy place the prophet in an impossible situation; what is left is only refusal.

Miriam and the Problem of a Woman Prophet

The other prophet to consider as a limit case is Miriam, perhaps the best-known female prophet in the Hebrew Bible. Moses' sister saves Moses' life as a baby (Exod. 2; this sister is generally taken as Miriam, though she is unnamed in the text). Miriam leads the women in song and dance after the crossing of the Sea of Reeds and the destruction of Pharaoh and his army (Exod. 15). She is equally famous, however, for her jealousy of her brother Moses, for which she is punished with scale disease and temporarily exiled from the Israelite camp in the wilderness. Given this study's focus on the unstable masculinity of the prophetic body, what can we say of the body of Miriam? How do the findings about gender, sexuality, and embodiment relate to *her* body?

Miriam is both a prophet and a woman; her gender is often problematic. The paradigmatic acts that constitute a woman in the text—motherhood, as well as sexual relations with men—are missing in Miriam's story. Her gender is therefore a subject of some unease. The only real place where her body comes to the fore is Numbers 12, where she is afflicted with scale disease. This scene is hardly subtle. Instead, it offers an aggressive lesson (with a side of misogyny, as Aaron escapes unpunished) on the consequences of speaking against Moses. Just as the bodies of Israel and Gomer express Hosea's masculine anxiety over prophecy, the affliction of Miriam's body tells of the power of *Moses* as prophet.[25]

While pleading for Miriam to be spared, Aaron compares her to a stillborn, "whose flesh is half consumed as it comes out of its mother's womb" (Num. 12:12). His words bring together a number of themes that circle around the female body in the biblical text. Maternity is linked to death; what should not be said (at least by women) corresponds to what should not be born. The female body is represented as multiply polluted, simultaneously associated with disease, birth, and (fetal) death.[26] Claudia Camp reads this narrative as activating gender difference to reconstitute a number of binaries in the text, as well as to validate the intimate relations between men, here Moses and Aaron.[27] This masculine intimacy is both close and erotic; it is also threatening. Miriam must be afflicted—"*made* strange," to use Camp's phrase—in order to repair relations between men while also offering an "ideological cover-up" for male intimacy.[28] This incident with the female prophetic body at once parallels and diverges from the norms of the male body. The transformation and the suffering of her body make a new sort of *masculinity* possible—but with limited benefit for the *female* prophet. Though Miriam is a prophet, her suffering body resembles the women that prophecy uses to "think with," from Israel and Gomer in Hosea to the late wife of Ezekiel. Here again, the female body provides ground to negotiate masculine crises. Miriam is made to suffer for a masculine transformation to occur. This is the same old problem of thinking with women, at their expense.

There is also the question of Miriam's voice. Miriam's punishment in Numbers 12 underscores the problematic dimension of female vocality (cf. above, chapter 3), even for as unsettled and unsettling a medium as prophetic speech. Beyond this scene, Miriam does not leave behind many words. She sings a song at the crossing of the sea, but its contents are lost. Instead, it is Moses' song (really, the "Song of the Sea," a much older text) that is preserved.[29] And yet in this way, is Miriam's experience so different from Dora's? Dora's words, after all, are lost, except for a few stray remarks preserved in Freud's case study. The example of Miriam tells us something about which voices texts choose to censor, about who is authorized to speak, to sing, even—in the case of Jeremiah, for example—simply to scream. Here, it is appropriate to recall Carson on the gender of sound: "Female sound is bad to hear both because the quality of a woman's voice is objectionable and because women say what should not be said."[30] Bringing together the vocalizations of the male prophets with the silencing of Miriam, it becomes clear that a man crying like a woman is still less threatening than a woman herself.

The song that Miriam sings, and that the text silences, is sung at edge of the sea. Miriam saves Moses by means of water, watching the basket that carries him down the Nile and into the hands of Pharaoh's daughter. And, as Camp notes, Miriam dies in a place *without* water, causing an impurity that cannot be cleansed; her death scene is likewise followed by a controversy over water.[31] In Camp's reading, water, boundaries, and women are all linked together as markers of otherness. And fluidity, I have suggested, offers one possibility for reconfiguring and reimagining the prophetic body. Yet Miriam's body does not seem to be a fluid body. Instead, she is associated with fluidity in other ways, through relations of location and contiguity. (This is true as well of Zipporah, who meets Moses at a well and subsequently saves his life by drawing blood.) Fluidity presents a realm of possibility that simultaneously excludes the feminine, even as it draws on a textual imaginary of the female body.

Male prophets use femininity to think through prophecy and masculinity; the female prophet is accorded no such opportunity, with either male or female bodies to "think with." Instead, Miriam's role is to watch—to watch Moses in the waters of the Nile, to watch Moses lead the congregation in song, to watch the camp of the Israelites from without, while exiled from its borders. Miriam shares in the experience of bodily suffering, via her scale disease, but her true suffering is the suffering of displacement. The same prophecy that transforms and unmans masculine bodies leaves no space for feminine ones. Thus Miriam as limit case shows us that prophecy, in all its radical and transformative flux, is still bound up in the male body. Its questions of embodiment, as well as its promises of subversion and transformation, remain masculine ones.

From Queer Refusal to Queer Pain

The figures of Jonah and Miriam each contribute to, and complicate, the queer prophetic body. The disturbance of the body is observable in both narratives, though it plays out in somewhat different ways. Prophetic speech is difficult for both—Jonah must be strictly instructed on what to say (he does, however, complain freely), while Miriam's speech leads her to exclusion and bodily suffering (Jon. 4; Num. 12). Jonah is made into a sign for the sailors, and later exposed before Yahweh by the destruction of his shelter. He is not, however, unambiguously unmanned. While I have suggested that other prophetic texts express, if only temporarily, an openness to transformation or reconfiguration of the male body, in Jonah the primary stance is one of refusal. Jonah resists being a prophet; even as he reconfigures his physical trajectory (first to Tarshish, then to Nineveh), he refuses to reorient his desires. Instead of the open or transformed body, he offers a body of refusal—and yet this, too, may be a queer body, as I have shown. The refusal, including the refusal of happiness, is a key prophetic stance.

In the case of Miriam, the reconfiguration of masculinity is an already impossible task; Miriam is a prophet, but not a man. As *nêbî'â*, or "female prophet," she stands at the collision point of irreconcilable norms of gender and prophecy. Indeed, if Jonah introduces refusal as a new form of queer orientation toward transformation—one that we might consider, for example, with respect to Jeremiah's complaints in the Confessions—Miriam's narrative is one that forces us to return to the problem of pain. There is the pain of women, forced to suffer so that their bodies may speak the prophetic truth. There is also the pain that the prophet complains of in his own body (as in Jeremiah), or that goes unspoken (Ezekiel, lying on his side). To this we may add the pain and tribulation of Jonah: thrown overboard, interned in a fish, burned by the sun. That Jonah's great indignation is reserved for the final, seemingly minor, suffering caused by the destruction of the plant points to the comic economy of the text, as well as, perhaps, to the accumulation of pains that constitute a prophetic life. In Miriam's case, meanwhile, there is the pain of disease, and even more so, of exclusion and marginalization. There is even greater suffering here.

The case of Miriam raises another issue related to pain, and queer pain in particular—the question of legibility. As a "female prophet," Miriam is largely *illegible*. The *nêbî'â*, the female prophet, is difficult to think under competing norms of prophecy and gender. Her body and her experiences are unreadable under the norms that the biblical text constructs for bodies. Miriam's exclusion from the community in Numbers 12 is only the culmination of a series of markings of her female prophetic body as illegible and her life as unlivable. This issue of illegible bodies and unlivable lives is one that has been taken up by queer theory. In *Undoing Gender*, Judith Butler discusses the way certain forms of queer life are marked as unlivable. This is the result of a crisis of recognition, an inability or refusal to grant recognition—to render legible—bodies and lives. Butler writes,

> There is a certain departure from the human that takes place in order to start the process of remaking the human. I may feel that without some recognizability I cannot live. But I may also feel that the terms by which I am recognized make life unlivable.[32]

Though she is not writing of Miriam, Butler's words describe her; they seem to offer another version of Miriam's own complaint in Numbers 12. The difficulty, even unlivability, of Miriam's life is given bodily form in her scale disease, just as it assumes social form in her exclusion. Ilana Pardes has described Miriam as a figure akin to Virginia Woolf's "Shakespeare's sister" in *A Room of One's Own*.[33] Adding to this description, I would suggest that even an emphasis on the queerness of the prophetic body is not sufficient to redeem Miriam from this position. Shakespeare's sister, after all, ends up dead at a crossroads.[34] Miriam dies in the wilderness without descendants; her death is an occasion of contamination for the people. The queer potentiality of the prophetic body is not enough, at least in the case of a female prophet.

Nor are the questions of illegibility and unlivability questions only for Miriam. More broadly, prophecy offers a process of remaking the body that relies on distancing from the (normative) categories of the human. Miriam, the female prophet of greatest significance in the biblical text, is here both extraordinary—there is no other prophet like Miriam, there are hardly any other female prophets—and exemplary. Repeatedly, the prophet "becomes, to a certain extent, unknowable" and "there is a certain departure from the human that takes place." For Moses, this is the literal transformation of his face; for Jonah, it is the assumption of his body into the larger form of the animal. "I may also feel that the terms by which I am recognized make life unlivable"—where is this truer than in Jeremiah's Confessions? Does not Jonah say the same to Yahweh? And this experience of the unlivability of prophecy, meanwhile, drives Hosea to the torture of the feminine and Ezekiel to mute immobility. Miriam exemplifies all this.

The prophetic body is a body undone, and gender in particular bears the weight of this undoing. For the male prophets, this opens a possibility for the transformation—perhaps even a radical transformation—of the male body. For Miriam, it is prophecy and its legacy that are undone. The female body is returned to the service of the masculine economy of prophecy. In addition to its consequences for gender, undoing suggests that pain is not secondary to the prophetic body, or to its transformation. Neither is it instrumental. Instead, the pain of the prophetic body is linked to larger questions of the legibility of the subject and the livability of life. Prophecy pushes the prophet to the very edges of the livable, and sometimes beyond. Miriam is left without descendants, either literal or symbolic. This is no accident. It is left to us to read from this loss.

Unstable Masculinity and Prophecy beyond Pain and Loss

As I have discussed with reference to Jonah, happiness is not a neutral good. In *The Promise of Happiness*, Ahmed has traced the ways in which discourses of happiness can become coercive.[35] Pushing back against the easy, if pervasive, assumption of happiness as an unquestionable good, she considers the ways in which certain subjects are commanded to be happy, and the costs of such demands. She notes that the demand to be happy can be especially brutal when levied against queer or other subjects outside the male white straight Enlightenment subject. As Ahmed argues, leaving a space for queer unhappiness, and for unhappy queers, is essential. In reading the queerness of the prophetic body, it is essential to remember the pain of prophecy, the ways in which it pushes life to the very boundaries of the livable. And yet I do not want to end with pain. It has been a repeated argument of this book that documenting pain and suffering is a necessary but not sufficient response to prophetic texts and prophetic bodies. This is perhaps clearest in the case of Hosea, where the violence against female bodies is both appalling and amply documented. Instead, I have sought to read beyond witnessing, to draw out other possibilities that inhere in the text.

Are We Not Men? has set forth a number of ways of understanding the prophetic body as open to transformation. In the case of Moses, I have suggested that the body of the prophet is at once deficient and glorious, refusing phallic masculinity and reconfiguring the very idea of a prophetic bodily norm. Moses' body functions as an assemblage. With respect to Hosea, I have traced the displacements of masculine anxiety onto the female body. This displacement, in addition to the pain it afflicts on the feminine, also suggests a curious extending of the body beyond the boundaries of a single individual. The body spreads, almost as a rhizome. In the Confessions of Jeremiah, I have proposed that this body and voice resemble the body and voice of the hysteric, displaying a curious crossing over of sound, flesh, and meaning. The unmanned body of Daniel Paul Schreber, meanwhile, offers an analog to the body of Ezekiel in the opening chapters of his book. This body offers a radical reconfiguration of pleasure and pain, presenting an autoerotic economy of what Schreber terms "soul-voluptuousness." In the case of Ezekiel, such voluptuousness is ultimately impossible, and the prophetic body is replaced with the architectural body of the Temple.

The body deployed against the normative. The body as force of desire. The body as hysteric. The body as autoerotic unmanning. The body as assemblage. The body as fluidity. Brought together, these various figurations of the prophetic body suggest a certain Deleuzian thread running through my descriptions of queer prophetic bodies. At this point, I am not interested in committing to arguing for the prophetic body as Deleuzian assemblage or desiring machine. Instead, I want simply to direct attention to the confluence of possibility, assemblage, and openness. Approaching the prophetic body from this perspective offers a new way to bring together—*to assemble*—its variant features. At the very least, thinking the prophetic body with Deleuze and Guattari offers a way of conceiving of the body that breaks with normative categories while also suggesting an alternative to hermeneutics of pain and suffering. Here, the body becomes a dynamic emergence, an assemblage and becoming. I have dwelt at length on the pain of the prophetic body, from Ezekiel's sign acts to Jeremiah's complaints to Moses' many bodily anguishes. But it is also possible to read these moments primarily as signs of *intensity*. Certain strands of affect theory suggest that the affect precedes the assignation of meaning.[36] Taking this seriously with respect to the prophets is one way to move beyond a practice of documenting pain, toward a more complex understanding of the body and its functioning. Tarlin begins to offer such a reading in his description of Ezekiel as caught in masochistic ecstasy. I have called for readers to attend to prophetic pain; I wish now to suggest, as well, that we look prior to pain for traces of intensity. Does Moses' face cause him suffering before the people are frightened of it? What might Isaiah's naked body experience?

Attending to intensity and affect suggests the possibility of a Deluezian prophetic body. This reading of the prophetic body coexists uneasily with Butler's reading of unintelligibility and grief (as, indeed, Butler's work coexists uneasily with forms of queer theory informed by Deleuze and Guattari).[37] There is no singular narrative here. Instead, there are multiple orientations, multiple queernesses, multiple trajectories.

The prophetic body is at once disabled and powerful, vulnerable and restorative, its power extending beyond the boundaries of life itself (which does not mean that this life should not be grievable, or be grieved). Moses' many parts fit together not as a narrative, but as an assemblage. The prophetic body as "undone" opens a space to think through prophecy as mutually implicated, frequently illegible, and often worthy of grief; the prophetic body as Deleuzian assemblage and becoming opens alternative possibilities. Nor are these the only forms of understanding that are possible. Instead, this chapter has brought together a number of trajectories and tendencies that crisscross and connect the bodies of the prophets. I have chosen in this chapter to name the prophetic body as queer in order to draw together the multiple bodies in this text while also leaving space for thinking critically about the differences that sexuality, embodiment, and desire all bring.

The queer body of the prophet is a body frequently positioned in pain; it may also possess, or create, its own economy of pleasure. Like the prophetic word that animates it, this body is frequently unpredictable, pursuing new trajectories or destabilizing old ones. It is excessive, hysterical, unmanned, opened. It instrumentalizes women and is frequently implicated in violence, as its object or perhaps its agent. The fate of each prophetic body is different, reflecting the multiple trajectories of the prophetic body. What they share, instead, is a queerness. Prophecy destabilizes masculinity, prophecy undoes the body, and this undoing opens new possibilities of being and becoming.

6

Final Reflections

IT IS A difficult thing to be a prophet; it is a difficult thing to have a body. And to be a prophet while inhabiting a body is an especially difficult, even terrible, thing. Prophecy places outrageous demands upon the prophet. While the initial entry of Yahweh's word may be sweet, its tenure in the prophetic body is filled with bitterness and suffering. Sometimes this suffering is visibly inscribed or transfigured on the prophet (as with Moses' glowing face). At other points it is only made known by the prophet's cries of pain, or hinted at through silence. In each case, prophecy violates the prophet's body; consent is not a category to which prophets are entitled. There is simply Yahweh's desire, Yahweh's word, and the necessary entry of the prophet's body into prophecy, willing or otherwise. Little wonder that Samuel, once dead, does not wish to be disturbed to be returned to the struggles of prophecy (1 Sam. 28:15). Little wonder that Jonah flees from the prophetic word (Jon. 1).

The bodily experiences of the prophet can be almost unspeakable—and yet they demand to be spoken. What sort of prophetic corporeality do we find in the biblical text, and how do we understand it? In seeking answers to these questions, this book has surveyed a wide range of prophetic bodies. I have argued that the body is essential to prophecy, which at once depends upon and transforms the prophet's corporeality. This transformation is alternately ontological, phenomenological, and material. In some cases, the entire body is transformed. At other moments, a specific body part is the object of attention and transformation. As we survey the texts, it becomes apparent that the bodies of the prophets are not identical or interchangeable; each experiences prophecy in its own way. Still, examining the bodies together can prove useful both to illuminate individual quirks of embodiment and to bring together a more comprehensive picture of the prophetic body.

I have also argued throughout this volume that the prophetic body is a queer body, though without insisting too adamantly on a particular meaning of this term. To the contrary, I have made use of multiple meanings, sometimes even activating contradictory definitions in reference to a single prophetic body or biblical text. This choice is intentional. My aim has been to give some sense of the sheer breadth of the term "queer," and to show how these multiple meanings figure across the prophetic bodies and prophetic texts. The queer prophetic body is not one body—it is multiple, in bodies, meanings, and significations. At moments, it seems to herald new configurations of gender and sexuality. At others, it is queer only insofar as it is unsettling and strange. If we are to think of the "prophetic body" as a unified concept, then it is essential to remember that this unity is one of assemblage and affinity, not of a single ideal type. The prophetic body is assembled, produced, and repeatedly reimagined. To return for one last time to Deleuze and Guattari, the question is not *Is it true?* but rather *Does it work?*[1]

The chapters assembled here have revealed different forms of the prophetic body, and different ways of negotiating masculinity, embodiment, and prophecy. Chapter 1 considered Moses and the body of the prophet who serves as a model for all others. Moses' body, despite its exemplarity, is also filled with difficulty. Frequently, bodily weakness threatens to subvert or contravene the prophet's actions; he is likewise often terrifying to those he is supposed to serve. It is only in death that the prophet's body is restored—or perhaps, rendered more perfect than it ever was. Taken together, these features point to Moses' body as at once troubled and essential, disturbed and disturbing, a queer potentiality that threatens the norms of embodiment.

The body of Hosea does not figure as directly as Moses' body in the biblical text, even in the famous passages involving his marriage. Instead, as chapter 2 has demonstrated, Hosea 1–3 is organized around structures of displacement. Prophecy makes demands upon the body, including the demand that it be opened by the divine word. This opening has implications both sexual and painful, which figure in the text in multiple ways. In the opening chapters of Hosea, this image of opening is displaced onto the female body. In this way, Hosea 1–3 resembles a possession film: its internal logic is that of *The Exorcist* or *Witchboard*, with Hosea's wife Gomer and the feminized Israel in the role of the acted-upon female body. To turn again to Carol Clover, "For a space to be created in which men can weep without being labeled feminine, women must be relocated to a space where they will be made to wail uncontrollably; for men to be able to relinquish emotional rigidity, control, women must be relocated to a space in which they will undergo a flamboyant psychotic break."[2] Israel and Gomer suffer in many ways, even as the anxieties of male embodiment remain unsatisfied.

Neither Jeremiah nor Ezekiel enacts the same structure of displacement onto the female body as do the marriage texts in Hosea. Instead, these two prophets engage the difficulties of prophetic embodiment in different ways. In the case of Jeremiah—and in particular, Jeremiah's Confessions, the focus of chapter 3—the displacement is internal to the prophet's own body. The problematics of masculinity and embodiment become, for Jeremiah, problems of the voice. Jeremiah uses sound in ways that structurally resemble hysteria. Though hysteria is typically associated with feminine sound, Jeremiah's hysterical vocalizations challenge the category of the masculine. His voice is thus also a queer voice. This suggests a new way of understanding the prophetic body, one that begins with the instability and promise of sound and leads to the reconfigurations of voice, gender, and body. While Jeremiah's reconfiguration of masculinity is primarily limited to the voice, there are, meanwhile, no such limitations placed on Ezekiel. Instead, as I have argued in chapter 4, the theophany and sign acts of Ezekiel 1–5 represent a radical reconfiguration of the body of the prophet. Drawing on the *Memoirs* of Daniel Paul Schreber as well as queer-theoretical work on the prophet, I have suggested that Ezekiel experiences an "unmanning" of his body. The prophetic body temporarily becomes a queer autoerotic economy that defies the ordinary practice of biblical masculinity. This transgression, while radical, cannot last; in the final chapters of the book of Ezekiel, the prophet's reimagined body is replaced by the radical reconfiguration of the space of the reconstructed Temple and the new Jerusalem.

These various prophetic bodies came together at last in chapter 5, which set forth in detail the argument that what the texts share is the general figure of a queer prophetic body. Queerness takes multiple forms; the prophetic body is queer both in its relation to norms of embodiment and, more specifically, in its configurations of masculinity, male embodiment, gender, and desire. To call the prophetic body *queer* brings together these various narratives of embodiment, tracing their continuities while also opening a space to consider their differences. It is also instructive insofar as it begins to teach us a new way of thinking and reading prophetic texts and bodies. If "orientation" is a practice of habituation, as Sara Ahmed argues, then intentionally assuming a reading practice organized around the queer prophetic body can have consequences for our orientations toward texts more generally.[3]

The queer prophetic body is a strange and disturbed body; it is likewise disturbing, troubling norms and categories of identity. It is also a body whose performance of gender, sexuality, and desire may break from certain biblical norms of masculinity, figuring this body as queer in another way. Throughout *Are We Not Men?* I have proposed a number of ways of understanding this body, often drawing on intertexts such as the repressed male character at the center of horror films, the sounds and cries of the hysteric, and the "unmanned" psychotic. The prophet is absent, and perhaps also present as fluidity and fluid potential.

Indeed, even more than queerness, it is instability that unites these prophetic bodies. Masculinity, never a fully stable category, is broken down and transformed in all sorts of ways in the narratives and poetry of the prophets.

To speak of prophetic masculinity is to speak of a category disturbed. At moments, this disturbance seems to open a space of possibility for reconfiguring new ways of being for the male body. There are glimmers of where this instability may lead in Ezekiel's prostrate form and in Moses' gleaming face. But while prophecy may usher in the possibility of transformation, the objects of this transformation are limited to men. Miriam may be a prophet, but when her body transforms, it is only as punishment—the temporary affliction of scale disease. We do not know if Yahweh's word enters into Miriam. We do not know how, except in this moment, her body is touched by prophecy. This is no accidental omission. It is left to us to read from this absence, to consider the question of gender along with sexuality, to offer new ways of thinking and imagining.

It is a difficult thing to be a prophet; it is a difficult thing to have a body. The body is pained, violated, and pushed into extremity by the demands of prophecy. But prophecy, too, is challenged and even transformed by the body. Because prophecy relies on bodies—in the case of the Hebrew Bible, almost entirely male bodies—prophecy cannot be disembodied or neutral. Prophecy happens on and through male bodies, but the central work of prophecy is not upholding norms of masculinity. Instead, the prophetic body offers a space of resistance to, if not outright critique of, the biblical norms of masculinity and embodiment.

The prophets are many things, but disembodied neutral male subjects are not one of them. Rather, they are torn between pleasure and pain, between meaning and its shattering. The bodies of the prophets offer the possibility of a different sort of organization of masculinity, a masculinity that begins with an open body, with opened registers of voice, and with a move beyond directional, effective performance into messy, inchoate embodiment. This is the hope, the danger, and the promise of the Hebrew prophetic body.

Notes

INTRODUCTION

1. This translation and others from the Hebrew Bible are my own. When relevant, I have noted meaningful differences between the Greek Septuagint and the Hebrew Masoretic text in the footnotes.

2. For example, Hans Wildberger, *Isaiah 13–27: A Commentary*, ContC (Minneapolis, MN: Fortress, 1997), 293–94.

3. Elaine Scarry, *The Body in Pain: The Making and Unmaking of the World* (New York: Oxford University Press, 1987), 4.

4. Daniel L. Smith-Christopher, "Ezekiel in Abu Ghraib: Rereading Ezekiel 16:37–39 in the Context of Imperial Conquest," in *Ezekiel's Hierarchical World: Wrestling with a Tiered Reality*, ed. Stephen L. Cook and Corrine L. Patton, SBLSym 31 (Atlanta, GA: SBL, 2004); Cynthia R. Chapman, *The Gendered Language of Warfare in the Israelite-Assyrian Encounter*, HSM 62 (Winona Lake, IN: Eisenbrauns, 2004), 26–27, 160–61; Wildberger, *Isaiah 13–27*, 294.

5. Sara Ahmed, *Queer Phenomenology: Orientations, Objects, Others* (Durham, NC: Duke University Press, 2006), 161.

6. Here we might think as well of what Halberstam terms "the queer art of failure." Judith Halberstam, *The Queer Art of Failure* (Durham, NC: Duke University Press, 2011). On the unintelligibility of the sign acts to their intended audience, see further my discussion of Ezekiel's sign acts in chapter 4.

7. Timothy R. Koch, "Cruising as Methodology: Homoeroticism and the Scriptures," in *Queer Commentary and the Hebrew Bible*, ed. Ken Stone, JSOTSup 334 (Cleveland, OH: Pilgrim, 2001), 176.

8. See further chapter 1.

9. De Lauretis also sought to direct attention to issues such as race and class. Teresa De Lauretis, "Queer Theory: Lesbian and Gay Sexualities: An Introduction," ed. Teresa De Lauretis, *Differences: A Journal of Feminist Cultural Studies* 3, no. 2

(1991): iii–xviii. On queer theory and feminist biblical studies, see further Rhiannon Graybill, "Surpassing the Love of Women: From Feminism to Queer Theory in Biblical Studies," in *Feminist Interpretation of the Hebrew Bible in Retrospect*, ed. Susanne Scholz, vol. 3, *Methods* (Sheffield: Sheffield Phoenix Press, 2016), 304–325.

10. Gilles Deleuze and Félix Guattari, *Anti-Oedipus: Capitalism and Schizophrenia*, trans. Robert Hurley and Mark Seem (Harmondsworth: Penguin, 2009), 109, italics original. For Deleuze and Guattari, this question is posed by desire. For a discussion, see further Brian Massumi, *A User's Guide to Capitalism and Schizophrenia: Deviations from Deleuze and Guattari* (Cambridge, MA: MIT Press, 1992), 8ff.

11. Ahmed, *Queer Phenomenology*, 4.

12. Ibid., 169, italics original.

13. I discuss Blake's text briefly in chapter 4.

14. Anne Carson, "The Book of Isaiah," in *Glass, Irony, and God* (New York: New Directions, 1995), 107.

15. Ibid., 108.

16. Ibid., 117–18, italics original.

17. Ahmed, *Queer Phenomenology*, 86.

18. Rhiannon Graybill, "Uncanny Bodies, Impossible Knowledge and Somatic Excess in Isaiah 29," *BCT* 7, no. 1 (2011): 21.

19. One body that does appear in Isaiah 40–55 is that of the Suffering Servant. However, I do not think that the Servant is a stand-in for the prophet. The speaker consistently refers to the Servant in the third person. There is also no indication that the prophet experiences in his own body the Servant's suffering—in contrast, for example, with the suffering of Jeremiah.

20. See further chapter 1.

21. See further chapter 2.

22. See further chapter 4.

23. For example, Howard Eilberg-Schwartz, *God's Phallus: And Other Problems for Men and Monotheism* (Boston: Beacon, 1995); Stephen D. Moore, *God's Gym: Divine Male Bodies of the Bible* (New York: Routledge, 1996); Stephen D. Moore and Janice Capel Anderson, eds., *New Testament Masculinities*, SBLSS 45 (Atlanta, GA: SBL, 2003); Colleen M. Conway, *Behold the Man: Jesus and Greco-Roman Masculinity* (New York: Oxford University Press, 2008); Ovidiu Creangă, ed., *Men and Masculinity in the Hebrew Bible and Beyond*, BMW 33 (Sheffield: Sheffield Phoenix Press, 2010); Susan E. Haddox, *Metaphor and Masculinity in Hosea*, SiBL 141 (New York: Peter Lang, 2011); Roland Boer, *The Earthy Nature of the Bible: Fleshly Readings of Sex, Masculinity, and Carnality*, BibleWorld (New York: Palgrave Macmillan, 2012); Ovidiu Creangă and Peter-Ben Smit, *Biblical Masculinities Foregrounded*, HBM 62 (Sheffield: Sheffield Phoenix Press, 2014).

24. For example, Stuart Macwilliam, *Queer Theory and the Prophetic Marriage Metaphor in the Hebrew Bible*, BibleWorld (Sheffield and Oakville, CT: Equinox, 2011).

25. Luce Irigaray, *Sexes and Genealogies*, trans. Gillian C. Gill (New York: Columbia University Press, 1993), 117.
26. Luce Irigaray, *Speculum of the Other Woman*, trans. Gillian C. Gill (Ithaca, NY: Cornell University Press, 1985), 133.
27. John Berger, *Ways of Seeing* (London: Penguin, 1990), 47.
28. Furthermore, it is essential that an opening to queer reading and to the queer (male) gaze does not tacitly endorse an erasure of the feminine. Laurel Schneider and Deryn Guest have offered important reminders to this end, which help steer the project of this book. See Laurel C. Schneider, "Yahwist Desires: Imagining Divinity Queerly," in *Queer Commentary and the Hebrew Bible*, ed. Stone, 210–27; Deryn Guest, *When Deborah Met Jael: Lesbian Biblical Hermeneutics* (London: SCM, 2005); Deryn Guest, *Beyond Feminist Biblical Studies*, BMW 47 (Sheffield: Sheffield Phoenix Press, 2012).
29. Though see Haddox, *Metaphor and Masculinity in Hosea*; Jonathan Stökl and Corrine L. Carvalho, *Prophets Male and Female: Gender and Prophecy in the Hebrew Bible, the Eastern Mediterranean, and the Ancient Near East*, AIL 15 (Atlanta, GA: SBL, 2013); David J. A. Clines, "He-Prophets: Masculinity as a Problem for the Hebrew Prophets and Their Interpreters," in *Sense and Sensitivity: Essays on Reading the Bible in Memory of Robert Carroll*, ed. Robert P. Carroll, Alastair G. Hunter, and Philip R. Davies, 311–27, JSOTSup 348 (Sheffield: Sheffield Academic Press, 2002); C. J. Patrick Davis, "Jeremiah, Masculinity and His Portrayal as the 'Lamenting Prophet,'" in *Men and Masculinity in the Hebrew Bible and Beyond*, ed. Creangă, 189–210; Ken Stone, "'You Seduced Me, You Overpowered Me, and You Prevailed': Religious Experience and Homoerotic Sadomasochism in Jeremiah," in *Patriarchs, Prophets and Other Villains*, ed. Lisa Isherwood, 101–9, Gender, Theology, and Spirituality (London: Equinox, 2007); David J. Halperin, *Seeking Ezekiel: Text and Psychology* (University Park: Pennsylvania State University Press, 1993). Additional relevant sources are discussed in the following chapters.
30. For example, Athalya Brenner, ed., *A Feminist Companion to the Latter Prophets*, FCB (Sheffield: Sheffield Academic Press, 1995); Julie Galambush, *Jerusalem in the Book of Ezekiel: The City as Yahweh's Wife*, SBLDS 130 (Atlanta, GA: Scholars, 1992); S. Tamar Kamionkowski, *Gender Reversal and Cosmic Chaos: A Study in the Book of Ezekiel*, JSOTSup 368 (Sheffield: Sheffield Academic Press, 2003); Gerlinde Baumann, *Love and Violence: Marriage as Metaphor for the Relationship Between YHWH and Israel in the Prophetic Books* (Collegeville, MN: Liturgical Press, 2003); Susan E. Haddox, "Engaging Images in the Prophets: Feminist Scholarship on the Book of the Twelve," in *Feminist Interpretation of the Hebrew Bible in Retrospect*, ed. Susanne Scholz, vol. 1, *Biblical Books*, RRBS 5 (Sheffield: Sheffield Phoenix Press, 2013), 170–91; Stökl and Carvalho, *Prophets Male and Female*.
31. Clines, "He-Prophets," 311.
32. Isaiah, the other of the Major Prophets, also addressed above; I have also written about embodiment in Isaiah in Graybill, "Uncanny Bodies, Impossible Knowledge and Somatic Excess in Isaiah 29."

33. Brian Massumi, *Parables for the Virtual: Movement, Affect, Sensation* (Durham, NC: Duke University Press, 2002), 19–20.

34. Ibid., 46–56.

35. Ahmed criticizes Massumi for insisting on the "autonomy of affect." Sara Ahmed, *The Promise of Happiness* (Durham, NC: Duke University Press, 2010), 214–15; Massumi, *Parables for the Virtual*, 23–45. For Ahmed's argument about sticky affect, see *Promise of Happiness*, 21–50; Sara Ahmed, *The Cultural Politics of Emotion*, 2nd ed. (New York: Routledge, 2014), 11–15, 89–92. Whether or not affect itself is sticky, I suggest that texts, whether biblical or theoretical, often come to us "sticky."

36. Irigaray, *Speculum of the Other Women*, 166, italics original.

37. Ezekiel does not fully abstain from drinking, but rather drinks a limited and small amount, at precise intervals.

38. For an elaboration of this argument with reference to Hebrew prophecy and Moses in particular, see the section "Fluidity, Openness, and a New Mosaic Masculinity" in chapter 1.

CHAPTER 1

1. Lamentations Rabbah Petihta 24, XXIV.ii.2.

2. Virginia Burrus, "Mapping as Metamorphosis: Initial Reflections on Gender and Ancient Religious Discourses," in *Mapping Gender in Ancient Religious Discourses*, ed. Todd Penner and Caroline Vander Stichele, BIS 84 (Boston: Brill, 2007), 4.

3. In the words of Daniel Boyarin, "the world was divided into the screwers—all male—and the screwed—both male and female." Daniel Boyarin, "Are There Any Jews in 'The History of Sexuality'?" *Journal of the History of Sexuality* 5, no. 3 (1995): 333.

4. See Robert W. Connell and James W. Messerschmidt, "Hegemonic Masculinity: Rethinking the Concept," *Gender and Society* 19, no. 6 (2005): 832.

5. Ibid., 846–47.

6. On this question, see Susan E. Haddox, "Favoured Sons and Subordinate Masculinities," in *Men and Masculinity in the Hebrew Bible and Beyond*, ed. Creangă, 4–5; David J. A. Clines, "Dancing and Shining at Sinai: Playing the Man in Exodus 32–34," in *Men and Masculinity in the Hebrew Bible and Beyond*, ed. Creangă, 55; Harold C. Washington, "Violence and the Construction of Gender in the Hebrew Bible: A New Historicist Approach 1," *BibInt* 5, no. 4 (1997): 326.

7. Clines has suggested several other features that constitute hegemonic masculinity, including persuasive speech, musical skill, and male beauty; see David J. A. Clines, *Interested Parties: The Ideology of Writers and Readers of the Hebrew Bible* (Sheffield: Sheffield Academic Press, 1995), 212–43.

8. Thomas Hentrich, "Masculinity and Disability in the Bible," in *This Abled Body: Rethinking Disabilities in Biblical Studies*, ed. Hector Avalos, Sarah J. Melcher, and Jeremy Schipper, 73–87, SBLSS 55 (Atlanta, GA: SBL, 2007); Carole R. Fontaine, "'Be Men, O Philistines' (1 Sam. 4:9): Iconographic Representations and Reflections on Female Gender as Disability in the Ancient World," in *This Abled Body*, ed. Avalos, Melcher, and Schipper, 61–72.

9. Mark K. George, "Masculinity and Its Regimentation in Deuteronomy," in *Men and Masculinity in the Hebrew Bible and Beyond*, ed. Creangă, 64–82.

10. See Clines, *Interested Parties*, 221–23. While male beauty is sometimes noted in the text—Joseph, David, and Absalom are key examples, as well as the male lover in the Song of Songs—it does not bear a straightforward relationship to masculine power. See Stuart Macwilliam, "Ideologies of Male Beauty and the Hebrew Bible," *BibInt* 17, no. 3 (2009): 265–87.

11. Boer, *Earthy Nature of the Bible*, 72.

12. For example Clines, "Dancing and Shining at Sinai." The study of Moses' masculine performance, though without a particular focus on masculine embodiment, has also been undertaken by Brian C. DiPalma, "Deconstructing Masculinity in Exodus 1–4," in *Men and Masculinity in the Hebrew Bible and Beyond*, ed. Creangă, 36–53.

13. To facilitate readability for a wider audience, all Hebrew terms in the body of the text are transliterated. When required for clarity, Hebrew and Greek appear in the notes.

14. Macwilliam makes a similar point about the function of male beauty in the biblical narrative. Macwilliam, "Ideologies of Male Beauty and the Hebrew Bible," 285.

15. Ibid., 278.

16. S. Levin, "The Speech Defect of Moses," *Journal of the Royal Society of Medicine* 85, no. 10 (1992): 632–33.

17. For a good overview of the theories, see Jeffrey H. Tigay, "'Heavy of Mouth' and 'Heavy of Tongue': On Moses' Speech Difficulty," *BASOR*, no. 231 (October 1978): 57–67.

18. This is the most common explanation. It occurs in LXX, the Syriac text, and a number of ancient and modern interpretations. William H. C. Propp, *Exodus 1–18*, AYB 2 (New Haven, CT: Yale University Press, 1999), 210–11. For a contemporary example, see Marc Shell, *Stutter* (Cambridge, MA: Harvard University Press, 2005), 102–36.

19. For example, Levin, "Speech Defect of Moses." See also Propp, *Exodus 1–18*, 211.

20. See, for example, S. D. Luzzatto, *Commentary to the Pentateuch* (Tel Aviv: Dvir, 1965). Quoted in Tigay, "'Heavy of Mouth' and 'Heavy of Tongue,'" 63n4. This position also occurs in Philo, Ignatius, and Cyprian, among other ancient sources, as Tigay notes.

21. Jeremy Schipper, *Disability Studies and the Hebrew Bible: Figuring Mephibosheth in the David Story*, LHB/OTS 441 (London: T. & T. Clark, 2009), 73.

22. On this point, see further Mladen Dolar, *A Voice and Nothing More* (Cambridge, MA: MIT Press, 2006), 12–33. On prophecy and stuttering, see as well Herbert Marks, "On Prophetic Stammering," in *The Book and the Text: The Bible and Literary Theory*, ed. Regina M. Schwartz, 60–80 (Oxford: Blackwell, 1990).

23. See Propp's comments on E and P in Propp, *Exodus 1–18*, 211.

24. Julia Kristeva, *Powers of Horror: An Essay on Abjection* (New York: Columbia University Press, 1982), 2–3.

25. Ibid., 71ff.

26. While leprosy is the most commonly offered explanation, it is almost certainly not what is meant by the biblical text. LXX translates with λέπρα for the disease and λεπρός for the sufferer, both related to the meaning of *scaly*. This word is used by the Greek medical authors to refer to a number of conditions and also furnishes the root for the English *leprosy*; it does not refer specifically to Hansen's disease (caused by *mycobacterium leprae*). Furthermore, leprosy was likely unknown in the Near East until brought by Alexander's armies. Jacob Milgrom, *Leviticus 1–16: A New Translation with Introduction and Commentary*, AYB 3 (New York: Doubleday, 1991), 816–26. Milgrom also notes that Rabbinic Hebrew treats ṣāraʿat as referring to multiple diseases (776).

27. Ibid., 817.

28. Propp, *Exodus 1–18*, 210. The number of instances, however, is strictly limited.

29. On Exod. 17:8–16 as a narrative about Moses' weakness and inadequacy, see Bernard P. Robinson, "Israel and Amalek : The Context of Exodus 17:8–16," *JSOT* 10, no. 32 (1985): 16, 19.

30. Shell, *Stutter*, 109–11, cf. 188–89.

31. Ibid., 107.

32. Clines argues that Moses' transformation also increases his sexual desirability. Clines, "Dancing and Shining at Sinai," 60–61.

33. In the Vulgate, Exod. 33:29 reads, *cumque descenderet Moses de monte Sinai tenebat duas tabulas testimonii et ignorabat quod cornuta esset facies sua ex consortio sermonis Dei*. This literal translation gave rise to the idea that Moses had horns.

34. Seth L. Sanders, "Old Light on Moses' Shining Face," *VT* 52, no. 3 (2002): 404.

35. Ibid., 405.

36. Howard Eilberg-Schwartz has argued that the horns are a masculinizing addition, symbolizing the male deity (often associated with bulls) and counterbalancing the feminizing effect of the veil. Eilberg-Schwartz, *God's Phallus*, 145.

37. On the intimacy of the voice, see Dolar, *A Voice and Nothing More*, 86.

38. Gen. 49:11 contains a related hapax legomenon, סות, "garment." Phoenician contains the related forms סות, "garment," and סוית, which may perhaps mean "veil" (the precise meaning is unclear). See further Gary A. Rendsburg, "Hebrew Philological Notes (I)," *HS* 40, no. 1 (1999): 27–32.

39. While the Middle Assyrian laws require women to cover their heads, in other periods, no evidence of such a law exists. See Michelle I. Marcus, "Dressed to Kill: Women and Pins in Early Iran," *Oxford Art Journal* 17, no. 2 (1994): 7–8; M. Stol, "Women in Mesopotamia," *Journal of the Economic and Social History of the Orient* 38, no. 2 (1995): 123. The *requirement* for women to cover their heads comes later, appearing in the New Testament and the Talmud. See Alicia J. Batten, "Clothing and Adornment," *BTB* 40, no. 3 (2010): 155–56.

40. Theodore W. Jennings, *Jacob's Wound: Homoerotic Narrative in the Literature of Ancient Israel* (New York: Continuum, 2005), 256. On the interpretive history of the veil as feminizing, see Brian Britt, *Rewriting Moses: The Narrative Eclipse of the Text*, JSOT Sup 402, GCT 14 (London and New York: T. & T. Clark, 2004), 98, 113–14.

41. It is also possible to read לח as a variant of לחי, "cheek" or "jawbone." In this case, the emphasis is on Moses' exemplary physical condition, even as an old man. There is also perhaps a degree of refutation of the strangeness of Moses' face emphasized prior.

42. Eilberg-Schwartz, *God's Phallus*, 146; W. F. Albright, "The 'Natural Force' of Moses in the Light of Ugaritic," *BASOR*, no. 94 (April 1944): 32–35.

43. On the straightening of orientations, see Ahmed, *Queer Phenomenology*, 85–86.

44. Saul M. Olyan, *Disability in the Hebrew Bible: Interpreting Mental and Physical Differences* (New York: Cambridge University Press, 2008), 18–19.

45. See, to begin, Avalos, Melcher, and Schipper, *This Abled Body*; Schipper, *Disability Studies and the Hebrew Bible*; Olyan, *Disability in the Hebrew Bible*; Rebecca Raphael, *Biblical Corpora: Representations of Disability in Hebrew Biblical Literature*, LHB/OTS 445 (New York: T. & T. Clark, 2008).

46. Nyasha Junior and Jeremy Schipper, "Mosaic Disability and Identity in Exodus 4:10; 6:12, 30," *BibInt* 16, no. 5 (2008): 429, 441.

47. Ibid., 440.

48. Fontaine, "Be Men, O Philistines," 69.

49. Hentrich, "Masculinity and Disability in the Bible," 75.

50. Olyan, *Disability in the Hebrew Bible*, 128. Olyan further suggests that disability is more commonly associated with poverty or foreignness.

51. See discussion in Introduction.

52. See Roland Boer, "Yahweh as Top: A Lost Targum," in *Queer Commentary and the Hebrew Bible*, ed. Stone, 75–105, for an imaginative version of this reading.

53. Jasbir K. Puar, *Terrorist Assemblages: Homonationalism in Queer Times* (Durham, NC: Duke University Press, 2007), 205.

54. Puar, *Terrorist Assemblages*, 215.

55. See Brian Massumi, *The Power at the End of the Economy* (Durham, NC: Duke University Press, 2014), 68.

56. In LXX, Zipporah says, Ἔστη τὸ αἷμα τῆς περιτομῆς τοῦ παιδίου μου, "May the blood of my son's circumcision stand." Propp, *Exodus 1–18*, 189.

57. חתן means "male relative by marriage," hence, either bridegroom or son-in-law.

58. Exod. 4:20.

59. Ned. 3:9, quoted in Christopher B. Hays, "'Lest Ye Perish in the Way': Ritual and Kinship in Exodus 4:24–26," *HS* 48 (2007): 40.

60. William H. C. Propp, "That Bloody Bridegroom (Exodus IV 24–6)," *VT* 43, no. 4 (1993): 505.

61. Hans Kosmala, "The 'Bloody Husband,'" *VT* 12, no. 1 (1962): 24.

62. Hays, "Lest Ye Perish in the Way," 45–46.

63. Eilberg-Schwartz, *God's Phallus*, 60–64.

64. Eilberg-Schwartz argues, "The sexual body of a father God is troubling for the conception of masculinity," especially because "when a man confronts a male God, he is put into the female position so as to be intimate with God." Ibid., 1, 137.

65. This argument is pervasive in Irigaray's work; see, e.g., Irigaray, *Sexes and Genealogies*, 13; *Speculum of the Other Woman*.

66. Luce Irigaray, *The Forgetting of Air in Martin Heidegger*, trans. Mary Beth Mader (Austin: University of Texas Press, 1999), 30. The capitalization (original to the English translation) reflects Heidegger's usage.

67. Irigaray makes this argument at multiple points and in multiple ways. For an argument with reference to the elements, another of Irigaray's key themes, see *Forgetting of Air in Martin Heidegger*, 12, 63–67, 129; on air as a fluid, see 41, 85–86. In another work drawing on the elements, she makes a similar argument about fluidity and openness with respect to water: Luce Irigaray, *Marine Lover of Friedrich Nietzsche*, trans. Gillian C. Gill (New York: Columbia University Press, 1991).

68. Irigaray, *Speculum of the Other Woman*, 200.

69. Amy Hollywood, "'That Glorious Slit': Irigaray and the Medieval Devotion to Christ's Side Wound," in *Luce Irigaray and Premodern Culture: Thresholds of History*, ed. Elizabeth D. Harvey and Theresa Krier (Abingdon and New York: Routledge, 2004), 105, 119–21.

70. Elizabeth A. Grosz, *Volatile Bodies: Toward a Corporeal Feminism* (Bloomington: Indiana University Press, 1994), 198.

71. Ibid., 200.

72. Ibid., 202.

73. Ibid., 201. While I would push back against Grosz's reading of transgender embodiment here, her larger point about the open, permeable, reconfigured masculinity is well worth taking seriously.

74. Grosz is not the only scholar to build on Irigaray in this way. More recently, Britt-Marie Schiller has used Irigaray's work to formulate an "incomplete masculine" that, in its openness, rejects phallicism as a "fortress of emotional self-sufficiency and impenetrability." Britt-Marie Schiller, "The Incomplete Masculine: Engendering the Masculine of Sexual Difference," in *Thinking with Irigaray*, ed. Mary C. Rawlinson, Sabrina L. Horn, and Serene J. Khader, SUNY Series in Gender Theory (Albany: State University of New York Press, 2012), 131.

75. For an analysis of the queerness of all-male spaces and genealogies, though of a different text, see Roland Boer, "Of Fine Wine, Incense, and Spices: The Unstable Masculine Hegemony of the Book of Chronicles," in *Men and Masculinity in the Hebrew Bible and Beyond*, ed. Creangă, 20–35.

76. Clines, "He-Prophets," 314.

CHAPTER 2

1. The woman in Isaiah 8:3 is generally but not always taken as his wife; she is described in the text as a "female prophet" (נביאה).

2. The meaning of this term will be discussed in greater detail below.

3. See, for example, T. Drorah Setel, "Prophets and Pornography: Female Sexual Imagery in Hosea," in *Feminist Interpretation of the Bible*, ed. Letty M. Russell, 85–95 (Louisville, KY: Westminster John Knox Press, 1985); Renita J. Weems, *Battered Love: Marriage, Sex, and Violence in the Hebrew Prophets*, OBT (Minneapolis, MN: Fortress, 1995); Athalya Brenner, "Pornoprophetics Revisited: Some Additional Reflections," *JSOT* 21, no. 70 (1996): 63–86.

4. The critical discussion of prophecy and pornography, or "pornoprophetics," represents biblical studies' response to, and appropriation of, the debates over feminism and pornography more generally. On this larger debate, see Andrea Dworkin, *Pornography: Men Possessing Women* (New York: Perigee, 1981); Andrea Dworkin and Catharine A. MacKinnon, *Pornography and Civil Rights: A New Day for Women's Equality* (Minneapolis, MN: Organizing Against Pornography, 1988); Nadine Strossen, "A Feminist Critique of 'the' Feminist Critique of Pornography," *Virginia Law Review* 79, no. 5 (1993): 1099–1190.

5. On performance art, see Yvonne Sherwood, "Prophetic Performance Art," *The Bible and Critical Theory* 2, no. 1 (2006): 1–4. In a somewhat different form, the argument also appears in David Stacey, *Prophetic Drama in the Old Testament* (London: Epworth, 1990). On the alienation effect, see Yvonne Sherwood, *The Prostitute and the Prophet: Hosea's Marriage in Literary-Theoretical Perspective*, JSOTSup 212, GCT 2 (Sheffield: Sheffield Academic Press, 1996), 103–06. For the economic reading, see Alice A. Keefe, *Woman's Body and the Social Body in Hosea 1–2* (London: Sheffield Academic Press, 2001); Gale A. Yee, *Poor Banished Children of Eve: Woman as Evil in the Hebrew Bible* (Minneapolis, MN: Augsburg Fortress, 2003), 81–110.

6. For example, Eve-Marie Becker and Jan Dochhorn, *Trauma and Traumatization in Individual and Collective Dimensions: Insights from Biblical Studies and Beyond* (Göttingen: Vandenhoeck & Ruprecht, 2014).

7. See, for example, Barbara Creed, *The Monstrous-Feminine: Film, Feminism, Psychoanalysis*, Popular Fictions Series (New York: Routledge and Kegan Paul, 1993); Cynthia Freeland, *The Naked and the Undead: Evil and the Appeal of Horror*, Thinking through Cinema (Boulder, CO: Westview, 2009); Barry Keith Grant, ed., *The Dread of Difference: Gender and the Horror Film*, 2nd ed., Texas Film and Media Studies (Austin: University of Texas Press, 2015); Isabel Cristina Pinedo, *Recreational Terror: Women and the Pleasures of Horror Film Viewing*, Interruptions (Albany: State University of New York Press, 1997). The feminist reading of horror films has also become a micro-industry of its own in the feminist blogosphere.

8. Carol J. Clover, *Men, Women, and Chain Saws: Gender in the Modern Horror Film* (Princeton, NJ: Princeton University Press, 1993).

9. Thus *BDB, HALOT, TWOT*. See further Phyllis Bird, "'To Play the Harlot': An Inquiry into an Old Testament Metaphor," in *Gender and Difference in Ancient Israel*, ed. Peggy L. Day, 75–94 (Minneapolis, MN: Fortress, 1989); Athalya

Brenner, *The Intercourse of Knowledge: On Gendering Desire and "Sexuality" in the Hebrew Bible*, BIS 26 (Leiden: Brill, 1997), 147–48.

10. One exception is the use of the infinite form to describe the actions of the Israelites with the Moabite women in Numbers 25:1. Here as well, however, there is an association with female licentiousness. See as well Bird, "To Play the Harlot," 77.

11. See further Yvonne Sherwood, "Boxing Gomer: Controlling the Deviant Woman in Hosea 1–3," in *Feminist Companion to the Latter Prophets*, ed. Brenner, 101–25.

12. 2:2–13 in the Greek, the NRSV, and most English translations. This chapter follows the Hebrew numbering of verses in chapter 2.

13. In addition, when David gives raisin cakes to the Israelites upon the arrival of the Ark of the Covenant in Jerusalem, he sends them home to eat them—the raisin cake, it seems, is too powerful to be eaten in public, perhaps because of its aphrodisiacal properties (2 Sam. 6). The moment is already too close to a dangerous bodily openness as David, dancing and singing, exposes himself before the people.

14. Hebrew בעל, pl.בעלים . *Baʿal* is both the name of a rival northwest Semitic storm god and the Hebrew word for "husband" or "master"—meanings that the text plays on.

15. Andersen and Freedman write, "It is clear from Gen. 9:22–23 that ʿerwâ is a euphemism for genitals," cf. Leviticus 18. Francis I. Andersen and David Noel Freedman, *Hosea*, AYB 24 (Garden City, NY: Doubleday, 1996), 246.

16. Her genitals: נבלתה; נבלות + feminine possessive suffix. The term is a *hapax legomenon*. *HALOT* gives "shame" as well as "pudenda" (664); *BDB* has "immodesty" and "shamelessness." Wolff compares the term to Akkadian *baltu*, "genitalia," and translates "genitals"; Andersen and Freedman urge restraint, noting that the root נבל has a basic meaning of "fool" and settling on "lewdness" as a compromise. LXX translates τὴν ἀκαθαρσίαν αὐτῆς, "her uncleanliness."

17. Read תְּקַטֵּר for תַּקְטִיר.

18. For example, Weems, *Battered Love*, passim.

19. Because the second person feminine singular (2fs) and third person feminine singular (3fs) are identical in the imperfect, "she" may also be translated "you" (fs) in this verse.

20. *Supra* Note 14 above.

21. For example, Isaiah 6; Freud makes a similar point in his reading of Dora. See further my discussion of Freud, hysteria, and somatic compliance in chapter 3.

22. Clover, *Men, Women, and Chain Saws*, 5.

23. Ibid., 19.

24. Ibid., 19.

25. Eve Kosofsky Sedgwick, *Touching Feeling: Affect, Pedagogy, Performativity*, Series Q (Durham, NC: Duke University Press, 2002), 138–41.

26. In analyzing the slasher film, Clover introduces the now-famous figure of the Final Girl to horror criticism and then, via Wes Craven and others, to horror films themselves. The Final Girl, often the sole survivor of the slasher film, is a woman or, often, teenage girl who bears an androgynous name, avoids sexual contact (a clear

marker of death in the slasher film), survives the killer, and ultimately kills him, usually with a phallic weapon. This final girl represents "a physical female and a characterological androgyne," providing a point of identification for adolescent male viewers." Clover, *Men, Women, and Chain Saws*, 63.

27. Ibid., 61.
28. William Peter Blatty, *The Exorcist* (New York: Harper, 1971); William Friedkin, dir., *The Exorcist*, Horror (Warner Bros., 1973).
29. Clover, *Men, Women, and Chain Saws*, 87–88.
30. David M. Halperin, "Why Is Diotima a Woman?," in *One Hundred Years of Homosexuality: And Other Essays on Greek Love*, New Ancient World (New York: Routledge, 1990), 113–51.
31. Clover, *Men, Women, and Chain Saws*, 105.
32. Ibid., 70.
33. Susan E. Haddox, "(E)Masculinity in Hosea's Political Rhetoric," in *Israel's Prophets and Israel's Past: Essays on the Relationship of Prophetic Texts and Israelite History in Honor of John H. Hayes*, ed. John Haralson Hayes, Brad E. Kelle, and Megan Bishop Moore, LHB/OTS 446 (New York: T. & T. Clark, 2006), 187; Haddox, *Metaphor and Masculinity in Hosea*.
34. Ken Stone, *Practicing Safer Texts: Food, Sex and Bible in Queer Perspective*, Queering Theology Series (London: T. & T. Clark International, 2004), 110.
35. Ibid., 125.
36. The biblical adultery laws take into account only the marital status of the woman, not the man; this is in keeping with the text's intense interest in regulating and safeguarding paternal lines of descent.
37. Eilberg-Schwartz, *God's Phallus*, 137.
38. Clover, *Men, Women, and Chain Saws*, 105.
39. See further Stone, *Practicing Safer Texts*, 177.
40. Clover, *Men, Women, and Chain Saws*, 105.
41. "Her Body, Himself," a study of the slasher film, is the first chapter in Clover, *Men, Women, and Chain Saws*.

CHAPTER 3

1. Dolar, *A Voice and Nothing More*, 59.
2. Geoffrey Hartman, "Jeremiah 20:7–12: A Literary Response," in *The Biblical Mosaic: Changing Perspectives*, ed. Robert Polzin and Eugene Rothman, SBLSS (Philadelphia, PA: Fortress, 1982), 193–194.
3. Sigmund Freud and Josef Breuer, *Studies in Hysteria*, trans. Nicola Luckhurst (New York: Penguin, 2004); Sigmund Freud, *Dora: An Analysis of a Case of Hysteria*, ed. Philip Rieff (New York: Collier, 1963). The case study itself is entitled "Fragment of an Analysis of a Case of Hysteria."

4. See for example; Elaine Showalter, *The Female Malady: Women, Madness, and English Culture, 1830–1980* (New York: Pantheon, 1985); Martha Noel Evans, *Fits and Starts: A Genealogy of Hysteria in Modern France* (Ithaca, NY: Cornell University Press, 1991); Susan Bordo, *Unbearable Weight: Feminism, Western Culture, and the Body* (Berkeley: University of California Press, 1993), 45–70.

5. Kathleen O'Connor offers a slightly different division of the texts into six distinct Confessions (11:18–12:6; 15:10–21; 17:14–18; 18:18–23; 20:7–13; 20:14–18). See A. R. Pete Diamond, *The Confessions of Jeremiah in Context: Scenes of Prophetic Drama*, JSOTSup 45 (Sheffield: Sheffield Academic Press, 1987); Kathleen M. O'Connor, *The Confessions of Jeremiah: Their Interpretation and Their Role in Chapters 1–25*, SBLDS 94 (Atlanta, GA: Scholars, 1987). Happily, the ordering of the Confessions is the same in both MT and LXX.

6. Thus, William Holladay calls the passages "complaints," William McKane prefers "laments," and A. R. Diamond hedges, referring to the "so-called confessions" and "the texts generally known as the confessions. See William Lee Holladay, *Jeremiah: A Commentary on the Book of the Prophet Jeremiah*, Hermeneia (Philadelphia, PA: Fortress, 1986), 358; William McKane, *A Critical and Exegetical Commentary on Jeremiah*, ICC (Edinburgh: T. & T. Clark, 1986), xcii; Diamond, *Confessions of Jeremiah in Context*, 11.

7. It is worth noting that this Augustine, portrayed by the Confessions, is an eminently literary construction; see Isaac Miller, "St. Augustine, the Narrative Self, and the Invention of Fiction," *Qui Parle* 8, no. 2 (1995): 54–82.

8. *you showed me*: reading with MT; LXX reads εἶδον = ראיתי, "I saw."

9. *destroy the tree with its fruit*: the phrase is difficult. Reading with MT, I take בלחם to refer to the fruit of the tree; see O'Connor, *Confessions of Jeremiah*, 9n5.

10. *Calamitous day*: reading with MT אנוש יום; LXX has καὶ ἡμέραω ἀωθρώπου, reflecting the corruption of אֱנוֹשׁ to אֱנוֹשׁ, "man."

11. Rhiannon Graybill, "'Hear and Give Ear': The Soundscape of Jeremiah." Forthcoming, *JSOT* 40, no. 4 (2016): 467–490.

12. Reading with MT; LXX reads "because I will laugh with my bitter speech, I will call upon faithlessness and restlessness." See Diamond, *Confessions of Jeremiah in Context*, 251.

13. For a thorough discussion of possible readings of this passage, see David J. A. Clines and David M. Gunn, "'You Tried to Persuade Me' and 'Violence! Outrage!' in Jeremiah XX 7–8," *VT* 28, no. 1 (1978): 20–27; David J. A. Clines and David M. Gunn, "Form, Occasion and Redaction in Jeremiah 20," *ZAW* 88, no. 3 (2009): 390–409.

14. Hartman, "Jeremiah 20:7–12," 104.

15. *my heart*: reading with MT; missing from G, perhaps through homoioarcton with ב and כ. As Diamond writes, "If MT is an explanatory gloss, it is difficult to see the motivation since the meaning was already clear." Diamond, *Confessions of Jeremiah in Context*, 251n3.

16. *all of them curse me*: reading MT but correcting for word misdivision.

17. Reading with MT, following O'Connor, *Confessions of Jeremiah*, 11n24. LXX is expansionary.

18. *a pit*: reading MT *qere* שׁוחה, "pit." LXX λόγον, "word," translates MT *ketib* שׁיחה, "conversation" (with interchange of שׂ and שׁ).

19. *dried-up well*: אכזב, a substantivized adjective. The Hebrew contains an untranslatable double sense of lying or deceit and a dried-up water source.

20. See, e.g., L. Juliana M. Claassens, *Mourner, Mother, Midwife: Reimagining God's Delivering Presence in the Old Testament* (Louisville, KY: Westminster John Knox Press, 2012), 26–31.

21. See Yael Shemesh, "'Do Not Bare Your Heads and Do Not Rend Your Clothes' (Leviticus 10:6)," in *Leviticus and Numbers*, ed. Athalya Brenner and Archie Chi Chung Lee, Texts @ Contexts (Minneapolis, MN: Fortress, 2013), 48–49.

22. Carson, "The Gender of Sound," in *Glass, Irony and God*, 133.

23. Dolar, *A Voice and Nothing More*, 59.

24. Barbara Bakke Kaiser, "Poet as 'Female Impersonator': The Image of Daughter Zion as Speaker in Biblical Poems of Suffering," *JR* 67, no. 2 (1987): 182. Kaiser also discusses Lamentations, following its traditional association with the prophet.

25. For example Angela Bauer-Levesque, *Gender in the Book of Jeremiah: A Feminist-Literary Reading*, SiBL 5 (New York: P. Lang, 1999), 159–163. See also Bauer-Levesque, 63–66, for a specific discussion of Kaiser.

26. Kaiser, "Poet as 'Female Impersonator,'" 174.

27. While this story is frequently repeated, it relies upon a probable misreading of the ancient evidence. See Helen King, "Once upon a Text: Hysteria from Hippocrates," in *Hysteria beyond Freud*, ed. Sander L. Gilman, 3–40 (Berkeley: University of California Press, 1993).

28. Freud and Breuer, *Studies in Hysteria*, 236.

29. Mark S. Micale, *Hysterical Men: The Hidden History of Male Nervous Illness* (Cambridge, MA: Harvard University Press, 2009), 239–240, 259–260.

30. Jan Goldstein, "The Uses of Male Hysteria: Medical and Literary Discourse in Nineteenth-Century France," *Representations*, no. 34 (1991): 134–65; Micale, *Hysterical Men*.

31. Daniel Boyarin, "Freud's Baby, Fliess's Maybe: Male Hysteria, Homophobia, and the Invention of the Jewish Man," *GLQ: A Journal of Lesbian and Gay Studies* 2 (1995): 118.

32. Mary E. Mills, *Alterity, Pain, and Suffering in Isaiah, Jeremiah, and Ezekiel*, LHB/OTS 479 (New York: T. & T. Clark, 2007), 121.

33. On hysterical narrative, see Elaine Showalter, "On Hysterical Narrative," *Narrative* 1, no. 1 (1993): 24–35.

34. Freud, *Dora*, 15, 32–33.

35. Carson, *Glass, Irony and God*, 128–29.

36. Freud and Breuer, *Studies in Hysteria*, 52

37. Ibid., 61.

38. Ibid., 66.

39. Ibid., 51–52.

40. Ibid., 96n1. The capercaillie is a type of grouse.

41. Ibid., 32.

42. Freud, *Dora*, 16, 23.

43. Freud and Breuer, *Studies in Hysteria*, 28–29.

44. Ibid., 34.

45. Ibid., 25, italics in original.

46. Ibid., 281.

47. I have preserved minimal punctuation to indicate verse divisions.

48. The passage does not include, for example, a clarifying particle such as לאמר, often translated "saying."

49. Freud and Breuer, *Studies in Hysteria*, 51–52. See as well Marks, "On Prophetic Stammering," 71–72.

50. Dolar, *A Voice and Nothing More*, 132.

51. Carson, *Glass, Irony and God*, 128.

52. As Steven Marcus notes, "As it [analysis] unwinds, and it becomes increasingly evident that Dora is not responding favorably to Freud, it also becomes clear that Freud is not responding favorably to this response, and that he does not in fact like Dora very much." Steven Marcus, "Freud and Dora: Story, History, Case History," in *In Dora's Case: Freud—Hysteria—Feminism*, ed. Charles Bernheimer and Claire Kahane, Gender and Culture (New York: Columbia University Press, 1985), 89.

53. Freud, *Dora*, 15, 111–12; Hannah S. Decker, *Freud, Dora, and Vienna 1900* (New York: Free Press, 1991), 101–2.

54. Felix Deutsch, "A Footnote to Freud's 'Fragment of an Analysis of a Case of Hysteria,'" in *In Dora's Case*, ed. Bernheimer and Kahane, 43.

55. For example, variously, Maria Ramas, "Freud's Dora, Dora's Hysteria: The Negation of a Woman's Rebellion," *Feminist Studies* 6, no. 3 (1980): 472–510; Toril Moi, "Representation of Patriarchy: Sexuality and Epistemology in Freud's 'Dora,'" *Feminist Review* 9 (autumn 1981): 60–74; Hélène Cixous and Catherine Clément, *The Newly Born Woman* (Minneapolis: University of Minnesota Press, 1986); Jane Gallop, *The Daughter's Seduction: Feminism and Psychoanalysis* (Ithaca, NY: Cornell University Press, 1984), chapter 9.

56. See Paul H. Ornstein's comments in "Discussion" (pp. 51–70) in Evelyne Albrecht Schwaber, *The Transference in Psychotherapy: Clinical Management* (New York: International Universities Press, 1985), 63.

57. Marcus, "Freud and Dora," 61.

58. Mills, *Alterity, Pain, and Suffering in Isaiah, Jeremiah, and Ezekiel*, 111.

59. Freud and Breuer, *Studies in Hysteria*, 264.

60. Ibid., 25.

61. See the recounting and critical analysis of this story in Daniel Boyarin, *Unheroic Conduct the Rise of Heterosexuality and the Invention of the Jewish Man* (Berkeley: University of California Press, 1997), 313–14.

62. Christopher Reeves, "Breuer, Freud and the Case of Anna O: A Re-Examination," *Journal of Child Psychotherapy* 8, no. 2 (1982): 203–14; Mikkel Borch-Jacobsen, *Remembering Anna O.: A Century of Mystification* (New York: Routledge, 1996).

63. Borch-Jacobsen, *Remembering Anna O.*, 34.

64. Sigmund Freud, J. Moussaieff Masson, and Wilhelm Fliess, *The Complete Letters of Sigmund Freud to Wilhelm Fliess, 1887–1904* (Cambridge, MA: Belknap Press of Harvard University Press, 1985), 227. See also the discussion in Clément, "The Guilty One," pp. 12–14, in Cixous and Clément, *Newly Born Woman*, 3–59.

65. Freud, *Dora*, 12, 17, 18. On the gendered power dynamics, see Moi, "Representation of Patriarchy," 192–93.

66. Stone, "You Seduced Me, You Overpowered Me, and You Prevailed," 104–5.

67. Ibid., 106. cf. Sandie Gravett, "Reading 'Rape' in the Hebrew Bible: A Consideration of Language," *JSOT* 28, no. 3 (2004): 279–99.

68. Stone, "You Seduced Me, You Overpowered Me, and You Prevailed," 108. On Yahweh as top, see also Boer, "Yahweh as Top."

69. See "masochism" in Jean Laplanche and J.-B. Pontalis, *The Language of Psycho-Analysis* (New York: W. W. Norton, 1973), 244–45. See as well Clover, *Men, Women, and Chain Saws*, 215–18.

70. Karmen MacKendrick, *Counterpleasures,* SUNY Series in Postmodern Culture (Albany: State University of New York Press, 1999), 112.

71. Jan Goldstein, "The Uses of Male Hysteria: Medical and Literary Discourse in Nineteenth-Century France," *Representations* 34 (spring 1991): 134–65.

72. Ibid., 134–35.

73. Ibid., 156–57. See as well Elaine Showalter, "Critical Cross-Dressing: Male Feminists and the Woman of the Year," *Raritan* 3, no. 2 (1983): 130–49.

74. Cixous in Cixous and Clément, *Newly Born Woman*, 154.

75. Ibid.

76. E.g., Goldstein, "Uses of Male Hysteria."

77. Ahmed, *Promise of Happiness*, 88–120.

78. Clément in Cixous and Clément, *Newly Born Woman*, 155.

79. Ibid.

80. Ibid., 157.

CHAPTER 4

1. William Blake, *The Complete Poetry and Prose of William Blake*, trans. David V. Erdman, commentary by Harold Bloom. Revised ed. (New York: Random House, Inc., 1988), 39.

2. Ezekiel's actions are referred to as functioning as a "sign" (אות) in Ezekiel 4:3. For this reason, I will generally use "sign act" or "sign acts" to refer to the somatic performances in the text. Cf. Kelvin G. Friebel, *Jeremiah's and Ezekiel's Sign-Acts: Rhetorical Nonverbal Communication*, JSOTSup 283 (Sheffield: Sheffield

162 Notes

Academic Press, 1999); Daniel Isaac Block, *The Book of Ezekiel, Chapters 25–48*, NICOT (Grand Rapids, MI: W. B. Eerdmans, 1997).

The actions are also known as "symbolic actions" (*Symbolische Handlungen*) following Georg Fohrer, *Die Symbolischen Handlungen der Propheten*, AThANT 25 (Zürich: Zwingli-Verlag, 1953). Other terms include "prophetic acts" (*actes prophétiques*) (Samuel Amsler, "Les prophètes et la communication par les actes," in *Werden und Wirken des altes Testament: Festschrift für Claus Westermann zum 70. Geburtstag*, ed. Ranier Albertz, 194–201 [Göttingen: Vandenhoeck und Ruprecht, 1980]); "acts of power" (Thomas W. Overholt, "Seeing Is Believing: The Social Setting of Prophetic Acts of Power," *JSOT* 7, no. 23 [1982]: 3–31); and "prophetic drama" (Stacey, *Prophetic Drama in the Old Testament*). See further Friebel, *Jeremiah's and Ezekiel's Sign-Acts*, 11–13.

3. MT adds עליה, "against it," via assimilation to prior clauses in the verse; LXX and V omit.

4. Joseph Blenkinsopp, *Ezekiel*, Interpretation (Louisville, KY: Westminster John Knox Press, 1990), 37.

5. LXX has τέταρτον, identifying four acts of destruction (cf. also 5:12).

6. Over a century ago, Bernhard Duhm, Hermann Gunkel, and Johannes Lindblom identified ecstasy as part of prophetic subjectivity; Gustav Hölscher offers the fullest argument for ecstatic acting as a key prophetic practice. For an overview of the history of the ecstasy or trance argument, see David L. Petersen, "Ecstasy and Role Enactment," in *"The Place Is Too Small for Us": The Israelite Prophets in Recent Scholarship*, ed. Robert P. Gordon, SBTS 5 (Winona Lake, IN: Eisenbrauns, 1995), 279.

For a performance perspective, see William Doan and Terry Giles, *Prophets, Performance, and Power: Performance Criticism of the Hebrew Bible* (New York: T. & T. Clark, 2005), 61. Yvonne Sherwood argues for understanding prophecy as a form of performance art (Sherwood, "Prophetic Performance Art"); see also Theresa Hornsby, "Ezekiel Off-Broadway," *BCT* 2, no. 1 (2006): 2.1–2.8.

The pathology argument can be traced at least to August Klostermann, "Ezechiel: Ein Beitrag zu besserer Würdigung seiner Person und seiner Schrift," *Theologische Studien und Kritiken* 50 (1877): 391–439. Also worth noting is Edwin C. Broome, "Ezekiel's Abnormal Personality," *JBL* 65, no. 3 (1946): 277–92, which argues that the prophet was a paranoid schizophrenic, and Halperin, *Seeking Ezekiel*, which offers a book-length revival of the argument.

7. Moses Maimonides, *The Guide of the Perplexed*, trans. Shlomo Pines (Chicago: University of Chicago Press, 1963), 2:46. Quoted in Friebel, *Jeremiah's and Ezekiel's Sign-Acts*, 22n31.

8. For an account of Schreber's biography, see Zvi Lothane, *In Defense of Schreber: Soul Murder and Psychiatry* (Hillsdale, NJ: Analytic, 1992).

9. Lothane notes that the German title is better translated "the great thoughts of a nervous patient" but that the English title given by the original translators persists. Ibid., 1–2.

10. Daniel Paul Schreber, *Memoirs of My Nervous Illness*, trans. Ida Macalpine and Richard A. Hunter (New York: New York Review Books, 2000), 46, 59–61. The translators of the English edition of Schreber's memoirs, Ida Macalpine and Richard A. Hunter, write, "*Entmannung*. The authorized translation of Freud (1911) uses the term 'emasculation.' We have chosen 'unmanning' because its primary meaning is 'to remove from the category of men,' which is what Schreber intended. Only its fourth definition in the Oxford English Dictionary is given as castration. Emasculation, on the other hand, has castration as its primary meaning, i.e. rendering sterile. From the pages immediately following, as well as Schreber's further text, it is quite obvious that he meant transformation by an evolutionary process into a reproductive woman which was to render him fertile. Schreber himself stresses this by usually putting 'change into a woman' in brackets after 'unmanning'" (Ibid., 447.). I have followed the translators' practice here.

11. חשמל. A gleaming substance whose precise identification remains uncertain. It is sometimes translated "amber" or "electrum".

12. Thomas Hentrich describes the "Israelites' imagination of YHWH as the perfect (male) human." Hentrich, "Masculinity and Disability in the Bible," 79.

13. See Eilberg-Schwartz, *God's Phallus*, 1 and passim; Moore, *God's Gym*, 79.

14. Sigmund Freud, "The Uncanny," in *The Uncanny*, ed. Adam Phillips, trans. David McClintock, 121–62, The Penguin Freud (New York: Penguin, 2003), 139–40; Irigaray, *Speculum of the Other Woman*, 47.

15. See Sigmund Freud, "Fetishism," in *The Complete Psychological Works of Sigmund Freud*, ed. and trans. James Strachey, vol. 21, *The Future of an Illusion, Civilization and Its Discontents, and Other Works*, 147–57 (London: Hogarth and the Institute for Psychoanalysis, 1961).

16. Following LXX. MT expands to אשר־תמצה אכול "what you have found, eat," prior to "eat this scroll"; a gloss following Jeremiah 15:16. See Walther Eichrodt, *Ezekiel: A Commentary*, OTL (Philadelphia, PA: Westminster John Knox Press, 2003), 60.

17. In a somewhat different reading, Boer describes the scene as "auto-fellatio." I would note, however, that the scroll comes to Ezekiel from Yahweh and does not appear identical with Ezekiel's own scribal productions. Boer, *Earthy Nature of the Bible*, 67–68.

18. Kamionkowski, *Gender Reversal and Cosmic Chaos*, 68.

19. Ibid.

20. Reading with LXX; MT adds אל־גוים, "to nations." See Walther Zimmerli, *Ezekiel: A Commentary on the Book of the Prophet Ezekiel: Chapters 1–24*, vol. 1, Hermeneia (Philadelphia, PA: Fortress, 1979), 89n3; Moshe Greenberg, *Ezekiel 1–20: A New Translation with Introduction and Commentary*, AYB 22 (Garden City, NY: Doubleday, 1983), 66.

21. Reading with LXX; MT begins the verse "The sons are brazen-faced and tough-hearted. I am sending you to them," a secondary expansion influenced by Isaiah and Jeremiah (Zimmerli, *Ezekiel 1–20*, 90n4.)

22. סרבים (plural; sing. סרב), likely "nettles," is a *hapax legomenon*. See Greenberg, *Ezekiel 1-20*, 66 for discussion.

23. There is also a reference here to the repeated description of the Israelites as a stiff-necked people (Exod. 32:2, 33:3, 5, 34:9; Deut. 9:6, 13; 2 Chron. 30:8)

24. Moore, *God's Gym*, 76–108.

25. For another articulation of the continuity in chapters 1–5, see Margaret S. Odell, "You Are What You Eat: Ezekiel and the Scroll," *JBL* 117, no. 2 (1998): 229–48.

26. Stone, "You Seduced Me, You Overpowered Me, and You Prevailed," 108.

27. Jan William Tarlin, "Utopia and Pornography in Ezekiel: Violence, Hope, and the Shattered Male Subject," in *Reading Bibles, Writing Bodies: Identity and the Book*, ed. Timothy K. Beal and David M. Gunn, Biblical Limits (London: Routledge, 1997), 182.

28. Ibid., 179.

29. MacKendrick, *Counterpleasures*, 102.

30. "A Medical Expert's Report to the Court of 9th December 1899 by Dr. Weber," in Schreber, *Memoirs of My Nervous Illness*, 333.

31. Schreber, *Memoirs of My Nervous Illness*, 19–20.

32. Ibid., 96 and passim.

33. Ibid., 33–37.

34. Ibid., 59–61. On the translation of "unmanning" (*Entmannung*), see note 10, above.

35. Freud's treatment of the specifics of the case is sometimes clumsy, and a number of scholars have noted that his theory of paranoia as repressed homosexuality does not grow out of Schreber's specific case, but rather seems superimposed upon it. See C. Barry Chabot, *Freud on Schreber: Psychoanalytic Theory and the Critical Act* (Amherst: University of Massachusetts Press, 1982), 34.

36. See Sigmund Freud, "Psycho-Analytic Notes on an Autobiographical Account of a Case of Paranoia (*Dementia Paranoides*) (1911)," in *The Complete Psychological Works of Sigmund Freud*, ed. and trans. James Strachey, vol 12, *The Case of Schreber, Papers on Technique, and Other Works*, 3–83, new ed. (London: Vintage, 2001); Jacques Lacan, *The Psychoses, 1955–1956* (New York: W. W. Norton, 1993); Elias Canetti, *Crowds and Power* (New York: Farrar, Straus and Giroux, 1984), 434–64; Deleuze and Guattari, *Anti-Oedipus*, 1–21; Gilles Deleuze and Félix Guattari, *A Thousand Plateaus: Capitalism and Schizophrenia*, trans. Brian Massumi (London: Continuum, 2004), 149–66, 288–89. For readings by de Certeau, Lingis, Lyotard, and others, see as well the collection by David B. Allison et al., *Psychosis and Sexual Identity: Toward a Post-Analytic View of the Schreber Case* (Albany: State University of New York Press, 1988).

37. Lucy Bregman, "Religion and Madness: Schreber's Memoirs as Personal Myth," *Journal of Religion and Health* 16, no. 2 (1977): 120.

38. Schreber, *Memoirs of My Nervous Illness*, 141–151.

39. Ibid., 258.

40. Mills, *Alterity, Pain, and Suffering in Isaiah, Jeremiah, and Ezekiel*, 104.

41. Scarry, *Body in Pain*, 47–48.

42. Ibid., 48.

43. Friebel, *Jeremiah's and Ezekiel's Sign-Acts*, 226–27; Blenkinsopp, *Ezekiel*, 37–38.

44. Kristeva, *Powers of Horror*, 3.

45. Scarry, *The Body in Pain*, 38, 53–54, and passim.

46. Ibid., 27.

47. Ibid., 12–13.

48. Ibid., 13.

49. Schreber, *Memoirs of My Nervous Illness*, 15–16.

50. Ibid., 15.

51. Stacey, *Prophetic Drama in the Old Testament*, 266.

52. Franz Kafka, "A Hunger Artist," in *Franz Kafka: The Complete Stories*, ed. Nahum N Glatzer (New York: Schocken, 1995), 268–77.

53. Schreber, *Memoirs of My Nervous Illness*, 23 and passim.

54. Daniel L. Smith-Christopher, *A Biblical Theology of Exile*, OBT (Minneapolis, MN: Fortress, 2002), 77, 76.

55. Smith-Christopher, "Ezekiel in Abu Ghraib," 149.

56. Kamionkowski, *Gender Reversal and Cosmic Chaos*, 74. Kamionkowski's reading of Schreber is perhaps too reliant on Freud's case study, though this is understandable, as Schreber is little more than an aside in her argument.

57. Schreber, *Memoirs of My Nervous Illness*, 142.

58. Eilberg-Schwartz, *God's Phallus*, 137–138.

59. Ibid., 137–196; Stephen D. Moore, *God's Beauty Parlor: And Other Queer Spaces in and around the Bible*, Contraversions (Stanford, CA: Stanford University Press, 2002), 21–89.

60. Deleuze and Guattari, *Anti-Oedipus*, 2.

61. Ibid., 2.

62. Ibid., 17.

63. Ibid., 9–15; Deleuze and Guattari, *A Thousand Plateaus*, 149–166.

64. Jonathan Kemp, "Schreber and the Penetrated Male," in *Deleuze and Queer Theory*, ed. Chrysanthi Nigianni and Merl Storr, Deleuze Connections (Edinburgh: Edinburgh University Press, 2009), 150.

65. Jill Marsden, "Cyberpsychosis: The Feminization of the Postbiological Body," in *Cyberpsychology*, ed. Ángel J. Gordo-López and Ian Parker (New York: Routledge, 1999), 69.

66. Ibid., 70.

67. Ibid., 71.

68. Ibid.; Luce Irigaray, *This Sex Which Is Not One*, trans. Catherine Porter with Carolyn Burke (Ithaca, NY: Cornell University Press, 1985). Irigaray discusses the Schreber case, with different conclusions than Marsden, in Luce Irigaray, "The Virginity of President Schreber," in *Sexuality and Medicine: Bodies, Practices, Knowledges*, ed. Paul A. Komesaroff, Philipa Rothfield, and John Wiltshire, 243–69 (Bloomington, IN: Xlibris, 2003).

69. Tarlin, "Utopia and Pornography in Ezekiel," 182.

70. Ibid.

71. Albert Spaulding Cook, *The Burden of Prophecy: Poetic Utterance in the Prophets of the Old Testament* (Carbondale: Southern Illinois University Press, 1996), 86.

72. Mills, *Alterity, Pain, and Suffering in Isaiah, Jeremiah, and Ezekiel*, 104–7; 1 Corinthians 6:19–20.

73. Christl Maier, *Daughter Zion, Mother Zion: Gender, Space, and the Sacred in Ancient Israel* (Minneapolis, MN: Fortress, 2008).

74. Ibid., 111.

75. Bennett Simon, "Ezekiel's Geometric Vision of the Restored Temple: From the Rod of His Wrath to the Reed of His Measuring," *HTR* 102, no. 4 (2009): 428.

76. Roland Boer, *Knockin' on Heaven's Door*, Biblical Limits (New York: Routledge, 1999), 107.

CHAPTER 5

1. Gerhard von Rad, *Old Testament Theology*, vol. 2, trans. D. M. G. Stalker, OTL (Louisville, KY: Westminster John Knox Press, 1965) 33n1. Luther's original phrasing is "sie haben eine seltsame Weise zu reden"; see Martin Luther, *D. Martin Luthers Werke*, Kritische Gesamtausgabe, vol. 19 (Weimar: Herman Böhlaus Nachfolger, 1897), 350.

2. Stalker thanks a "Professor Eudo C. Mason."

3. See in particular chapter 4.

4. This approach to the prophetic body invokes recent feminist and queer work on alternatives to intersectionality and identity politics. See Massumi, *Parables for the Virtual*, 8; Jasbir Puar, "Rethinking Homonationalism," *International Journal of Middle East Studies* 45, no. 2 (2013): 336–39.

5. Lee Edelman, *No Future: Queer Theory and the Death Drive*, Series Q (Durham, NC: Duke University Press, 2004), 43.

6. Ahmed, *Queer Phenomenology*, 3.

7. Tarlin, "Utopia and Pornography in Ezekiel," 176.

8. Michel Poizat, "'The Blue Note' and 'The Objectified Voice and the Vocal Object,'" *Cambridge Opera Journal* 3, no. 3 (1991): 210.

9. See further my discussion in chapter 3.

10. Cook, *Burden of Prophecy*, 1.

11. This use of women is not limited to the Bible, or to prophetic texts. Peter Brown, for example, has traced similar practices in late antique Christian texts. Peter Brown, *The Body and Society: Men, Women, and Sexual Renunciation in Early Christianity*, 2nd ed. (New York: Columbia University Press, 2008), 153. For another example, see Elizabeth A. Clark, "Ideology, History, and the Construction of 'Woman' in Late Ancient Christianity," *Journal of Early Christian Studies* 2, no. 2 (1994): 155–84.

12. Roland Boer, "Too Many Dicks at the Writing Desk, or How to Organize a Prophetic Sausage-Fest," *TS* 16, no. 1 (2010): 95–108.

13. David J. Halperin, for example, sets forth the case for Ezekiel's misogyny in *Seeking Ezekiel*. On queer biblical commentary and the erasure of women, see Schneider, "Yahwist Desires." Deryn Guest's work offers an alternate model of negotiating feminist and queer concerns; see *Beyond Feminist Biblical Studies*.

14. Irigaray, *Forgetting of Air in Martin Heidegger*, 41, 85–86. See also my chapter 1, note 67.

15. See as well Grosz, *Volatile Bodies*, 202; Schiller, "Incomplete Masculine.'" [cutting the sentence "This is discussed further in my chapter 5.

16. Yvonne Sherwood, *A Biblical Text and Its Afterlives: The Survival of Jonah in Western Culture* (Cambridge: Cambridge University Press, 2000), 15. For a number of readings of the fish's belly as the womb, see Dennis G. Shulman, "Jonah: His Story, Our Story; His Struggle, Our Struggle: Commentary on Paper by Avivah Gottlieb Zornberg," *Psychoanalytic Dialogues* 18, no. 3 (2008): 329–64.

17. Note, however, the specific reference in Jonah 2:3 (2:2 Eng.) is to בטן שאול "the belly of Sheol."

18. Eilberg-Schwartz, *God's Phallus*, 92.

19. One additional possibility for reconceiving gender in Jonah comes from Maria Kassel, who reads Jonah's time in the fish as a version of the Sumerian myth of the Descent of Inanna, thus positioning the male prophet in the role of the goddess. Maria Kassel, "Jonah: The Jonah Experience—for Women Too?," in *Feminist Biblical Interpretation: A Compendium of Critical Commentary on the Books of the Bible and Related Literature*, ed. Luise Schottroff, Marie-Theres Wacker, and Martin Rumscheidt, trans. Lisa E. Dahill, 411–20 (Grand Rapids, MI: W. B. Eerdmans, 2012).

20. I am grateful to Steven L. McKenzie and John Kaltner for conversations about Jonah, which revealed these points.

21. Ahmed, *The Promise of Happiness*, chapter 3, especially 89, 120. Compare as well Ahmed's discussion of the "feminist killjoy" (65–66) and the "angry black woman" (66–67).

22. Ibid., 13.

23. Ibid., 61, 91.

24. Ibid., 86.

25. Propp, *Exodus 1–18*, 210; see further my discussion in chapter 1.

26. Claudia V. Camp, *Wise, Strange, and Holy: The Strange Woman and the Making of the Bible*, JSOTSup 320, GCT 9 (Sheffield: Sheffield Academic Press, 2000), 253.

27. Ibid., 242.

28. Ibid., 256.

29. See Esther Fuchs, "Prophecy and the Construction of Women: Inscription and Erasure," in *A Feminist Companion to Prophets and Daniel*, ed. Athalya Brenner, FCB (Second Series) (London: Sheffield Academic Press, 2001), 54.

30. Carson, *Glass, Irony and God*, 133.

31. Camp, *Wise, Strange, and Holy*, 249, 256.

32. Judith Butler, *Undoing Gender* (New York: Routledge, 2004), 3–4.

33. Ilana Pardes, *Countertraditions in the Bible: A Feminist Approach* (Cambridge, MA: Harvard University Press, 1993), 6.
34. Virginia Woolf, *A Room of One's Own* (Orchard Park, NY: Broadview, 2001), 58. At least according to Woolf. Shakespeare's sister, including the circumstances of her death, is Woolf's invention.
35. Ahmed, *Promise of Happiness*, 8.
36. Massumi, *Parables for the Virtual*, 6–8, 22–28.
37. See Anna Hickey-Moody and Mary Lou Rassmussen, "The Sexed Subject in-between Deleuze and Butler," in *Deleuze and Queer Theory*, ed. Nigianni and Storr, 37–53.

CHAPTER 6

1. Deleuze and Guattari, *Anti-Oedipus*, 109.
2. Clover, *Men, Women, and Chain Saws*, 105.
3. Ahmed, *Queer Phenomenology*, 17, 85–86.

Bibliography

Ahmed, Sara. *Queer Phenomenology: Orientations, Objects, Others*. Durham, NC: Duke University Press, 2006.

Ahmed, Sara. *The Cultural Politics of Emotion*. 2nd ed. New York: Routledge, 2014.

Ahmed, Sara. *The Promise of Happiness*. Durham, NC: Duke University Press, 2010.

Albright, W. F. "The 'Natural Force' of Moses in the Light of Ugaritic," *BASOR*, no. 94 (April 1944): 32–35.

Allison, David B., Prado De Oliveira, Mark S. Roberts, and Allen S. Weiss. *Psychosis and Sexual Identity: Toward a Post-Analytic View of the Schreber Case*. Albany: State University of New York Press, 1988.

Amsler, Samuel. "Les prophètes et la communication par les actes." In *Werden und Wirken des altes Testament: Festschrift für Claus Westermann Zum 70. Geburtstag*, edited by Ranier Albertz, 194–201. Göttingen: Vandenhoeck und Ruprecht, 1980.

Andersen, Francis I., and David Noel Freedman. *Hosea*. AYB 24. Garden City, NY: Doubleday, 1996.

Avalos, Hector, Sarah J. Melcher, and Jeremy Schipper, eds. *This Abled Body: Rethinking Disabilities in Biblical Studies*. SBLSS 55. Atlanta, GA: SBL, 2007.

Batten, Alicia J. "Clothing and Adornment." *BTB* 40, no. 3 (2010): 148–59.

Bauer-Levesque, Angela. *Gender in the Book of Jeremiah: A Feminist-Literary Reading*. SiBL 5. New York: P. Lang, 1999.

Baumann, Gerlinde. *Love and Violence: Marriage as Metaphor for the Relationship Between YHWH and Israel in the Prophetic Books*. Collegeville, MN: Liturgical Press, 2003.

Becker, Eve-Marie, and Jan Dochhorn. *Trauma and Traumatization in Individual and Collective Dimensions: Insights from Biblical Studies and Beyond*. Göttingen: Vandenhoeck und Ruprecht, 2014.

Berger, John. *Ways of Seeing*. London: Penguin, 1990.

Bird, Phyllis. "'To Play the Harlot': An Inquiry into an Old Testament Metaphor." In *Gender and Difference in Ancient Israel*, edited by Peggy L. Day, 75–94. Minneapolis, MN: Fortress, 1989.

Blake, William. *The Complete Poetry and Prose of William Blake*. Translated by David V Erdman, Commentary by Harold Bloom. Revised edition. New York: Random House, Inc., 1988.

Blatty, William Peter. *The Exorcist*. New York: Harper, 1971.

Blenkinsopp, Joseph. *Ezekiel*. Interpretation. Louisville, KY: Westminster John Knox Press, 1990.

Blenkinsopp, Joseph. *Isaiah 40–55*. AYB 19A. New Haven, CT: Yale University Press, 2002.

Block, Daniel Isaac. *The Book of Ezekiel, Chapters 25–48*. NICOT. Grand Rapids, MI: W. B. Eerdmans, 1997.

Boer, Roland. *Knockin' on Heaven's Door: The Bible and Popular Culture*. Biblical Limits. New York: Routledge, 1999.

Boer, Roland. *The Earthy Nature of the Bible: Fleshly Readings of Sex, Masculinity, and Carnality*. BibleWorld. New York: Palgrave Macmillan, 2012.

Boer, Roland. "Of Fine Wine, Incense, and Spices: The Unstable Masculine Hegemony of the Book of Chronicles." In *Men and Masculinity in the Hebrew Bible and Beyond*, edited by Ovidiu Creangă, 20–35. BMW 33. Sheffield: Sheffield Phoenix Press, 2010a.

Boer, Roland. "Too Many Dicks at the Writing Desk, or How to Organize a Prophetic Sausage-Fest." *TS* 16, no. 1 (2010b): 95–108.

Boer, Roland. "Yahweh as Top: A Lost Targum." In *Queer Commentary and the Hebrew Bible*, edited by Ken Stone, 75–105. JSOTSup 334. Cleveland, OH: Pilgrim, 2001.

Borch-Jacobsen, Mikkel. *Remembering Anna O.: A Century of Mystification*. New York: Routledge, 1996.

Bordo, Susan. *Unbearable Weight: Feminism, Western Culture, and the Body*. Berkeley: University of California Press, 1993.

Boyarin, Daniel. "Are There Any Jews in 'The History of Sexuality'?" *Journal of the History of Sexuality* 5, no. 3 (1995): 333–55.

Boyarin, Daniel. "Freud's Baby, Fliess's Maybe: Male Hysteria, Homophobia, and the Invention of the Jewish Man." *GLQ: A Journal of Lesbian and Gay Studies* 2 (1995): 115–47.

Boyarin, Daniel. *Unheroic Conduct the Rise of Heterosexuality and the Invention of the Jewish Man*. Berkeley: University of California Press, 1997.

Bregman, Lucy. "Religion and Madness: Schreber's Memoirs as Personal Myth." *Journal of Religion and Health* 16, no. 2 (1977): 119–35.

Brenner, Athalya, ed. *A Feminist Companion to Prophets and Daniel*. FCB (Second Series). Sheffield: Sheffield Academic Press, 2002.

Brenner, Athalya, ed. *A Feminist Companion to the Latter Prophets*. FCB (First Series). Sheffield: Sheffield Academic Press, 1995.

Brenner, Athalya. *The Intercourse of Knowledge: On Gendering Desire and "Sexuality" in the Hebrew Bible*. BIS 26. Leiden: Brill, 1997.

Brenner, Athalya. "Pornoprophetics Revisited: Some Additional Reflections." *JSOT* 21, no. 70 (1996): 63–86.

Britt, Brian. *Rewriting Moses: The Narrative Eclipse of the Text*. JSOTSup 402, GCT 14. London and New York: T. & T. Clark, 2004.

Broome, Edwin C. "Ezekiel's Abnormal Personality." *JBL* 65, no. 3 (1946): 277–92.

Brown, Peter. *The Body and Society: Men, Women, and Sexual Renunciation in Early Christianity*. 2nd ed. New York: Columbia University Press, 2008.

Burrus, Virginia. "Mapping as Metamorphosis: Initial Reflections on Gender and Ancient Religious Discourses." In *Mapping Gender in Ancient Religious Discourses*, edited by Todd Penner and Caroline Vander Stichele, 1–10. BIS 84. Boston: Brill, 2007.

Butler, Judith. *Undoing Gender*. New York: Routledge, 2004.

Camp, Claudia V. *Wise, Strange, and Holy: The Strange Woman and the Making of the Bible*. JSOTSup 320. Gender, Culture, Theory 9. Sheffield: Sheffield Academic Press, 2000.

Canetti, Elias. *Crowds and Power*. New York: Farrar, Straus and Giroux, 1984.

Carson, Anne. *Glass, Irony and God*. New York: New Directions, 1995.

Chabot, C. Barry. *Freud on Schreber: Psychoanalytic Theory and the Critical Act*. Amherst: University of Massachusetts Press, 1982.

Chapman, Cynthia R. *The Gendered Language of Warfare in the Israelite-Assyrian Encounter*. HSM 62. Winona Lake, IN: Eisenbrauns, 2004.

Cixous, Hélène, and Catherine Clément. *The Newly Born Woman*. Minneapolis: University of Minnesota Press, 1986.

Claassens, L. Juliana M. *Mourner, Mother, Midwife: Reimagining God's Delivering Presence in the Old Testament*. Louisville, KY: Westminster John Knox Press, 2012.

Clark, Elizabeth A. "Ideology, History, and the Construction of 'Woman' in Late Ancient Christianity." *Journal of Early Christian Studies* 2, no. 2 (1994): 155–84.

Clines, David J. A. "Dancing and Shining at Sinai: Playing the Man in Exodus 32–34." In *Men and Masculinity in the Hebrew Bible and Beyond*, edited by Ovidiu Creangă. BMW 33. Sheffield: Sheffield Phoenix Press, 2010.

Clines, David J. A. "He-Prophets: Masculinity as a Problem for the Hebrew Prophets and Their Interpreters." In *Sense and Sensitivity: Essays on Reading the Bible in Memory of Robert Carroll*, edited by Robert P. Carroll, Alastair G. Hunter, and Philip R. Davies, 311–27. JSOTSup 348. Sheffield: Sheffield Academic Press, 2002.

Clines, David J. A. *Interested Parties: The Ideology of Writers and Readers of the Hebrew Bible*. Sheffield: Sheffield Academic Press, 1995.

Clines, David J. A., and David M. Gunn. "Form, Occasion and Redaction in Jeremiah 20." *ZAW* 88, no. 3 (2009): 390–409.

Clines, David J. A., and David M. Gunn. "'You Tried to Persuade Me' and 'Violence! Outrage!' in Jeremiah XX 7–8." *VT* 28, no. 1 (1978): 20–27.

Clover, Carol J. *Men, Women, and Chain Saws: Gender in the Modern Horror Film.* Princeton, NJ: Princeton University Press, 1993.

Connell, Robert W., and James W. Messerschmidt. "Hegemonic Masculinity: Rethinking the Concept." *Gender and Society* 19, no. 6 (2005): 829–59.

Conway, Colleen M. *Behold the Man: Jesus and Greco-Roman Masculinity.* New York: Oxford University Press, 2008.

Cook, Albert Spaulding. *The Burden of Prophecy: Poetic Utterance in the Prophets of the Old Testament.* Carbondale: Southern Illinois University Press, 1996.

Creangă, Ovidiu, ed. *Men and Masculinity in the Hebrew Bible and Beyond.* BMW 33. Sheffield: Sheffield Phoenix Press, 2010.

Creangă, Ovidiu, and Peter-Ben Smit, eds. *Biblical Masculinities Foregrounded.* HBM 62. Sheffield: Sheffield Phoenix Press, 2014.

Creed, Barbara. *The Monstrous-Feminine: Film, Feminism, Psychoanalysis.* Popular Fictions Series. New York: Routledge and Kegan Paul, 1993.

Davis, C. J. Patrick. "Jeremiah, Masculinity and His Portrayal as the 'Lamenting Prophet.'" In *Men and Masculinity in the Hebrew Bible and Beyond*, edited by Ovidiu Creangă, 189–210. BMW 33. Sheffield: Sheffield Phoenix Press, 2010.

Decker, Hannah S. *Freud, Dora, and Vienna 1900.* New York: Free Press, 1991.

De Lauretis, Teresa. "Queer Theory: Lesbian and Gay Sexualities: An Introduction." Edited by Teresa de Lauretis. *Differences: A Journal of Feminist Cultural Studies* 3, no. 2 (1991): iii–xviii.

Deleuze, Gilles, and Félix Guattari. *Anti-Oedipus: Capitalism and Schizophrenia.* Translated by Robert Hurley and Mark Seem. Harmondsworth: Penguin, 2009.

Deleuze, Gilles, and Félix Guattari. *A Thousand Plateaus: Capitalism and Schizophrenia.* Translated by Brian Massumi. London: Continuum, 2004.

Deutsch, Felix. "A Footnote to Freud's 'Fragment of an Analysis of a Case of Hysteria.'" In *In Dora's Case: Freud—Hysteria—Feminism*, edited by Charles Bernheimer and Claire Kahane, 35–43. Gender and Culture. New York: Columbia University Press, 1985.

Diamond, A. R. Pete. *The Confessions of Jeremiah in Context: Scenes of Prophetic Drama.* JSOTSup 45. Sheffield: Sheffield Academic Press, 1987.

DiPalma, Brian C. "Deconstructing Masculinity in Exodus 1–4." In *Men and Masculinity in the Hebrew Bible and Beyond*, edited by Ovidiu Creangă, 36–53. Sheffield: Sheffield Phoenix Press, 2010.

Doan, William, and Terry Giles. *Prophets, Performance, and Power: Performance Criticism of the Hebrew Bible.* New York: T. & T. Clark, 2005.

Dolar, Mladen. *A Voice and Nothing More.* Cambridge, MA: MIT Press, 2006.

Dworkin, Andrea. *Pornography: Men Possessing Women.* New York: Perigee, 1981.

Dworkin, Andrea, and Catharine A. MacKinnon. *Pornography and Civil Rights: A New Day for Women's Equality.* Minneapolis, MN: Organizing Against Pornography, 1988.

Edelman, Lee. *No Future: Queer Theory and the Death Drive.* Series Q. Durham, NC: Duke University Press, 2004.

Eichrodt, Walther. *Ezekiel: A Commentary.* OTL. Philadelphia, PA: Westminster John Knox Press, 2003.

Eilberg-Schwartz, Howard. *God's Phallus: And Other Problems for Men and Monotheism.* Boston: Beacon, 1995.

Evans, Martha Noel. *Fits and Starts: A Genealogy of Hysteria in Modern France.* Ithaca, NY: Cornell University Press, 1991.

Fohrer, Georg. *Die Symbolischen Handlungen der Propheten.* AThANT 25. Zürich: Zwingli-Verlag, 1953.

Fontaine, Carole R. "'Be Men, O Philistines' (1 Samuel 4:9): Iconographic Representations and Reflections on Female Gender as Disability in the Ancient World." In *This Abled Body*, edited by Hector Avalos, Sarah J. Melcher, and Jeremy Schipper, 61–72. SBLSS 55. Atlanta, GA: SBL, 2007.

Freeland, Cynthia. *The Naked and the Undead: Evil and the Appeal of Horror.* Thinking through Cinema. Boulder, CO: Westview, 2009.

Freud, Sigmund. *Dora: An Analysis of a Case of Hysteria.* Edited by Philip Rieff. New York: Collier, 1963.

Freud, Sigmund. "Fetishism." In *The Complete Psychological Works of Sigmund Freud*, edited and translated by James Strachey, vol. 21, *The Future of an Illusion, Civilization and Its Discontents, and Other Works*, 147–57. London: Hogarth and the Institute for Psychoanalysis, 1961.

Freud, Sigmund. "Psycho-Analytic Notes on an Autobiographical Account of a Case of Paranoia (*Dementia Paranoides*) (1911)." In *The Complete Psychological Works of Sigmund Freud*, edited and translated by James Strachey, vol. 12, *The Case of Schreber, Papers on Technique, and Other Works*, 3–83. New edition. London: Vintage, 2001.

Freud, Sigmund. "The Uncanny." In *The Uncanny*, edited by Adam Phillips, translated by David McClintock, 121–62. The Penguin Freud. New York: Penguin, 2003.

Freud, Sigmund, and Josef Breuer. *Studies in Hysteria.* Translated by Nicola Luckhurst. New York: Penguin, 2004.

Freud, Sigmund, J. Moussaieff Masson, and Wilhelm Fliess. *The Complete Letters of Sigmund Freud to Wilhelm Fliess, 1887–1904.* Cambridge, MA: Belknap Press of Harvard University Press, 1985.

Friebel, Kelvin G. *Jeremiah's and Ezekiel's Sign-Acts: Rhetorical Nonverbal Communication.* JSOTSup 283. Sheffield: Sheffield Academic Press, 1999.

Friedkin, William, dir. *The Exorcist.* Horror. Warner Brothers, 1973.

Fuchs. "Prophecy and the Construction of Women: Inscription and Erasure." In *A Feminist Companion to Prophets and Daniel*, edited by Athalya Brenner, 54–69. FCB (Second Series). London: Sheffield Academic Press, 2001.

Galambush, Julie. *Jerusalem in the Book of Ezekiel: The City as Yahweh's Wife.* SBLDS 130. Atlanta, GA: Scholars, 1992.

Gallop, Jane. *The Daughter's Seduction: Feminism and Psychoanalysis*. Ithaca, NY: Cornell University Press, 1984.

George, Mark K. "Masculinity and Its Regimentation in Deuteronomy." In *Men and Masculinity in the Hebrew Bible and Beyond*, edited by Ovidiu Creangă, 64–82. Sheffield: Sheffield Phoenix Press, 2010.

Goldstein, Jan. "The Uses of Male Hysteria: Medical and Literary Discourse in Nineteenth-Century France." *Representations* 34 (spring 1991): 134–65.

Grant, Barry Keith, ed. *The Dread of Difference: Gender and the Horror Film*. 2nd ed. Texas Film and Media Studies. Austin: University of Texas Press, 2015.

Gravett, Sandie. "Reading 'Rape' in the Hebrew Bible: A Consideration of Language." *JSOT* 28, no. 3 (2004): 279–99.

Graybill, Rhiannon. "'Hear and Give Ear!': The Soundscape of Jeremiah." *JSOT* 40, no. 4 (2016): 467–90.

Graybill, Rhiannon. "Surpassing the Love of Women: From Feminism to Queer Theory in Biblical Studies." In *Feminist Interpretation of the Hebrew Bible in Retrospect. III. Methods*, edited by Susanne Scholz, 304–25. Sheffield: Sheffield Phoenix Press, 2016.

Graybill, Rhiannon. "Uncanny Bodies, Impossible Knowledge and Somatic Excess in Isaiah 29." *BCT* 7, no. 1 (2011): 16–28.

Greenberg, Moshe. *Ezekiel 1–20: A New Translation with Introduction and Commentary*. AYB 22. Garden City, NY: Doubleday, 1983.

Grosz, Elizabeth A. *Volatile Bodies: Toward a Corporeal Feminism*. Bloomington: Indiana University Press, 1994.

Guest, Deryn. *Beyond Feminist Biblical Studies*. BMW 47. Sheffield: Sheffield Phoenix Press, 2012.

Guest, Deryn. *When Deborah Met Jael: Lesbian Biblical Hermeneutics*. London: SCM, 2005.

Haddox, Susan E. "(E)Masculinity in Hosea's Political Rhetoric." In *Israel's Prophets and Israel's Past: Essays on the Relationship of Prophetic Texts and Israelite History in Honor of John H. Hayes*, edited by John Haralson Hayes, Brad E. Kelle, and Megan Bishop Moore, 174–200. LHB/OTS 446. New York: T. & T. Clark, 2006.

Haddox, Susan E. "Engaging Images in the Prophets: Feminist Scholarship on the Book of the Twelve." In *Feminist Interpretation of the Hebrew Bible in Retrospect. 1. Biblical Books*, edited by Susanne Scholz, 170–91. RRBS 5. Sheffield: Sheffield Phoenix Press, 2013.

Haddox, Susan E. "Favoured Sons and Subordinate Masculinities." In *Men and Masculinity in the Hebrew Bible and Beyond*, edited by Ovidiu Creangă, 2–19. Sheffield: Sheffield Phoenix Press, 2010.

Haddox, Susan E. *Metaphor and Masculinity in Hosea*. SiBL 141. New York: Peter Lang, 2011.

Halberstam, Judith. *The Queer Art of Failure*. Durham, NC: Duke University Press, 2011.

Halperin, David J. *Seeking Ezekiel: Text and Psychology*. University Park: Pennsylvania State University Press, 1993.

Halperin, David M. "Why Is Diotima a Woman?" In *One Hundred Years of Homosexuality: And Other Essays on Greek Love.*, 113–51. New Ancient World. New York: Routledge, 1990.

Hartman, Geoffrey. "Jeremiah 20:7–12: A Literary Response." In *The Biblical Mosaic: Changing Perspectives*, edited by Robert Polzin and Eugene Rothman, 184–95. SBLSS. Philadelphia, PA: Fortress, 1982.

Hays, Christopher B. "'Lest Ye Perish in the Way': Ritual and Kinship in Exodus 4:24–26." *HS* 48 (2007): 39–54.

Hentrich, Thomas. "Masculinity and Disability in the Bible." In *This Abled Body: Rethinking Disabilities in Biblical Studies*, edited by Hector Avalos, Sarah J. Melcher, and Jeremy Schipper, 73–87. SBLSS 55. Atlanta, GA: SBL, 2007.

Hickey-Moody, Anna, and Mary Lou Rassmussen. "The Sexed Subject in-between Deleuze and Butler." In *Deleuze and Queer Theory*, edited by Chrysanthi Nigianni and Merl Storr, 37–53. Deleuze Connections. Edinburgh: Edinburgh University Press, 2009.

Holladay, William Lee. *Jeremiah: A Commentary on the Book of the Prophet Jeremiah.* Hermeneia. Philadelphia, PA: Fortress, 1986.

Hollywood, Amy. "'That Glorious Slit': Irigaray and the Medieval Devotion to Christ's Side Wound." *Luce Irigaray and Premodern Culture: Thresholds of History*, edited by Elizabeth D. Harvey and Theresa Krier, 105–25. Abingdon and New York: Routledge, 2004.

Hornsby, Theresa. "Ezekiel Off-Broadway." *BCT* 2, no. 1 (2006): 2.1–2.8.

Irigaray, Luce. *The Forgetting of Air in Martin Heidegger.* Translated by Mary Beth Mader. Austin: University of Texas Press, 1999.

Irigaray, Luce. *Marine Lover of Friedrich Nietzsche.* Translated by Gillian C. Gill. New York: Columbia University Press, 1991.

Irigaray, Luce. *Sexes and Genealogies.* Translated by Gillian C. Gill. New York: Columbia University Press, 1993.

Irigaray, Luce. *Speculum of the Other Woman.* Translated by Gillian C. Gill. Ithaca, NY: Cornell University Press, 1985.

Irigaray, Luce. *This Sex Which Is Not One.* Translated by Catherine Porter with Carolyn Burke. Ithaca, NY: Cornell University Press, 1985.

Irigaray, Luce. "The Virginity of President Schreber." In *Sexuality and Medicine: Bodies, Practices, Knowledges*, edited by Paul A. Komesaroff, Philipa Rothfield, and John Wiltshire, 243–69. Bloomington, IN: Xlibris, 2003.

Jennings, Theodore W. *Jacob's Wound: Homoerotic Narrative in the Literature of Ancient Israel.* New York: Continuum, 2005.

Junior, Nyasha, and Jeremy Schipper. "Mosaic Disability and Identity in Exodus 4:10; 6:12, 30." *BibInt* 16, no. 5 (2008): 428–41.

Franz Kafka, "A Hunger Artist." In *Franz Kafka: The Complete Stories*, edited by Nahum N. Glatzer, 268–77. New York: Schocken, 1995.

Kaiser, Barbara Bakke. "Poet as 'Female Impersonator': The Image of Daughter Zion as Speaker in Biblical Poems of Suffering." *JR* 67, no. 2 (1987): 164–82.

Kamionkowski, S. Tamar. *Gender Reversal and Cosmic Chaos: A Study in the Book of Ezekiel.* JSOTSup 368. Sheffield: Sheffield Academic Press, 2003.

Kassel, Maria. "Jonah: The Jonah Experience—for Women Too?" In *Feminist Biblical Interpretation: A Compendium of Critical Commentary on the Books of the Bible and Related Literature*, edited by Luise Schottroff, Marie-Theres Wacker, and Martin Rumscheidt, translated by Lisa E. Dahill, 411–20. Grand Rapids, MI: W. B. Eerdmans, 2012.

Keefe, Alice A. *Woman's Body and the Social Body in Hosea 1–2.* JSOTSup 338; GCT 14. London: Sheffield Academic Press, 2001.

Kelso, Julie. "Reading the Silence of Women in Genesis 34." In *Redirected Travel: Alternative Journeys and Places in Biblical Studies*, edited by Roland Boer and Edgar W. Conrad, 85–109. JSOTSup 382. New York: T. & T. Clark International, 2003.

Kemp, Jonathan. "Schreber and the Penetrated Male." In *Deleuze and Queer Theory*, edited by Chrysanthi Nigianni and Merl Storr, 150–67. Deleuze Connections. Edinburgh: Edinburgh University Press, 2009.

King, Helen. "Once upon a Text: Hysteria from Hippocrates." In *Hysteria beyond Freud*, edited by Sander L. Gilman, 3–40. Berkeley: University of California Press, 1993.

Klostermann, August. "Ezechiel: Ein Beitrag zu besserer Würdigung seiner Person und seiner Schrift." *Theologische Studien und Kritiken* 50 (1877): 391–439.

Koch, Timothy R. "Cruising as Methodology: Homoeroticism and the Scriptures." In *Queer Commentary and the Hebrew Bible*, edited by Ken Stone, 169–80. JSOTSup 334. Cleveland, OH: Pilgrim, 2001.

Kosmala, Hans. "The 'Bloody Husband.'" *VT* 12, no. 1 (1962): 14–28.

Kristeva, Julia. *Powers of Horror: An Essay on Abjection.* European Perspectives. New York: Columbia University Press, 1982.

Lacan, Jacques. *The Psychoses, 1955–1956.* New York: W. W. Norton, 1993.

Laplanche, Jean, and J.-B. Pontalis. *The Language of Psycho-Analysis.* New York: W. W. Norton, 1973.

Levin, S. "The Speech Defect of Moses." *Journal of the Royal Society of Medicine* 85, no. 10 (1992): 632–33.

Lothane, Zvi. *In Defense of Schreber: Soul Murder and Psychiatry.* Hillsdale, NJ: Analytic, 1992.

Luzzatto, S. D. *Commentary to the Pentateuch.* Tel Aviv: Dvir, 1965.

MacKendrick, Karmen. *Counterpleasures.* SUNY Series in Postmodern Culture. Albany: State University of New York Press, 1999.

Macwilliam, Stuart. "Ideologies of Male Beauty and the Hebrew Bible." *BibInt* 17, no. 3 (2009): 265–87.

Macwilliam, Stuart. *Queer Theory and the Prophetic Marriage Metaphor in the Hebrew Bible.* BibleWorld. Sheffield and Oakville, CT: Equinox, 2011.

Maier, Christl. *Daughter Zion, Mother Zion: Gender, Space, and the Sacred in Ancient Israel*. Minneapolis, MN: Fortress, 2008.

Maimonides, Moses. *The Guide of the Perplexed*. Translated by Shlomo Pines. 2 vols. Chicago: University of Chicago Press, 1963.

Marcus, Michelle I. "Dressed to Kill: Women and Pins in Early Iran." *Oxford Art Journal* 17, no. 2 (1994): 3–15.

Marcus, Steven. "Freud and Dora: Story, History, Case History." In *In Dora's Case: Freud—Hysteria—Feminism*, edited by Charles Bernheimer and Claire Kahane, 56–92. Gender and Culture. New York: Columbia University Press, 1985.

Marks, Herbert. "On Prophetic Stammering." In *The Book and the Text: The Bible and Literary Theory*, edited by Regina Schwartz, 60–80. Oxford: Blackwell, 1990.

Marsden, Jill. "Cyberpsychosis: The Feminization of the Postbiological Body." In *Cyberpsychology*, edited by Ángel J. Gordo-López and Ian Parker, 59–76. New York: Routledge, 1999.

Massumi, Brian. *A User's Guide to Capitalism and Schizophrenia: Deviations from Deleuze and Guattari*. Cambridge, MA: MIT Press, 1992.

Massumi, Brian. *Parables for the Virtual: Movement, Affect, Sensation*. Durham, NC: Duke University Press, 2002.

Massumi, Brian. *The Power at the End of the Economy*. Durham, NC: Duke University Press, 2014.

McKane, William. *A Critical and Exegetical Commentary on Jeremiah. Commentary on Jeremiah XXVI–LII*. ICC. Edinburgh: T. & T. Clark, 1996.

Micale, Mark S. *Hysterical Men: The Hidden History of Male Nervous Illness*. Cambridge, MA: Harvard University Press, 2009.

Milgrom, Jacob. *Leviticus 1–16: A New Translation with Introduction and Commentary*. AYB 3. New York: Doubleday, 1991.

Miller, Isaac. "St. Augustine, the Narrative Self, and the Invention of Fiction." *Qui Parle* 8, no. 2 (1995): 54–82.

Mills, Mary E. *Alterity, Pain, and Suffering in Isaiah, Jeremiah, and Ezekiel*. LHB/OTS 479. New York: T. & T. Clark, 2007.

Moi, Toril. "Representation of Patriarchy: Sexuality and Epistemology in Freud's 'Dora.'" *Feminist Review* 9 (autumn 1981): 60–74.

Moore, Stephen D. *God's Beauty Parlor: And Other Queer Spaces in and around the Bible*. Contraversions. Stanford, CA: Stanford University Press, 2002.

Moore, Stephen D. *God's Gym: Divine Male Bodies of the Bible*. New York: Routledge, 1996.

Moore, Stephen D., and Janice Capel Anderson, eds. *New Testament Masculinities*. SBLSS 45. Atlanta, GA: SBL, 2003.

O'Connor, Kathleen M. *The Confessions of Jeremiah: Their Interpretation and Their Role in Chapters 1–25*. SBLDS 94. Atlanta, GA: Scholars, 1987.

Odell, Margaret S. "You Are What You Eat: Ezekiel and the Scroll." *JBL* 117, no. 2 (1998): 229–48.

Olyan, Saul M. *Disability in the Hebrew Bible: Interpreting Mental and Physical Differences*. New York: Cambridge University Press, 2008.

Overholt, Thomas W. "Seeing Is Believing: The Social Setting of Prophetic Acts of Power." *JSOT* 7, no. 23 (1982): 3–31.

Pardes, Ilana. *Countertraditions in the Bible: A Feminist Approach*. Cambridge, MA: Harvard University Press, 1993.

Petersen, David L. "Ecstasy and Role Enactment." In *"The Place Is Too Small for Us": The Israelite Prophets in Recent Scholarship*, edited by Robert P. Gordon, 279–88. SBTS 5. Winona Lake, IN: Eisenbrauns, 1995.

Pinedo, Isabel Cristina. *Recreational Terror: Women and the Pleasures of Horror Film Viewing*. Interruptions. Albany: State University of New York Press, 1997.

Poizat, Michel. "'The Blue Note' and 'The Objectified Voice and the Vocal Object.'" *Cambridge Opera Journal* 3, no. 03 (1991): 195–211.

Propp, William H. C. *Exodus 1–18*. AYB 2. New Haven, CT: Yale University Press, 1999.

Propp, William H. C. "That Bloody Bridegroom (Exodus IV 24–6)." *VT* 43, no. 4 (1993): 495–518.

Puar, Jasbir. "Rethinking Homonationalism." *International Journal of Middle East Studies* 45, no. 2 (2013): 336–39.

Puar, Jasbir. *Terrorist Assemblages: Homonationalism in Queer Times*. Durham, NC: Duke University Press, 2007.

Ramas, Maria. "Freud's Dora, Dora's Hysteria: The Negation of a Woman's Rebellion." *Feminist Studies* 6, no. 3 (1980): 472–510.

Raphael, Rebecca. *Biblical Corpora: Representations of Disability in Hebrew Biblical Literature*. LHB/OTS 445. New York: T. & T. Clark, 2008.

Reeves, Christopher. "Breuer, Freud and the Case of Anna O: A Re-Examination." *Journal of Child Psychotherapy* 8, no. 2 (1982): 203–14.

Rendsburg, Gary A. "Hebrew Philological Notes (I)." *HS* 40, no. 1 (1999): 27–32.

Robinson, Bernard P. "Israel and Amalek : The Context of Exodus 17:8–16." *JSOT* 10, no. 32 (1985): 15–22.

Sanders, Seth L. "Old Light on Moses' Shining Face." *VT* 52, no. 3 (2002): 400–406.

Scarry, Elaine. *The Body in Pain: The Making and Unmaking of the World*. New York: Oxford University Press, 1987.

Schiller, Britt-Marie. "The Incomplete Masculine: Engendering the Masculine of Sexual Difference." In *Thinking with Irigaray*, edited by Mary C. Rawlinson, Sabrina L. Horn, and Serene J. Khader, 131–51. SUNY Series in Gender Theory. Albany: State University of New York Press, 2012.

Schipper, Jeremy. *Disability Studies and the Hebrew Bible: Figuring Mephibosheth in the David Story*. LHB/OTS 441. London: T. & T. Clark, 2009.

Schneider, Laurel C. "Yahwist Desires: Imagining Divinity Queerly." In *Queer Commentary and the Hebrew Bible*, edited by Ken Stone, 210–27. JSOTSup 334. Cleveland, OH: Pilgrim, 2001.

Schreber, Daniel Paul. *Memoirs of My Nervous Illness*. Translated by Ida Macalpine and Robert A. Hunter. New York: New York Review, 2000.

Schwaber, Evelyne Albrecht. *The Transference in Psychotherapy: Clinical Management.* New York: International Universities Press, 1985.

Sedgwick, Eve Kosofsky. *Touching Feeling: Affect, Pedagogy, Performativity.* Series Q. Durham, NC: Duke University Press, 2002.

Setel, T. Drorah. "Prophets and Pornography: Female Sexual Imagery in Hosea." In *Feminist Interpretation of the Bible,* edited by Letty M. Russell, 85–95. Louisville, KY: Westminster John Knox Press, 1985.

Shell, Marc. *Stutter.* Cambridge, MA: Harvard University Press, 2005.

Shemesh, Yael. "'Do Not Bare Your Heads and Do Not Rend Your Clothes' (Leviticus 10:6)." In *Leviticus and Numbers,* edited by Athalya Brenner and Archie Chi Chung Lee, 33–54. Texts @ Contexts. Minneapolis, MN: Fortress, 2013.

Sherwood, Yvonne. *A Biblical Text and Its Afterlives: The Survival of Jonah in Western Culture.* Cambridge: Cambridge University Press, 2000.

Sherwood, Yvonne. "Boxing Gomer: Controlling the Deviant Woman in Hosea 1–3." In *A Feminist Companion to the Latter Prophets,* edited by Athalya Brenner, 101–25. FCB (First Series). Sheffield: Sheffield Academic Press, 1995.

Sherwood, Yvonne. "Prophetic Performance Art." *BCT* 2, no. 1 (2006): 1–4.

Sherwood, Yvonne. *The Prostitute and the Prophet: Hosea's Marriage in Literary-Theoretical Perspective.* JSOTSup 212; GCT 2. Sheffield: Sheffield Academic Press, 1996.

Showalter, Elaine. "Critical Cross-Dressing: Male Feminists and the Woman of the Year." *Raritan* 3, no. 2 (1983): 130–49.

Showalter, Elaine. "On Hysterical Narrative." *Narrative* 1, no. 1 (1993): 24–35.

Showalter, Elaine. *The Female Malady: Women, Madness, and English Culture, 1830–1980.* New York: Pantheon, 1985.

Shulman, Dennis G. "Jonah: His Story, Our Story; His Struggle, Our Struggle: Commentary on Paper by Avivah Gottlieb Zornberg." *Psychoanalytic Dialogues* 18, no. 3 (2008): 329–64.

Simon, Bennett. "Ezekiel's Geometric Vision of the Restored Temple: From the Rod of His Wrath to the Reed of His Measuring." *HTR* 102, no. 4 (2009): 411–38.

Smith-Christopher, Daniel L. *A Biblical Theology of Exile.* OBT. Minneapolis, MN: Fortress, 2002.

Smith-Christopher, Daniel L. "Ezekiel in Abu Ghraib: Rereading Ezekiel 16:37–39 in the Context of Imperial Conquest." In *Ezekiel's Hierarchical World: Wrestling with a Tiered Reality,* edited by Stephen L. Cook and Corrine L. Patton. SBLSym, no. 31. Atlanta, GA: SBL, 2004.

Stacey, David. *Prophetic Drama in the Old Testament.* London: Epworth, 1990.

Stökl, Jonathan, and Corrine L. Carvalho. *Prophets Male and Female: Gender and Prophecy in the Hebrew Bible, the Eastern Mediterranean, and the Ancient Near East.* AIL 15. Atlanta, GA: SBL, 2013.

Stol, M. "Women in Mesopotamia." *Journal of the Economic and Social History of the Orient* 38, no. 2 (1995): 123–44.

Stol, Marten, and F. A. M Wiggermann. *Birth in Babylonia and the Bible: Its Mediterranean Setting.* Cuneiform Monographs 14. Groningen: Styx, 2000.

Stone, Ken. *Practicing Safer Texts: Food, Sex and Bible in Queer Perspective.* Queering Theology Series. London: T & T Clark International, 2004.

Stone, Ken. "'You Seduced Me, You Overpowered Me, and You Prevailed': Religious Experience and Homoerotic Sadomasochism in Jeremiah." In *Patriarchs, Prophets and Other Villains*, edited by Lisa Isherwood, 101–9. Gender, Theology, and Spirituality. London: Equinox, 2007.

Strossen, Nadine. "A Feminist Critique of 'the' Feminist Critique of Pornography." *Virginia Law Review* 79, no. 5 (1993): 1099–1190.

Tarlin, Jan William. "Utopia and Pornography in Ezekiel: Violence, Hope, and the Shattered Male Subject." In *Reading Bibles, Writing Bodies: Identity and the Book*, edited by Timothy K. Beal and David M Gunn, 175–83. Biblical Limits. London: Routledge, 1997.

Tigay, Jeffrey. "'Heavy of Mouth' and 'Heavy of Tongue': On Moses' Speech Difficulty." *BASOR*, no. 231 (October 1978): 57–67.

von Rad, Gerhard. *Old Testament Theology*, vol. 2. Translated by D. M. G. Stalker. OTL. Louisville, KY: Westminster John Knox Press, 1965.

Washington, Harold C. "Violence and the Construction of Gender in the Hebrew Bible: A New Historicist Approach 1." *BibInt* 5, no. 4 (1997): 324–63.

Weems, Renita J. *Battered Love: Marriage, Sex, and Violence in the Hebrew Prophets.* OBT. Minneapolis, MN: Fortress, 1995.

Wildberger, Hans. *Isaiah 13–27: A Commentary.* ContC. Minneapolis, MN: Fortress, 1997.

Wolff, Hans Walter, *Hosea: A Commentary on the Book of the Prophet Hosea*, Hermeneia (Philadelphia: Augsburg Fortress, 1973), 37 note 52.

Woolf, Virginia. *A Room of One's Own.* Orchard Park, NY: Broadview, 2001.

Yee, Gale A. *Poor Banished Children of Eve: Woman as Evil in the Hebrew Bible.* Minneapolis, MN: Augsburg Fortress, 2003.

Zimmerli, Walther. *Ezekiel: A Commentary on the Book of the Prophet Ezekiel: Chapters 1–24.* Vol. 1. Hermeneia. Philadelphia, PA: Fortress, 1979.

Index

Index of Biblical References